Gift ✓

D1065309

HAUNTED BY GOD

HAUNTED
BY
GOD

JAMES McBRIDE DABBS

Foreword by Edgar T. Thompson

JOHN KNOX PRESS
Richmond, Virginia

WINGATE COLLEGE LIBRARY
WINGATE, N. C.

Library of Congress Cataloging in Publication Data

Dabbs, James McBride, 1896–1970.
   Haunted by God.

   Includes bibliographical references.
   1. Southern States—Civilization. 2. Southern
States—Religion. 3. Southern States—Race question.
I. Title.
F209.D13   917.5′03   72–1760
ISBN 0–8042–0822–0

© John Knox Press 1972
Printed in the United States of America

Preface

On the morning of May 30, 1970, James McBride Dabbs wrote the last page of his manuscript *Haunted by God*. As he stacked the pages on his desk, he said, "There it is. I've done all I'm going to do to it. I suppose a man can't put his entire philosophy of life into one book, but I've drawn more or less on everything I know for this one." Four hours later, as he was resting and talking contentedly, his voice suddenly trailed off in the middle of a sentence and he was gone.

There is no one really qualified to edit and sharpen the manuscript as he would have done it. Yet this had to be accomplished as well as possible without doing any violence to his style, which was so much a part of the man himself. Now, after months of intensive work on my own part and the very skillful assistance of the editorial staff of John Knox Press, I present this book.

The particular circumstances make it impossible for me to list here all those who helped him in many ways to think out the manuscript and to stay with it until he had done it all. The actual work depended upon much encouragement and urging from his friends and readers.

I am deeply grateful to Dr. Edgar T. Thompson of Duke University for the perceptive and scholarly Foreword, and to these friends who were kind enough to read the manuscript before I began work on it: Mr. Pat Watters of the Southern Regional Council; Dr. Bell I. Wiley, Professor of History, Emory University; Dr. Donald W. Shriver, Jr., Associate Professor of Religion, North Carolina State University, and Dr. James Luther Adams, Professor Emeritus, Harvard Divinity School.

Underlying all other assistance was that of the directors of the Rockefeller Foundation, whose confidence and financial support made the project possible.

EDITH M. DABBS

Rip Raps Plantation
Mayesville, South Carolina
June 8, 1972

56671

Foreword

> And God saw everything that He had made and, behold, it was very bad. On the seventh day, therefore, God could not rest. In the morning and evening He busied himself with terrible and beautiful concoctions and in the twilight of the seventh day He finished that which is of more import than the beasts of the earth and the fish of the sea and the lights of the firmament. And He called it Imagination because it was made in His own image; and those unto whom it is given shall see God.*

It was given to James McBride Dabbs.

I well remember the day when, with a friend, I visited James Dabbs and talked with him as he sat in his study in his beautiful old plantation home near Mayesville, South Carolina. Lean and spare and gray, of kindly face and faint smile, he sat there and told us about the history of the plantation, about his ancestry, about his kin (his brother lives nearby on another plantation), about books he had read, and about the book he was writing. Here now is that book, a draft of which he finished shortly before his death. It appears in print through the efforts of Mrs. Dabbs, a remarkable and talented lady in her own right.

The stuff of this book comes straight out of the life and experiences of the author. But raw experience is empty until it is filled out by steady reflection and imagination, and these James Dabbs was fully prepared to furnish. He had traveled, studied, and read widely, always, apparently, with a view to better understanding his native South. He consciously writes about himself as

---

*Russell Gordon Smith, *Fugitive Papers* (New York: Columbia University Press, 1930), p. 3.

a Southerner—a Southerner searching for fundamentals and not content merely to be reconstructed. One will note how often he uses the first person singular and plural; he fully identified himself with his people, both black and white.

I now know, after reading the manuscript, that the core ingredients of this book were present in the immediate situation as we talked to James Dabbs in his study and as, later in the afternoon, we strolled about the grounds of the old Presbyterian church nearby. There was the plantation setting, there was the family in the Big House and round about, and there was race as represented in the relationships of the black and white members of the plantation. All of these, together with the nearby church and the religion it represented, were brought together in the experience and thinking of James Dabbs in one rich mix. He began with the grass roots, with what he knew best, with what he himself had lived through, with what his ancestors had backgrounded, and he sought to make sense of it all and to determine what the real South is and had been, what it might have been, and what it still might be. In the manner of the prophets of the Old Testament, he is calling upon the people of this region to face up to their racial as well as their individual sins, and to repent; he is asking the church to make the call clear.

It has been said that the South is a history in search of a country worthy enough to have it—or worthy enough to have the history which its regional historians have claimed for it. Its historians, themselves often an integral part of the history about which they wrote, narrated stirring events, identified and glorified heroes and leaders, and debated the issues which separated Southerners from other Americans and about which Southerners also were divided. But they did not concern themselves overmuch with the sources of its code of manners and its *sittlichkeit*, with the institutional components of its plantation system, or with the flavor of its culture, as this word is anthropologically understood. In recent years our better historians have begun to turn their attention to the role of the South's great forest frontiers, to its country stores and commissaries, to its several "little races," and to the human history of its black people—matters lying outside the succession of political events and the parade of heroes and politicians. Perhaps this is the kind of history Flannery O'Connor had in mind when she wrote, "Behind our own history, deepening it at every point, has been another history"—an oral and folk history of common behavior and belief. As we turn more and more to the consideration of this "other history," we shall have to turn more and more to the work of such men as W. J. Cash and James Dabbs.

One will notice in this book how little concerned James Dabbs was with the jargon and procedures of professional historians and social scientists. There is no section on methodology, little mention of old or of newly discovered documents, no questionnaires, no statistics. The choice insights and distinctions in this book, especially in Part I, may not win the accolade of "knowledge" in a strictly scientific sense, but their cogency is part of that great and human tradition which includes such figures as Plato and de Tocqueville. This is the kind of knowledge which liberates us from the limitations of our own time and place by, paradoxically, pushing us deeper into our own time and place. James Dabbs does this by answering questions that many of the rest of us have not yet known how to ask. I think older Southerners will understand what I mean when I say this. His answers to our unformulated questions can lead us back to the way it used to be—and often still is. From the pages of this book nostalgic Southerners will learn that they *can* go home again—at least part way.

EDGAR T. THOMPSON

Professor Emeritus of Sociology
Duke University

Contents

PART
ONE

The Culture

I

Main Characteristics: A Summary

The Southerner, white or black, is the product of the experience of several centuries in the South. He brought with him certain national or regional traits, but these have been modified by his life here. For he is no longer an Englishman, a European, or an African. He is a new man, an American, but a special form of American, a Southern American, a Southerner. One thing that makes him so hard to define is that he is more or less an American. So, when we say that the Southerner has certain characteristics, we don't mean that other Americans necessarily lack these characteristics, we mean that they are more noticeable in the Southerner.

Another difficulty in defining the Southerner is that he is the result of the meeting of two distinct races, the white and the black, the European (including here the English) and the African. Out of this meeting and this longtime extensive and intensive association has come the Southerner. Not that the white Southerner and the black Southerner are entirely alike. Without raising here the question of possible racial differences, we can say that each group has been modified by the particular place it has held in society, the role it has played. Yet granting this, the overall influence of the culture—which they themselves of course created—has made the two groups so much alike that, in distinction from other Americans and other men, they can all be called Southerners. When in the following pages I refer to Southerners, I shall be referring to both white and black Southerners unless I state otherwise or the context makes it clear.

Finally, like all of us in this rapidly changing world, the Southerner is in the process of change. He becomes more American every day. In this process he is returning toward what the white Southerner was in the early days of the nation—the most passionate of all Americans. How far this change will go, whether at long last the Southerner will be indistinguishable from other Americans except as the citizen of the southern part of the country, we do not know. It is safe to guess that traits that have been so long in the learning will not entirely disappear in the near future.

There is first the Southerner's strong sense of place, both physical and social. He is always from somewhere—some state, some town, even—occasionally—some plantation. On Armistice Day in 1918, two American soldiers, one white, the other black, met on the street in Paris. Each felt that he knew the other. The black's reply to the question "Where are you from?" was, "Mr. Bob Jones' place." That didn't make sense until he explained that it was Mr. Bob Jones' place in Lee County, South Carolina, near St. Charles.

Not only is the Southerner from some place; he is also, especially if white, from parents and grandparents who came from some place. Again, he is often aware of a social place or role. This sense is rapidly fading with the increasing mobility of all Americans, but it still remains in attenuated form. When the black soldier said he was from Mr. Bob Jones' place, he suggested his entire social background. The nation has noticed that the South is the region where whites like the Negro "in his place." What it hasn't noticed is that Southerners generally like everyone in his place. They like an ordered social structure. In maintaining this, however, white Southerners have unfortunately insisted upon a fixed low place for the blacks.

An extension of this sense of place is the Southerner's interest in the concrete, the particular, the given. Not only is he attached to places; he is attached to particular aspects of those places and to particular people who live there. His thought also lingers about things and people. His general conclusions rest heavily upon illustrations. His conversation tends to stories and anecdotes. He isn't always sure what they mean. He would rather have you guess for yourself. Robert Penn Warren has remarked that the Southerner fears abstractions more than anything else; he fears that they may iron out and dispose of all the curious

WINGATE COLLEGE LIBRARY
WINGATE, N. C.

particularities of life. For it is the manifoldness of life, often even its contradictions, that mainly interests him. He would rather stay close to home in his thinking, as he has tended to stay close to things as they are, to the things he knows and loves—or maybe hates. There was one Populist revolt in the South, but generally the South has simply endured its ills.

The Southerner's thinking, therefore, tends to show a certain circular quality. He does not proceed straightforwardly, as other Americans tend to do, through a series of abstractions into a different and hoped-for future; rather, he circles in his thought the known object or place, considering it, remembering it. If he is thinking at all, it is concretely; he is musing, perhaps like a poet, upon the images in his mind's eye. Perhaps he has been more lazy than poetic, but he has always responded to the lures of the world with considerable acceptance. The known present has often, though not always, appealed to him more than the unknown future.

There is also in the South—and strangely—a sense of spaciousness. This stands in contrast to the Southerner's focus upon the local, upon things and people in place, and has served as a counterweight to that focus. It is connected with several things. First is the vast amount of long-unsettled land in the South. This is notable even in the coastal plain of the old Southern states. In 1906 my father, for reasons of health, left a settled place on a pre-Revolutionary highway and began all over again in the deep pine woods a mile away. Living for eighteen months in a "camp" was for us children reliving the American pioneering experience. This suggests the long continuation of the frontier in the South, with its physical spaciousness. Much of Mississippi was still frontier at the time of the Civil War, and the desolation of defeat reduced most of the South to frontier conditions. Again, the sense of spaciousness is related to the loose institutional structure of the South. Where there are few institutional ties, the individual has the sense of moving freely. A powerful institutional tie in the South has been the family, as well as the locus of the family, the plantation. It goes without saying that this sense of spaciousness was far more limited for the black. Indeed, as we shall see, it was limited also for the white by the very presence of the black.

The Southerner has his own sense of time. Time moves more slowly and less insistently here. There is a greater sense of leisure, a greater emphasis upon the present moment, a lesser emphasis upon future hopes and dreams. This is connected, of course, with the Southerner's stress upon the particular person or thing, the concrete object, as opposed to some abstraction of that object. Also, for a long time now heavy stress has been laid upon the past. Southerners have a sense of history, of the past continuing into the present. This goes for black Southerners as well as white. William Faulkner once remarked, "The past is not dead; it isn't even past."

Finally, there is the Southerner's strong sense of community allied with a paradoxical individualism. Indeed, the existence of communities in the South is itself paradoxical. David Bertelson argues in *The Lazy South* that the Southern colonists, unlike the New Englanders, never set out to build communities, and as a result became the most individualistic of all Americans. Whether they planned communities or not, and however individualistic they were or became, they developed somehow a strong sense of community. They developed a sense of belonging.

It is this sense of belonging that colors the inner life of the Southerner. This, however, is a subtle matter; it is not the first thing the outsider notices; indeed, the Southerner himself is often only vaguely aware of it. What the outsider probably notices first, beyond peculiarities of speech and movement, is the importance of the past to the Southerner—not only last year or last lifetime, but the day just past, with its experiences and anecdotes. The Southerner tends to move rather slowly into the future because his present is so enriched, or burdened, by the past. This concern for the past, this continuing attempt to link the present with the past, is what the outsider first becomes aware of.

But the intriguing thing to the student of the South—and the really significant thing—is that the Southerner seems to belong to the South and the South to him. This is felt even by the relatively few Southern whites who, angered by the repressions of the South, have left, vowing never to return. Their very anger indicates that they had a dream of the South which has not been fulfilled. It belongs even to those thousands of blacks who, lured by hope and driven by anger, have left the South. Most of them still make regular pilgrimages "down home," and even among the most militant of them "soul food" is stock Southern food, cherished alike by blacks, poor whites, and many well-to-do whites.

But those blacks who have left the South may be simply nostalgic for their childhood home, as *emigres* often are. Are we going to say that the millions who have remained in the South also belong to it and it to them? However impossible it seems, yes. Legally owned as slaves for some two centuries, more or less owned for another century, how could they have developed any sense of really belonging to this land or it to them? To answer this question is to begin to answer our main question: What is Southern culture? We shall have to take it up, therefore, as we go along. Suffice it to say here that, possibly even more than the whites, the blacks made the South. Insofar as it is their creation, they belong to it and it to them.

So far we have simply said that there was and to a degree still is a culture in the South, with subcultures, it is true, but with the regional culture strong enough to put its mark upon practically all those who have lived here. As a consequence, it has belonged to them and they to it.

It is difficult for the typical modern to understand this. For the more modern he is, the more he is alienated, the less does he belong—to his work, his profession, his country, even himself. In place of belonging to something worthy of attachment, he tends to feel that he is controlled by some alien power far stronger than himself. Therefore, his passionate cry is for freedom from the smothering system or for justice within it.

Freedom and justice are two basic ideals, especially in Christianity. A great wind of freedom blows through the New Testament. Apparently the early Christians felt they had been freed from the shackles of principalities and powers, even of mortality itself. As for justice, it was the passionate cry of the great prophets, and some philosopher has remarked of it that in a world where justice does not exist, it is a miracle that man has dreamed of it and continually seeks it. In the modern world multitudes are so patently bound—and so often unjustly—that they cry out for freedom and justice.

Yet there is something more. We do not want freedom just for itself, nor do we want simple, cold justice. We want freedom from tyrannical structures in order to belong to human structures. Absolute freedom, even were it possible, is a burden too great to be borne. For we are social creatures, and justice can exist only among men, within institutions. It is, however, an ideal, which, like all great ideals, is impossible of actualization but necessary for guidance. Exhibiting too little of it, institutions crumble or are destroyed. Therefore we always seek justice but never find it.

So it is with a culture. Men must live below the ideals of freedom and justice. But to say that Southerners belong to the South and the South to them is only to say that the South has been and to a degree is a culture. It does not define this culture or its members. In order to do this, we shall have to determine in what particular ways Southerners are bound to the South, and in order to understand these ways, we shall have to consider in some degree how they developed, that is, their history.

II

The Southerner as American

I assume in the United States one basic culture, originating mainly in European culture but different from it. I assume in the South the most distinctive variant of the American culture. If the South had won the Civil War, this variant might have become the American culture and the present American culture the variant. But the idea is impossible, for the South was fighting against the modern world and sooner or later was bound to be overcome by that world. Whether, when this occurred, its culture would remain a variant of the modern American culture or be absorbed and lost in it, it is too soon to say. We are still in the position of the Confederate veteran of about 1900, regaling his admiring grandson with tales of Civil War battles, most of which, as a matter of fact, the South won. Said the little boy, "Grandpa, the South won all the battles, but how did the war come out?" "Sonny," said the old man, "it's too soon yet to tell."

Now, more than seventy years later, it is still too soon to tell just what will be the fate of Southern culture in the larger American culture. Southerners become more American every day, but American whites generally begin to appear more Southern every day. Will Southerners become entirely American, only distinguishable as living within certain parallels of latitude?

If the culture of the South is the most distinctive variant of the larger American culture, we shall need, for purposes of clarity, to set it alongside that larger culture. It is my belief that the South began to be different, even though in subtle ways, with the Virginia settlement of 1607. I also think it to be the case that the larger American culture received a slight though ineffaceable mark with the landing at Plymouth in 1620 and the more important landing at Massachusetts Bay in 1630. Different, however slightly, from the beginning, the two groups, north and south, under the influence of religious ideas, of land and weather, and of the slow effect of time, became increasingly different for some three centuries. Within the last half century we have been drawing together. How far we shall follow this course no one knows.

Let me suggest, as briefly as I can, certain differences between the predominantly Puritan culture of early New England and the predominantly non-Puritan culture of the South.

The old division into Cavaliers and Roundheads was simplistic, meant to gratify the vanity of the South. Nevertheless, there is something to be seen in that comparison. There were, of course, Puritan settlers in the early South long before the coming of that mass of Scotch-Irish Presbyterians in the eighteenth century. There were also easy-living settlers in Massachusetts, best known among them Thomas Morton, who set up a Maypole, hilariously assisted by Indian squaws and good liquor. But Morton was a momentary distraction; he couldn't last in that Puritan air. Indeed, the Puritans couldn't last in the more seductive air of the South. The historian William Dodd tells us that in the 1640's John Winthrop helped send three ministers to southern Virginia to preach the "true gospel." Sir William Berkeley, then governor, persuaded the next assembly to denounce them. (Of course, religion and politics were all mixed up in the 1640's.) The Puritans retreated northward and settled in Maryland, but they took hundreds of converts with them, including the wealthy plantation owner Richard Bennet.[1]

Though there were Puritans, then, in the early South, the South was not concentratedly Puritan. Indeed, it was not concentratedly anything. Nor was it concentrated anywhere. One main tendency of its varied inhabitants was not to concentrate but to spread out loosely across the landscape. So, from their very beginnings, New England was a tightly structured and the South a loosely structured society.

When we begin to examine in more detail these two societies, we find several interesting differences. These are clearly seen in the different orientations to space and time. Both groups were strongly attracted to the New World, with its vast uncharted spaces. But the Southern settlers brought more of the Old

World, of the past, with them; the Puritans tended to detach themselves from the past. Recalling England as a corrupt society from which they had fled as from a wicked city, the Puritans were determined to set up in the New World a *new* England, wherein by the grace of God they would establish his kingdom, and from which, if things went well, they might return at some future date to England to bring salvation to the people there. With this determination they signed compacts and organized communities, the chief purpose of which was to see that the will of God was done.

The Southern settlers also came because they disliked life in England or in Europe. They would not otherwise have made the desperate gamble. But they neither agreed with one another in their likes and dislikes as much as the New Englanders did, nor were they as deeply opposed to the world they had left. The Puritans wanted a new world; the Southern settlers wanted more freedom, especially economic freedom from Old World restrictions. *New* England appropriately named itself; the first Southern settlement, Virginia, honored by its name England's greatest queen. We shall see continuing in the South this early accent upon the personal and the feminine. The New Englanders, far more than the Southerners, looked forward to a radically changed world and organized themselves to create this world. The Southerners looked forward to a better, freer world. "Better" certainly carried strong religious overtones, especially among the eighteenth-century Scotch-Irish settlers, but religious values were not so consciously or corporately sought as in New England. In the first Southern settlement, in Virginia, the lure of tobacco was too strong for a closely organized community. In spite of the efforts of the London Company and later of the Virginia House of Delegates, most men would not settle in towns, either for this-worldly or otherworldly reasons. The lure of tobacco was too great. Each man struck out on his own, up the creeks and rivers, risking his life for the chance of worldly gain.

Yet these same men, moving westward, were still willing to keep many of the forms of their earlier life in England. The Established Church of England was for decades their church. And when, with the passage of time, the plantations arose, they were more or less consciously modeled after the estates of the English landed gentry.

However, it isn't quite accurate to say that the Southern settler brought more of the past with him than did the New England settler. He brought it in a different form; he held it in his mind differently. The Puritan brought to America from his past a set of abstract ideas about the relation of man to man, of man to the physical world, of man to God. He came deeply dissatisfied with the expression these ideas had obtained in England. He came looking for a place and a time in which he might bring these abstract ideas into concrete practice.

I do not mean, of course, that the Puritan never remembered the actual English past with nostalgic longing. One of the classic passages in American literature is contained in William Bradford's account of the first Massachusetts autumn: "For summer being done, all things stand upon them with a wetherbeaten face; and the whole countrie, full of woods and thickets, represented a wild and savage heiw. If they looked behind them, ther was the mighty ocean which they had passed, and was now a main barr and goulf to seperate them from al the civill parts of the world." But out of this moment of nostalgia and almost self-pity, "they cried unto the Lord, and he heard their voice, and looked on their adversatie."

Yet in spite of natural longing for the past, they brought minds filled with goals, plans, and dreams of a new social order. It may be safe to say that Southern settlers were less concerned to extend and improve the social order. Thus they tended to bring more images and fewer abstract plans. This is simply to say that they remembered more, they planned less. Or, to put it still another way, they carried with them more of the past, less of the future.

Yet it is clear that in at least one matter they broke more sharply with the past than did the Puritans: they refused to build towns, whereas the Puritans repeated the English and European pattern. How shall we explain this?

What we are sure of is that the lure of the land—especially, in Virginia, the tobacco-growing land—drew men up along the creeks and rivers to lonely farms. There was no such lure for the

New England settlers. But it seems to me that behind this clear physical fact lay, subtly, a religious trait. The Puritans were what the name implies: they wished to purify themselves from the evils of the world. Therefore they separated themselves from the world and viewed it with continuous skepticism. The new England was to be conquered for the glory of God, but meanwhile its dark forests were the abode of Satan. Therefore the settlers organized themselves and drew together in towns. The Virginia settlers were more acceptive of the world. They had been more acceptive in England; they remained more acceptive in the New World. I do not mean to say that they had no sense of God or the devil in the world; they were seventeenth-century Englishmen. But they were less deeply impressed and oppressed with such a sense. The lure of the pleasant land drew them, even dangerously, toward the interior.

David Bertelson, in *The Lazy South,* makes much of the lure of the generally pleasant Southern land and climate. He discusses all this under the doctrine of allurement, according to which, he says, the South was settled and developed in the belief that all that society needed was opportunity. Opportunity itself would lure individuals onward, and a social order would incidentally occur. This attractionist doctrine, as he points out, is a variant of the economic doctrine of laissez-faire: every man works for his own interest, and a hidden hand shapes all these individual efforts into a social order. Says Bertelson: "The doctrine of allurement can be viewed as a very early expression of the idea of *laissez-faire.* . . . Only in the South (and the sugar islands) were attempts made to form whole societies in accordance with this notion. And these attempts worked—after a fashion." In contrast to the Southern settlers, "Both the Quakers and to an even greater degree the Puritans in New England founded societies based on communities of consent and common goals. Imbued with a sense of community and social purposefulness, these people were truly able to build cities in the wilderness."[2]

Out of these New England colonies and to a lesser degree out of the less strict but still prudent Middle Atlantic colonies sprang the dominant culture of the United States. The haunting question that arises is: How, out of these so carefully laid communities, have there appeared during three hundred years the great beehives of the North, where the sense of community has been almost shattered? And, contrariwise, how, out of the isolated, selfish settlements of the South, has there appeared a sense of community probably unmatched in the nation? This second question is ours. Of the first, I may simply hazard a guess. The Puritans, like other Protestants, were basically individualists: each man stood alone before God. They said that they organized themselves and built towns for the glory of God, as a step to bringing in his kingdom in America. Let us take them at their word. These towns were built, however, along an enormously rich hinterland, and were an effective instrument in conquering that hinterland. They were also instruments for conquering the wicked world and bringing it to heel. But this process brought enormous wealth to the conquerors, and with wealth came a turning from the heavenly to the earthly city. As this happened, the saints became Yankees; the individualism of their religion found expression in the individualism of their economic life. The structures built originally to keep men in the service of God became structures chiefly occupied with bringing wealth to the few who controlled them.

The central problem of this book, however, is the second question: How, out of the isolated, selfish settlements of the South, there appeared such an extraordinary community sense.

III

The Plantation

No matter how loosely structured the South has been, it has nevertheless been structured. Individuals were not related to one another atomistically but through institutions. The most important of these were the plantation, the family, and race—an institution based upon biological facts. Of these, the plantation was probably the most important; the strength of the family and the importance of race rested mainly upon the plantation.

To admit that the plantation was probably the most important institution in the South is for many people today to admit that nothing worthwhile was created in the South. The plantation is synonymous first with slavery, later with exploited Negro labor, today with the great landholdings of the Mississippi Delta—until recently plantations, now fast becoming mechanical and industrial farms. But perhaps this is the basic paradox of the South: that an institution created mainly for exploitation should have become, by the grace of God, we would say, one of the key institutions in creating a culture with a considerable degree of humanity. How this happened is a part of our story.

Certainly the plantation is done for now, both economically and humanly. But this does not mean that it never had any human value. That it had economic value is evidenced by the fact that it lasted as long as it did.

In placing the plantation at the heart of the South, I am following chiefly Edgar T. Thompson, Professor Emeritus of Sociology at Duke University, a student of the plantation in its worldwide expression. Says Thompson, "The civilization of the South really has to be understood in terms of an institution that came significantly upon the world after the sixteenth century, the plantation. The plantation has been the molecular unit, the very quintessence, of the South and of southernism. In a sense the plantation is the South writ small and the South is the plantation writ large."[1]

In allotting this primacy to the plantation, I am not falling into the error so often made by antebellum commentators on the South: the division of the South into three groups—the slave owners, the slaves, and the poor whites. This summary completely omits the great number of independent white farmers— usually called yeoman farmers—with no slaves or with only one or two, and also the tradesmen and mechanics of the towns and villages. Compared with the yeoman farmers, the true slave owners were a relatively small group. Yet the power and the lure of the plantation was such that a study of Tennessee in the decades just before the Civil War shows that visitors to that area saw only plantations. They were looking actually at the homes and lands of independent small farmers, but bemused by the plantation myth, they saw these as parts of large plantations.

The plantation did not come into existence in the South merely to satisfy the selfish ambitions of a few men who wished to become plantation owners. It appeared in widely scattered areas of the Western world at about the same time. To quote Thompson again, "Relatively cheap water transportation transformed the Atlantic Ocean into an inland sea, no larger than the Mediterranean once was, and gave the warmer lands in and surrounding the Caribbean and Gulf of Mexico territorial divisions of labor in the larger community of Western civilization as producers of agricultural staples for the markets of Europe." He adds in a note, "This region, of course, extended to the southwest from the distant markets of Western Europe across the Atlantic Ocean." But also, "Beyond the Elbe River in Germany there appeared large plantation-like estates producing for the same market centers." The latter may have developed on the model of the American plantation, or they may have developed independently in response to similar ecological and historical circumstances.[2]

Even though the Southern plantation arose in response to demands of the European market, it also satisfied a desire in the minds of at least the English settlers. For they remembered the great landed estates of England, and their own plantations at best became great landed estates. That the American landowner differed markedly from his English forerunner goes without saying, but he had at least somewhere in mind the English pattern. We have already remarked that the Southerner generally brought to the New World a mind filled more by solid images of the past than by vague plans for the future. The English estate was such an image. It is possible that from the beginning the plantations of the American South, though rising in response to the economic needs of Europe, also rose in response to an English ideal. Certainly in the long run they expressed this ideal, and as such became more humanly productive enterprises than they would have been without it.

The Southern plantation, then, was clearly the product of economic forces, less clearly of social ideals. The economic forces are evident in the settlement of Carolina during the last quarter of the seventeenth century. They appear but slightly in the settlement of Virginia two-thirds of a century earlier. There was a quality of sheer adventure in the settlement of Virginia that was hardly apparent in the later settlement of Carolina. The men who composed the London Company called themselves adventurers, and the people they sent out were also adventurers. Looking for gold and failing to find it, they stumbled upon tobacco. This captured the European market, the demand grew, and great tobacco plantations, the first plantations in the South, came into being. But the Lords Proprietor of Carolina were mainly businessmen who were determined to produce for the European market. The first ship that anchored in what was to become the Charleston harbor brought seeds of various kinds to be tried in the new soil and climate, with the purpose of determining what crops most needed by Europe could best be grown in the new province.

This was of course the accent in the England and Europe from which the seventeenth-century settlers came. The settlers did not find it strange, therefore, that certain lands were preempted and that large holdings were supposed to belong to men back in the homeland. But this acceptive attitude inevitably changed with the passage of time. Though there seemed to be an infinity of land, it tended to go to those who had the energy to settle and work it. In this free, expansive air the democratic spirit increased until finally, when the first democratic revolution—the American Revolution—came, it was hardly a revolution but a mere legitimation of already existing facts. The American forest and frontier had already accomplished the revolution.

Before this time the plantation had reached and passed its peak in Virginia and was rapidly reaching its peak in South Carolina. The point to note is that it had reached this central and commanding position through the acquiescence of the great majority of yeoman farmers, who never became plantation owners. They acquiesced partly because they hoped to become plantation owners themselves—the plantation had become the ideal —and partly because the plantation had become the economic and political center of power. As Thompson and others have pointed out, the plantation of the American South differed from that of South America in that there was a greater centralization of power within the former than within the latter. In South America the power of the plantation was offset by the power of a strongly centralized government, the Crown, and of the strongly centralized Roman Catholic Church. In the American South the government was always relatively weak—before the Revolution because of the growing democracy of the English government, and after the Revolution because the Americans desired a relatively weak government. As for the church, there was no comparison between the centralized Roman Catholic Church in South America and the separated and separating Protestant Church in North America. This situation left the plantations of the American South without real challenge.

So, says Thompson, "Planters dominated the state and filled its offices. The state universities and military academies trained their sons to succeed them as another generation of planters. The church gave moral sanction to the principle of rank order among kinds of men. Originally there was no manufacturing industry to compete for its labor; when such industry did develop it retained the paternalistic principle of the plantation. The small farm sometimes got in the way, but yeoman farmers and even poor whites aspired to become planters themselves."[3]

In the long run the Southern plantation became the chief source of power and prestige in the South. As such it not only gave power and prestige to its owners and their families but also demanded service and devotion from them. Legally a plantation, together with its slaves in antebellum days, belonged to its owner. In reality not only the slaves but even the owner and his family belonged to the plantation. He and they were parts of a large, ongoing enterprise located in space and time, an enterprise which demanded of all who were associated with it fairly steadfast attention and even concern. For it was their world, very imperfect, it is true, but with a large inclusiveness and even attraction.

We are now in the late twilight of the plantation; it becomes the mechanized farm or farming corporation. But I remember what my uncle did here at Rip Raps—and what I was supposed to do but didn't because between his lifetime and mine family and land had lost some of their compelling character. When my uncle graduated from college in the 1880's, he was offered a position in the department of mathematics. Undoubtedly he would have justified the confidence shown in him. Yet he chose to come back here to run the plantation for his widowed mother and intellectually and to a degree actually to bury himself in it. In 1916 I had inherited the plantation but had shown no clear intention of taking up the responsibility. An old ruling elder of my church exclaimed in disbelief, "What! James not coming back to the old place!" In his mind the old place demanded absolute allegiance. (I did return later, but only after a career in the world.)

Negroes also "belonged" to the plantation; a few of them belong still. Thirty years ago when Joseph Hampton moved to this place from the neighboring Cooper plantation, Tamar Weston was heard to remark, "He ain't got no business coming here. He belong to the Cooper people." Some economic concern may have been expressed in this remark, but undoubtedly there was more than economic concern. Exactly what was this *more*? Exactly how did Southerners of all ranks and both races belong to the plantation? If in the last twilight of the plantation some sense of belonging still exists, what must it have been when the institution incorporated both the power and the prestige of the South?

It is perhaps significant for the South that the plantation was not an institution carefully planned beforehand as were the town communities of New England. It arose rather as the expression of individual wills, themselves influenced by the vast material possibilities and needs of their times and by related institutions of commerce set up to meet those needs. In the course of its development, however, it took on certain social communal characteristics and finally became that institution which, with the attendant family, bound the South together loosely but tenaciously.

This comment is in partial answer to the question we raised earlier: How is it that the South, where in the beginning every man set out largely for himself, developed in the end a sense of community stronger even than that of New England, where men had covenanted together to form communities? Let us generalize by saying that the New Englanders took too seriously their ideals of the kingdom of God and the blessed community, not realizing how deeply modern and individualistic they really were, and not understanding, therefore, how they would use these communal institutions, built professedly for the glory of God but actually, as it turned out, for their individual profit. The Southern settler, usually with far vaguer ideals of the kingdom of God—they were, I think, too vague—set out to use this rich splendid world, which, he admitted, God had given him. But the world was such, and his temper, still enriched by the deep past, was such that in the end he built an institution which, whatever its other faults, expressed both social and economic ideals. As an institution it tended to make its members part of a community whose spiritual implications were certainly too vague but whose physical nature was rooted in earth (for the whites), in family, and in time.

IV

The Family

Beginning as an economic institution, soon crowned with the aura of the English estate, the plantation ended by becoming a rich social institution centered around the family. To quote Edgar Thompson, "white families, and particularly planter families, characteristically were united by the interweaving by marriage and other social ties into extensive kinship clans whose members often held membership in the same church."[1] In his opinion, it was the high degree of intermarriage in isolated communities that helped to give the South the strong sense of place it developed. One belonged not only to a geographical place but also to a kinship pattern. Such ties reached far and sometimes bound individuals and families together all across the South. One of the first questions the Southerner is apt to ask—or to think, because of the growing mobility of life even in the South—is, "Are you kin to so-and-so?"

Though the family feeling of the Southerner may have gained weight from its association with such a strong economic unit as the plantation, it was a force in its own right and added its strength to that of the plantation. One of the factors that has at least continued and strengthened it is, as Thompson says, isolation. The units of the South, plantations and small farms, were usually isolated in the woods or along the swamps; the South as a whole, because of its use of slavery and later its defeat in the Civil War, has often been isolated from the mainstream of American life. The most striking instance of Southern isolation appears in the Appalachians. Here settlers moving westward paused in the pleasant valleys, lingered too long, and were trapped in the ravines and up along the hillsides. The world passed them by, they intermarried, often within the same valley, sometimes across one or two ranges. Thus bound together by mountain walls and by close ties of kinship, they developed extremely strong family feelings and family animosities. The Kentucky feud between the Hatfields and the McCoys is famous.

Earlier than the isolated conditions, there were other influences which made for family cohesiveness. The first may have been extremely slight in the beginning, but it became stronger as other institutions encouraged its growth. This was the stronger social cohesiveness, the weaker individualism of the Southern settlers generally, as compared with the predominantly Puritan settlers of New England.

In apparent contradiction to this is the fact that the New England settlers organized towns, the Southern settlers did not. Bertelson cites this fact as proof that the New Englander was more social-minded, the Southerner a stronger individualist. It may be the other way around. Perhaps the Puritan organized definite communities because he sensed within himself—and feared—his individualistic thrust, especially in the boundless New World, and attempted to restrain this by making compacts with his neighbors. As we have already noted, the longtime effect was not to restrain him but to make the group far more efficient than the individual could ever have been in bringing the wilderness and Satan to heel. But conquering the wilderness, they domesticated Satan, brought him into the household and even the church, and made of him a gentleman indistinguishable from themselves.

The Southern settlers, fearing neither themselves nor the wilderness so much, felt less the need for towns that would provide self-restraint and wilderness control. They feared themselves less because they had withdrawn less from the old European groupings, were less individualistic, and trusted others and themselves more. This would appear, naturally, in a strong family sense.

Clifford Dowdey, in *The Great Plantation*, recounts the story of what he calls the Virginia Dynasty—that group of plantation owners who through intermarriage came to rule Virginia throughout the Colonial period and with lessening power into the nineteenth century. Among the first of these was Benjamin

Harrison II, who rose from a frontier position "to found a line that continued for generations in a public service which formed the background for the later Virginia Dynasty. . . . For Harrison, conforming to what was to become a Virginia tradition, the family was the thing."[2] His children, born too late to remember the frontier, grew up as members of the ruling class in an aristocratic republic, and all married into great Virginia families.

Harrison died in 1712, "patriarch of a most powerful clan, interlocked by marriage or friendship with the mighty." By about 1765 family had become of the first importance in Virginia. "Since everyone in the ruling class was kin to somebody else in it, the Virginia government was something like a large family, with all of a family's spites and jealousies, as well as the binding intimacies between some individuals."[3]

Allen Tate, discussing the South as a whole, refers specifically to Virginia and to his own state, Kentucky, an offshoot of Virginia. "The center of the South, then, was the family, no less for Robert E. Lee than for the people on Tate's Creek Pike; for Virginia was a great aggregate of families that through almost infinite ramifications of relationship was almost one family." It is also significant, Tate continues, "that the one original art of the South was domestic architecture, as befitted a family-centered society."[4]

But was not family feeling, evidently so strong in Virginia and the other Atlantic Seaboard states, distinctly weakened by the westward thrust of settlement, especially after the Revolution? The move to the frontier was basically an individualistic move away from reliance upon one's neighbors to reliance upon oneself. To the degree that it was this, it was also a weakening of family ties. However, the dangers of the frontier may have had at times the opposite effect, driving families even closer in upon themselves. In regard to this, Frank Owsley says: "Though families were frequently scattered by the westward migration, they more often than not migrated and settled together." In illustration of this, Owsley quotes from a letter of Senator Charles Tait of Georgia to his son James upon the occasion of their preparing to migrate to Alabama: "I wish you to go where you think it will be best for you to go—where you can be more prosperous and happy. I will go where you go and stay where you stay."[5]

There appeared in the eighteenth century another force in the South which, in the beginning at least, was unrelated to the plantation and must have had a strong effect upon the Southern family. This was the coming to America, mainly between 1717 and 1776, of some 200,000 Scotch-Irish. Though entering through the ports of Pennsylvania, most of these eventually drifted down and settled the Piedmont of the South. These people were mainly the descendants of Lowland Scots and had been on the frontier of northern Ireland for one to three generations. They certainly did not bring any clearly defined clan organization with them, yet this organization lay in their recent past, and it would have been strange indeed if they were not still deeply responsive to the attraction of near family, far family, and clan. They were generally a driving, ambitious people, and for those who succeeded, the family sense brought with them was soon strengthened by the possession of landed estates and the status that went with this. Stark Young says that they brought this sense of land with them. If so, it was merely strengthened by their ownership of land in America.

It is also probable that the ideals of the cultured South, fed so richly by the Greek and especially the Roman past, helped to focus the thought of at least the Southern leaders upon the family. We have already suggested that Southerners have always been more influenced than other Americans by their meditation upon images out of the past as opposed to the analytical formulation of plans for the future. Calhoun and a few others, recalling the free cities of Greece resting upon slavery, called the South a Greek democracy. But this was almost purely a political image picked up to defend slavery in the South. The ideal of intellectual freedom exemplified by Socrates and other great Greeks could never have had any deep appeal for Southerners. The Roman ideal did. The Southern plantation ideal, says Allen Tate, "was actually nearer to Republican Rome, a society which, like the South, was short in metaphysicians and great poets, and long in moralists and rhetoricians." This is suggested by the great number of Roman names that appear in the South. Tate even suggests that the Old South "was an aggregate of farms and plantations, presided over by [a] composite agrarian hero, Cicero Cincinnatus."[6]

The Roman ideal, in contrast to the Greek, gave high place to the family. Says Hannah Arendt: "The full development of the life of hearth and family into an inner and private space we owe to the extraordinary political sense of the Roman people who, unlike the Greeks, never sacrificed the private to the public, but on the contrary understood that these two realms could exist only in the form of coexistence."[7] Undoubtedly the cultural leaders of the South sensed this, whether they ever formulated it or not. In fact, the life of the plantation seems to be a striking illustration of public and private coexistence.

I realize that the position of woman in the South is an anomalous thing. Apparently she was both worshiped and scorned. But there seem grounds for the opinion that, at least on the plantation, the home presided over by the mistress coexisted powerfully with the farm and other public affairs presided over by the master. Within the house her word was law; she carried the keys and mapped the day's events. It has been suggested that this almost absolute control within the home was won at the cost of ceding all power beyond the home. Especially in the nineteenth century, when slavery came under increasing attack, the planter feared that his wife's sensitive nature might weaken the institution, and, therefore, to keep her out of the public affairs of the plantation, he yielded her almost absolute authority in its private affairs. But to the degree that this was so, it is an institutional expression of that too complete division between public and private which, as we shall see, is one of the basic weaknesses of the South.

The Greeks, according to Hannah Arendt, had no private life. Making a living belonged to slaves and women and was not life but the means to life. Life was what went on in the forum; life was political. The Romans, however, made the hearth important; they gave it its own gods. The Christians went on to say that the hearth was universal, and over it the one Father presided. The Protestants said this but did not as a rule believe it. The Catholics got as far as deifying the mother, but even they didn't understand what they'd done. The South, unfortunately, was Protestant, not

Catholic. Like all Protestants we were better at dividing than at uniting, at analysis than at synthesis. For many reasons we *did* give the home, the original synthesis, a high place in our scheme; we were Romans in this rather than Greeks. But for the most part we failed to become Christians and really to see in the home what we said we saw: the vital core of the universe. But I anticipate too much.

The Civil War, like any war, is filled with illustrations of family loyalty (and, in the border states especially, of tragic family division). I am not at all sure that Southerners showed such loyalty any more than Northerners did. It was the opinion of William L. Royall of Richmond that "The South was held together by personal loyalties, by ties of blood and kinship, that couldn't be lightly disregarded."[8] For this reason, he adds, it was impossible for Lee to have had Longstreet shot after Gettysburg. In Bryan's opinion, Lee in this instance placed personal devotion before national loyalty. Perhaps he did. He had left the Union to fight "for the local community which he could not abstract into fragments."[9] Perhaps here at Gettysburg he was still vague about the causes but clear about the human community of which he was a part; and Longstreet was both a part and an embodiment of that community.

To return to Southern family devotion during the Civil War, let me take a rather long passage from the writings of Bell I. Wiley, one of the most authoritative historians of the daily conduct of that war. He is telling the story of Jud and Cary Smith, Yale-educated brothers from Mississippi, and their father. "While in the act of lying down under fire, the younger, Cary, putting his hand under his coat found his inner garments covered with blood; and with only the exclamation 'What does this mean?' he died. Jud was so overwhelmed with grief that he spent the entire night muttering affectionate words over his brother's corpse. He passed the next day and night in unconsolable solitude. The third day was that of Malvern Hill, and when the first charge took place Jud kept going on after his comrades fell back under the murderous fire, and he was never seen or heard of again. After the father learned of the fate of his two sons he joined Price's army as a private soldier; when his regiment charged at Iuka, he followed the example set by Jud at Malvern Hill, and he likewise was never heard of again."[10]

Nathan Bedford Forrest, former slave trader and cavalry leader par excellence, was both in the combination of vocations and in the splendor of his military career a man not easily matched. Lytle, in commenting upon Forrest's deep interest in his men, his desire to save them even in the most terrible fights, and his grief at their deaths, says that these things all "maintained the feeling that the South was one big clan, fighting that the small man, as well as the powerful, might live as he pleased."[11]

If we consider the South since the Civil War, we shall find that though some families were ruined, dispersed, or destroyed by the war, perhaps the opposite effect was the most general and the strongest. Weakened, almost broken families were driven together for self-protection in the harsh new environment. Francis Simkins, in his *History of the South*, comments as follows: "In the decades after the Civil War the family was the core of Southern society; within its bounds everything worth while took place." And though "after 1910 there were changes in Southern domestic life," yet "there was no significant uprooting of family life."[12]

Margaret Jarman Hagood defends the family life even of the tenant farmer. She admits that "In tenant families the family pattern has to be based more upon personal relations than in owner families, where there are also ties to land, home, and various acquisitions." Yet she adds that "In no particular do the portrayals of certain fiction writers seem more unrepresentative than in their belittling of family ties."[13]

Let me cite one or two pertinent comments from the more recent past. John Temple Graves, a Southern columnist, speaking of the Scottsboro case of the 1930's, says: "I could only report to *The New Republic* that the Scottsboro decision had been set aside because the presiding judge was a man who was descended from General Donelson and who had sons through whom he, too, expected to be an ancestor, and who thought he owed it to the past and the future to be just although the heavens fell."[14]

That comment was made in 1943. Some ten years later Hodding Carter, of Greenville, Mississippi, also stressed the importance of family in the South. After admitting the overriding earthly importance but impersonal nature of a man's loyalty to his country, he adds: "The allegiance of the family to its individual members and the allegiance of the individual to the clan is a near and personal matter, and it is rooted especially deep in the soil of the South. I was raised to believe that whoever harmed my kinsman was also my enemy and whoever befriended him was a friend of mine." Later on he illustrates this by reference to the Percys of Mississippi, especially Will Percy. "His father's political enemies dared the Percys to appear in a hostile town. Young Will armed himself with an unfamiliar pistol. So did a handful of kinsmen. They went to the town, and his father was heard without molestation."[15]

Only one other comment needs to be made about family life in the South, but that is both important and difficult. What about the Negro family? Thinking mainly of the white family, we have said that for various reasons family life was extremely important. Everyone is aware that the slave system, even at its best, tended either to make impossible or greatly to disrupt normal family life. For the most part, marriages were considered unimportant; and, though the South made some effort to prevent the breaking up of families in the slave trade, little was officially accomplished. What good there was came from benevolent masters who, often against their own interests, refused to have their slave families broken up.

We do know that such cohesiveness as Negro families have had has been due primarily to the mother. This continues among most Negro families even today. However, as the father becomes a steady breadwinner and the family rises on the economic scale, the pattern begins to shift and to take on the more usual patriarchal form.

Though many scholars stress the matriarchal form of the Negro family, Hylan Lewis, in one of the best studies we have of Negro life in America, says in a note, "Again, we are dealing here with differences of emphasis rather than differences of kind because the picture here is but an exaggerated one of the role of the mother in the kinship system of 'Western Society.'"[16]

We have already seen how important the mistress of the plantation is within the walls of her home. Since historically most

American Negroes have lived on the plantation, it is possible that we see here some degree of imitation. Though the Negro mother could by no means control her affairs as the mistress of the plantation could hers, yet this was what she tried to do, and the relatively poor place granted by society to the man in her household helped her in the attempt.

Here we come to the moot point: To what degree, if any, did the Negro family gain cohesiveness by belonging, in the most general sense, to a cohesive white family? If we grant that belonging has any meaning in the South beyond the physical and the legal—and as I have said, I think it has—then we have to grant that the usual strength of the white family—plantation or farm—has done something to strengthen the Negro family. Or perhaps we should say simply the family.

For what it's worth, I add a picture of life in the South as reported by a British subject blockaded from the spring of 1860 to the summer of 1862. Catherine Hopley says: "There is that peculiar tie, 'I belong to you,' so very hard to comprehend by us English, the servants looking upon their masters as their natural protectors, and being themselves as free from all responsibilities. Their masters on their part grow up with corresponding sentiments. Even if the servants are useless and profitless, " 'they belong to me, their fathers and mothers nursed our fathers and mothers.' "[17] Even if Miss Hopley reported accurately, she undoubtedly reported about house servants alone.

V

The Black

If the plantation and its attendant family were two basic primary institutions shaping the South, chattel slavery was the third. Given the land, the climate, and the market, the plantation might have existed without slavery; there were such plantations in eastern Germany. Indeed, slavery was not recognized in Virginia until the 1660's; by that time tobacco plantations were already coming into existence, worked by indentured labor. But because of improved conditions in Europe, the flow of indentured labor declined. Furthermore, indentured labor was never highly satisfactory. In the land-rich New World it was hard to keep temporarily indentured Europeans from running away to the forest during the terms of their indentures, and impossible to keep them after their terms expired. The call of the free world was too strong.

Plantations, then, did exist without slavery, but it is very doubtful that without slavery they would have reached the peak of power they did in the American South. It is entirely safe to say that modern chattel slavery would not have existed without plantations. It is true that small farmers, yeoman farmers, did often own a slave or two. But the whole pressure of the European market, of the European and American slave trade, of the productive lands and climate of the South tended to make this a temporary situation. The small farmer was generally the big farmer, the plantation owner, on the make. At least in the new lands of America, therefore, slavery and the plantation depended upon each other.

It is bad enough to admit that the plantation was the primary institution that shaped the South, for plantations now are hopelessly outmoded and, indeed, like the institution of sharecropping, in disgrace. It is even worse to admit that another chief shaping institution of the South was slavery. To expect anything positive from the South with this background seems to be to expect the impossible. Perhaps that is just what we do when we consider the grace of God in the South.

According to James Sellers, it was indeed the settlers' misuse of God's great gift of the land that brought Negro slavery to the South. The land lay before them. It was their duty as Christians to use this gift of God. How could they best use it? The Negro slave seemed the best answer. But the gift was too lavish. "The Southerner," says Sellers in *The South and Christian Ethics,* "entered upon his ordeal of slaveholding because that was the way his good surroundings tempted him and got inside his own anxiety to live and show himself worthy of God's partnership."[1]

I can agree that God's chief gift to the South—its splendid land—became the Southerner's chief temptation. After all, we are always tempted by our greatest gifts. Jesus, supremely gifted, was tempted in that early experience in the desert to use his gifts for his own advancement rather than for the glory of God. It is always so. I cannot agree that the Southern settler generally began using this splendid gift for the glory of God and erred only in the means. This is what the Puritans said they themselves did; they said they were building the kingdom of God. The early Southern settlers were not predominantly Puritan; they were carving out fields primarily for themselves, secondarily, perhaps, for their old home, England (as against European powers).

Whatever may have been the motivation of the first slave owners, we are still inclined to cry out, *why?* The whole thing seems to us now, only three hundred years later, such a sad mistake. For England and most of Europe had rid themselves of slavery centuries before. Why, then, this turning backward? In spite of all the disasters of the last half century, most of us still live in the light of the eighteenth-century theory of progress: always upward. And certainly the adoption of slavery in the American colonies was a turning backward and downward.

Alas, we are still human, like the Romans, Greeks, and Babylonians. If our lives are improved over theirs, it is because we have built better social structures than they to guide, support, and restrain us. At the time of the American settlements, such structures had already been built in England and in most of Europe. In general, though the development varied greatly according to place and time, the European slave had become first a serf, then a peasant. But the great westward thrust of the sixteenth and seventeenth centuries was a new ball game. In the open lands of America, men began over. But not entirely, of course; this is impossible. That they have become over-individualistic, that the spirit of the wild, of limitless space, should at times have overcome them is no surprise. The lands they settled took their individualistic quality from them.

As we have already noted, the great need in the early settlements was for people to harvest the rich resources of the land. When Africans were first sold in the American colonies, in Virginia in 1619, they were doubtless sold by the Dutch captain as slaves, but were probably bought by the Virginians as indentured laborers, since it was to be more than forty years before slavery would be defined in Virginia. Slavery was, however, already endemic in Spanish and Portuguese South America.

Just as the plantation was created by the conjoined wills and efforts of American settlers and of European merchants and kingdoms, so was the slave trade developed. The Old World needed the raw products of the New. Both to increase these products and to make more money through increased transportation, Europe —especially Portugal, Holland, and England—developed the African slave trade. Further, as these countries gained in wealth, they gained in power. The ventures were not only economic; they were also political. As a consequence, the slave-operated plantations of North and South America and the Caribbean were not the business ventures of single colonials but the very heart of a vast mercantile system that extended throughout the lands bordering the Atlantic—Europe, Africa, North and South America.

Though the Southern plantation was a new creation—along with the European and South American plantations that grew up on the borders of the European economy—the introduction of slavery in support of this plantation was probably the most radical thing ever done by the North American settler (for during the Colonial period slavery was an American, not simply a Southern characteristic). During that period slavery existed in all the American colonies, though scatteringly in the North. In the sense of going backward to earlier roots, it was the most radical element of the American experiment. As far as the English were concerned—to a lesser degree as far as the Europeans were concerned—it was not a living though attenuated growth out of the immediate past, but a reaching back into a distant and already outmoded past and a dragging out of a supposedly dead element. Of course its adoption was not quite so simple as this. Slavery in North America followed in time slavery in Spanish and Portuguese South America and in the Caribbean, where the tradition of slavery still lingered from the European past. But in the English colonies of North America there was no tradition. Consequently, as we have said, it took the Virginians some fifty years after the introduction of the first Negro servants in 1619 to set forth in law the basic principles of slavery.

This radical departure from the immediate English past finally became localized in the South. By 1804 slavery had been outlawed in all the non-Southern states. The chief reason: it would not work there. There was more widespread and moral opposition to it there, but this was supported by the hard economic fact that it did not work. I do not say that in the matter of slavery there were no pure consciences in the North; I only say that most Northern consciences were impure. There were some pure consciences even in the South. For instance, toward the end of the eighteenth century, when it became apparent that the South would not abolish slavery, several Quaker groups left South Carolina for Ohio because of their objection to slavery. But the opposition of the few—those who left and those who remained—received little support from the many who benefited economically from slave labor or the many more who feared what would happen if the slaves were freed.

The striking thing about this radical backward reach into the dying world of slavery was that where it succeeded, as in the South, it carried its own conservatism with it. All the American colonies made this radical gambit. The Northern colonies dropped it because it clearly did not pay; the Southern colonies kept it because it seemed to pay. Keeping it, they had little further chance of being radical. They had tied themselves to an ancient and medieval institution unfitted for the modern world, and the longer they held it the more unfitted and unacceptable it became. From then on they would move slowly, far more slowly than their Northern counterparts, into the individualistic modern world.

As we shall see, with the apparent success and general acceptance of slavery the South felt increasingly the pull of the past, or at least of the existing situation, as against the pull of the future; the pull of place, both geographical and social, as against the pull of space; and the pull of the group as against the pull of the individual. If Americans have become over-individualistic and as a result alienated and cut off from larger social units, it must be said for the South that at least it tried, maybe most unwisely, to put off this unhappy day. When the South created the slave-operated plantation, it stopped. Centuries later, the plantation now entirely outmoded, it adopted Northern industrialism and urbanism. During the intervening centuries, however, the plantation had created the South. The tensions of the South had been centered in the plantation, operated first by Negro slaves, later by nominally free but actually bound Negro freemen.

VI

A Spacious Place

The main institutions of the South, then, were the plantation, the family, and race. But these institutions existed within space and time, and both gave to and received from space and time a certain coloring. For, though space and time are the universal accompaniments of human life, men respond to them differently, one individual or group in one way, another in another. Spengler comments upon the Faustian thrust of modern man into space, so opposed to the earlier Apollonian tendency to rest in space. Our recent moon flights are the best evidence of this.

The physical space surrounding a people, and even the quality of time—length of days and nights and seasons—affect the institutions they build, and then the institutions themselves shape the attitudes toward space and time of those who build them. I may feel that my response to space and time is my own, but it has been made my own by the people among whom I live and the institutions to which I belong.

There is no doubt that Southerners, white and black, respond distinctively to space and time. In considering the Southern view of space we shall be discussing both space itself and also that aspect or part of space referred to as *place* or *a place*. As we shall see, place has both physical and social connotations, and indeed in regard to space we can refer to vast physical spaces and to spaciousness of mind. In this study we shall ask what relation, if any, they have to one another in the South. Since the frontier has been very important in the South, we shall also consider the metaphorical racial and inner frontiers.

Let us consider first the combined effect upon the Southerner of the continuing frontier and of local places highly valued. I have entitled this chapter "A Spacious Place" in order to suggest in the Southerner a tension between interest in the spacious frontier and interest in the local, limited place.

As I have suggested, one of the basic concerns of the Southerner is his concern for place, both physical and social. First of all he wants to "place" the stranger: Where does he come from? What does he do? The second question refers to the part he plays in society: his role, his relationships. This includes his relations, his relatives, his kin. How does he belong to society? The Southerner feels he has a right to ask these questions. Beyond this he hesitates. What kind of man the stranger is, what his character is, he will have to wait and learn from experience. To some degree he feels he already knows, since he knows now where the stranger is from and something about his relations.

Allen Tate, referring to the importance of physical place in the Old South, says: "This preindustrial society meant, for people living in it, that one's identity had everything to do with land and material property, at a definite place, and very little to do with money. It was better for a person, however impoverished, of my name, to be identified with Tate's Creek Pike, in Fayette County, than to be the richest man in town without the identification of place."[1]

In this connection it is significant that the Southerner often refers to his home as "my place." He invites you to "come out to my place." Such language avoids the more intimate "home" for the more public "place." Its general use is an indication of the generally public nature of the Southerner. He establishes his identity by belonging to a place and by a place's belonging to him. In a recent book by a Southern novelist, the plantation home is called simply "The Place."

We have said that the chief places of the South were plantations. Theirs was the prestige and the power. We have not said that the far more numerous farms were unimportant. Their owners, the yeoman farmers, became increasingly important with the rising tide of democracy in the nineteenth century, and many of the effects of the Southerner's attachment to place can be seen as well among the small farmers as among the plantation owners, their families, and their dependents. The basic effect, which we shall consider later in more detail, is that by belonging to a place a man belongs not only to the other people who occupy that place and all the places around it, but also to the physical world, even to the whole expanse of nature beyond the farthest horizon, beyond sundown. He may seldom be aware of such belonging, but it gives a quality, however faint, to his nature.

We are raising here a basic question: How are men related to the natural world? For our purpose we make it more specific: If a man is deeply attached to a particular place, as the Southerner tends to be, is he also strongly attached to the extension of that place into surrounding space, that is, to space itself, as yet strange and unknown to him? Or is the opposite true—that the more deeply a man is attached to a particular place, the less interested he is in the rest of the world?

Now undoubtedly some men tend to stay at home, others to venture forth. In their thoughts some men tend to stay at home, to think conventionally, others to probe the frontiers. It is probably true that certain peoples at certain times tend to be adventurers. The Elizabethan Age has been referred to as "the spacious days of great Elizabeth"—spacious in both the outer and inner worlds.

But this does not answer our particular question. Suppose some men do prefer to remain at home, others to wander abroad. When the wanderer thinks of wandering, or actually wanders, how does he take the new land, either in imagination or in actuality? Is he a new man there, or the same man who left the old place? Or does he perhaps become a new man in the new environment?

It is clear that the new environment has some effect. As we have already shown, the new environment of America was one of the factors that rejuvenated the almost dead institution of slavery. Also, it has been remarked that in the westward movement of the plantation in the South, the code of behavior toward slaves tended to weaken, and slavery became more harsh. Frederick Jackson Turner has argued that the roots of democracy in America lie in the ever moving frontier. There has been some disagreement with this thesis, but no one has yet argued that the frontier, the open spaces, the unsettled places have no effect upon those who settle them.

Yet when the adventurer thinks of going, or when he actually goes, he carries the habits and attitudes of his life with him and tends to repeat in the new place what he has been doing in the old. If he has been primarily concerned to exploit the old, he will be primarily concerned to exploit the new. If he has cherished the old, he will cherish the new.

W. B. Yeats once remarked, "Only by the handle of the community can we pick up the world." That is to say, only as there is a human place here can we imagine and work for a human place everywhere. Émile Durkheim, seeking the origin of religion and of the sense of the sacred, says: "Extension, like duration, repeats itself indefinitely; if the portions which I touch have of themselves no sacred character, where did the others get theirs?"[2] From this point of view our dichotomy of place and space is misleading. Space is only place repeated indefinitely.

Finally, men seek only what they have found. Since life is filled with contingencies, they may find what they did not seek, but the man going out to the frontier is seeking there what he has come to value in the old place. If he values the fruits of exploitation, he will seek further exploitation; if he values the fruits of cooperation, he will seek further cooperation.

We now return to the plantation. The plantation, like any place, even the humblest clearing in the forest, was not only set in the larger and all-enveloping world of space; it was also at its best a spacious place within itself. This fusion of place and space says something about the culture of the South. Let us put aside for a little a question which has to be asked: Why did men build such spacious places at such great human cost? They did build them, of course. This means they wanted to, that such buildings, grounds, and estates satisfied some ideal. Say the worst thing first: that a part of the ideal was "conspicuous consumption," the desire to prove that one had arrived by a great spread of lawn and a high-columned piazza. Even so, this residential and landscape spaciousness both satisfied a community ideal and was beautiful in itself.

Whence came this ideal? Why, for instance, did it develop in the South and not in New England? For one thing, it suited the land—a sprawling, fertile land which, at the insistence of Europe, suggested plantations. And the great plantations suggested the plantation houses. Let us look for a moment at the lovely sprawling land.

There are glowing descriptions by promoters in England and by the Southern settlers themselves. The words of the promoters can be discounted, but even those who settled the new land described it with loving care. George Percy, remembering early Virginia, said that he "was almost ravished at the first sight" of "fair meadows and goodly tall trees with such fresh waters running through the woods."[3] In a public document much later, there is a phrase which sums up spring in the Carolina woods, with the wild flowers "perfuming the ambient air." Bishop Asbury, who rode the woods, has left loving descriptions: "Crossed Little Pee Dee at the Potato Bed Ferry. Beautiful deep sands, live oaks, lofty pines, palmetto swamps, with intermingled gums and cypress, variegated by evergreens of bay and laurel, and twining jessamine flinging its odors far and wide." Again: "Passed this day over expansive savannahs, charmingly decorated with late autumnal flowers."[4] Others wrote of the lure of the great pine forests, so open that "even small objects could be seen at a great distance, in the spring covered with grass and dotted with wild flowers," the "dark retreats and stately forests" of the historian Drayton. In his long travels William Bartram was especially impressed by these endless forests. "I soon entered a high forest, continuing the space of fifteen miles. . . . The ancient sublime forest, frequently intersected with extensive avenues, vistas and green lawns, opening to extensive savannahs and far-distant Rice plantations . . . captivates the senses by scenes of magnificence and grandeur." In what is now Alabama, Bartram entered a vast forest which continued above seventy miles, "the stately trees scatteringly planted by nature, arising straight and erect from the green carpet, embellished with varying grasses and flowering plants."[5]

Bartram noticed how the distant rice plantations fitted the picture—the extensive savannahs, vistas, and green lawns. So, in general, the Southern plantation was, like the farms, a part of the land. But only a part—not all. Much of the land even today is still woodland and swamp. In the South much of the land has never really become ours. It lies there between plantations and farms, either wild and untouched or despoiled by timbering or occasionally—and more frequently now—replanted in young trees. This wild or only partially tamed land has probably given us something of its wildness and its freedom. Even those humanly most bound, the blacks, found in the forests and swamps, in hunting and fishing, a temporary escape. That they could not escape completely from the bonds and duties of society is clear; yet there was always some hint of freedom there. I am not saying that for blacks and poor whites this made up for the restrictions they lived under; I am merely saying that this was one of the things, however slight, that gave to everyone the sense that this was his land. The feeling can be suggested by one illustration.

About 1906 my father, attempting to deal with the unsatisfactory labor situation, established on his farm a group of five or six Belgian immigrants. I shall never forget the men, dressed up on Sunday in boots and bright sashes, each carrying a shotgun, roaming the roads and woods. This was their "continental Sunday," but the striking thing from our point of view was their pleasure in carrying guns and shooting, often harmlessly, at birds and small animals, a privilege they had never had in thickly settled Europe, with its completely controlled woodlands. We in the South did not hunt on Sunday—we were not continental—but we could hunt and fish to some degree every day, and most especially on Saturday afternoon, which was everybody's day.

Whitman remarked somewhere that there seemed to be a strange kinship between the man and the land in the South, and he was thinking here, I believe, not so much of the woodlands as of the fields. But the fields in the South are usually small, the woods encroach on all sides, and the men who work the fields slip easily into the woods and back again. We are the land's to a greater degree than are most other Americans. We belong to it.

The plantations suited the sprawling land. In the same way the great plantation houses suited the great plantations. We shall see this trait of the fitting, the proper, appearing again and again in the South. It is an aesthetic element, an element heavily weighted with the public scene. Even the inner life, the life of the conscience, is often guided by a sense of the appropriate rather than a sense of the right.

As to these plantation houses and the lawns surrounding them, the question arises: To what degree were they merely the suggestion of the lovely, sprawling land, and to what degree did they express the vision of the creators themselves?

They certainly suited the land; I think we may say they also suited the natural bent of their creators. These men showed a strong tendency to accept and enjoy the world. In contrast to this, the stronger and more widespread Puritan strain in New England caused men to fear the world, to hold themselves away from it, and to use it for the glory of God. The distinction the Southern settler made between God and the world was probably more blurred; he didn't see quite so clearly God on one side and the devil on the other. The world was not so clearly and completely the home of the devil. The South was more suitable than New England for human settlement. It was more alluring. Herein lay its appeal, and herein lay its danger.

The appeal was recognized both by the Southern settlers themselves, as we have already seen, and occasionally by some of the men who settled the harsher shores of New England. In regard to the latter, David Bertelson quotes from a sermon (published in 1630) by the Reverend John White. It is a plea for the settlement of New England. Bertelson says: "This fear of a rich land is worth noting. Natural wealth ought not to constitute a danger to a people living up to their covenant obligations, but perhaps it was best not to be tempted by too great abundance."[6]

Undoubtedly, as Sellers says, the South was tempted by too great abundance, and in order to obtain this abundance more rapidly fell into the use of slave labor. But some of this abundance was spent to beautify, with house and lawn, the already attractive world—at too great human cost, of course, but the ideal was valid and to a degree Southern.

The plantation houses at their best are the clearest illustration we have that the Southern mind, in many ways strict and limited, was touched by liberality and spaciousness. For these houses and their locations were spacious places, ordered human habitations within the far-flung world. The best of them came

around 1750 in Virginia, around 1800 in Charleston, and between 1825 and 1850 in the Old Southwest. For all their splendor, they were still, at least in intention, homes, built for the
enjoyment of the world, not for its use.

Some years ago I drove across the South up into the Midwest. As we passed from Kentucky into Indiana, the farm scenes
changed. There were two marked differences: the farm houses
stood closer to the highway, and the barns were usually larger
and more pretentious than the homes. I realize that one reason
for placing the home closer to the highway in the Midwest is the
danger of being snowed in. But the Midwest was predominantly
settled by New Englanders, people with basic Puritan roots, who
by the time they moved west had become typical Yankees, and
their houses were also set close to the road in order to save land.
The large barns were built to hold the produce of that land. In
brief, the accent was upon production and a materially better
tomorrow, not upon living today. The Southern plantation
homes were built for living today.

I am aware that the majority of plantation homes were pretty
rough affairs—often log houses—and, generally speaking, the
newer the frontier, the rougher the house. Yet we judge a people
in part by their aims, not merely by their accomplishments. And
the aim of the South in this matter was beautiful homes set in
spacious grounds.

I am also aware that the number of farms was several times
the number of plantations. Yet, as we have already seen, the
plantation was the dominant ideal of the Southerner and the
main center of power within the South. The plantation house,
then, was a building set upon a hill, visible from afar. Its presence
says something about the Southern mind: a public mind, not
introspective; perhaps a showy mind, overly desirous of public
acclaim.

Finally, I am aware of the rows of slave cabins, not spacious
at all, cribbed and confined, somewhere near the Big House. This
is one of the paradoxes of the South—that the white Southerner,
keenly desirous of a spacious freedom for himself, should keep
blacks in slavery. Of course he didn't see it in quite such simple
terms as this. When he thought of it he saw it, as we shall have

occasion to consider further, as part of a hierarchical system in which every man had his place.

In the beginning, of course, even the Seaboard settlements lay on the frontier, and the hunters, trappers, and explorers who ventured westward into the endless forest were the frontiersmen of their day. These men moved as fast as, if not faster than, their Northern counterparts. As I wrote in an earlier study, "Even New York's 'bush runners' did not rival as explorers the Charles Town men, who, within a dozen years, were trading along the Coosa, seven hundred miles to the west, and, by 1705 [thirty-five years after Charles Town had been settled], had reached and crossed the Mississippi."[7]

Perhaps the sense of the frontier was strongest in the early days of the province of South Carolina. Indeed, that province was so important as a frontier that it came to be called the Southern Frontier—the frontier of England against France and especially Spain. The most dangerous war these colonists fought was the Yamasee War in 1715, a war with the Yamasee Indians fomented by Spain. The Carolinians were in desperate straits for a while, in danger of being swept into the Atlantic, pleading vainly for aid from England and from the other colonies. It has been suggested that this early experience as an outpost of empire helped to mark the character of the people with extreme independence and self-reliance. In 1733 the colony of Georgia was settled under the direction of Oglethorpe, in part to act as a buffer state between South Carolina and the Spanish.

It was not until after the Revolution that the settlers of the Atlantic Seaboard began to move in great numbers across the Appalachians into the great central valley. For the most part they had been restrained by edicts from Britain, the purpose of which had been to keep the settlers localized for better control and also to avoid conflict with France and Spain, who still owned most of the Mississippi Valley. With British control thrown off, the settlers poured in almost continuous streams westward across the Appalachians into the receding frontier.

But the westward trek in the South was considerably different from the same trek in the North, and this difference deepened the original difference between the Southern and the Northern settlers. As New Englanders moved west, they tended to move as communities, taking their towns with them. From these centers roads ran out into the surrounding countryside, the roads from one town usually meeting those from other towns. As a result, the frontier was rather effectively pushed ahead of western migration in the North.

In the South, by contrast, not towns but plantations and farms moved westward; and, as a rule, lying between these plantations and farms were forests and swamps, sometimes in fairly narrow strips, sometimes many miles deep. "As farmers and planters moved further into the Southwest," says Thompson, "their farms and plantations appeared as small clearings widely separated from each other by the forest. In the South, as in other plantation areas in the world, tales of wild beasts and wild game hunting form a substantial part of the lore of settlement and planting."[8] Almost always, therefore, the tame was surrounded by the wild, the place set in untamed space.

This is true in much of the South even today. Partridges still use under my study windows, and despite the dogs, an antlered buck sometimes walks across the yard. Yet the fields adjacent to this house may have been cleared as early as the 1750's, and the house itself was built in 1860.

Southerners, remaining during most of their history predominantly farmers, are naturally more aware of space than the predominantly urban and industrial dwellers of the North. Factories and cities also occupy space, but more narrowly and less significantly than do farms, for it is from space itself that comes much of the creative energy of the farm—the passing clouds, the far-driven rain, and the infinitely farther-driven sunlight.

The effect of the juxtaposition of the tame and the wild was a certain degree of order, balance, or moderation in the life of the Southerner. It is well to note this, since the Southerner is by reputation impulsive and disorderly. He may in part deserve this reputation, but the picture is overblown.

Wildness and tameness are closely interwoven in the Southerner—and gentleness and cruelty, the paradox Paul Green remarks. Indeed, as we shall see, the Southerner is a mass of paradoxes. W. J. Cash emphasized this in *The Mind of the South*. But paradoxes are apparent opposites that rest, however deeply, upon some unity. Institutionally the basic unity was the plantation, enriched by the extended family and endangered, though also made possible, by slavery.

Yet the plantation, as we shall see again when we come to discuss the Southerner's feeling for time, was divided from the beginning. It dragged up out of the rather distant past an outmoded form of labor, tried to dignify it by faint connotations of patriarchalism and feudalism, but generally used it like the mass labor of the dawning industrial world. Here in its central institution is the conflict that finally brought the South down in defeat.

From the point of view of the European market, the plantation, in the South the main center of order, was itself a frontier institution, lying along the far frontiers of that market and serving as organizing centers for those frontiers. And indeed, as we noted in speaking of the plantation houses, only a few of these houses were magnificent; many of them were rough log structures, treated at the same time as dwelling places and storage rooms, with saddles and other farm equipment thrown down in the halls or on the piazzas. I recall that even the plantation house I now occupy, built in 1860 on a rather spacious scale, in the 1920's had one room filled with wheat spread across the floor and another with salt pork. The salt marks still stain the floor. The tenant was only putting the house to normal plantation uses.

With the passage of time and with the westward movement of the plantation, this sense of belonging lost some of its richness and complexity and tended to become more a matter of legal relationships and sheer physical force. In other words, the trek of the plantation westward was a trek from a complex social organization toward a more individualistic enterprise. The early plantations of Virginia and the Carolinas were, from the point of view of Europe, frontier institutions; in like manner, the later plantations of the Old Southwest were, from the point of view of Virginia and Carolina, frontier institutions. Life was less settled, less conventional, less restrained there. There was more individualism, more sheer drive. In a sense there was a greater, though not necessarily better, freedom for the whites, a harsher slavery for the blacks. Such order as existed, therefore, became increasingly a compelled rather than an accepted order. That inner authority which had developed in the Atlantic Seaboard plantations never had the time to develop in the plantations of the Old Southwest.

Perhaps there was too much space in the Old Southwest for the settled places to control, and too little time to do it in. The wild, the individualistic, was too strong for the settled order. There was too much wildness, too deep a frontier. The Southerner from the beginning had, to his credit, accepted nature, but he had accepted it too easily and had been seduced by it. The wildness of the natural world had joined the wildness of the human spirit, and he had been led further and further astray. He was of course only following the individualistic lead of his fellow Americans. They had driven even more directly from the structured past into the atomic future. The tragedy of the Southerner was that the structure he tried to carry into the future, at its best hierarchy, at its worst chattel slavery, found itself in head-on conflict not only with the increasingly egalitarian tendency of the modern world, but also with that very tendency in himself as a modern man. In the long run he defeated himself.

We have spoken mainly of the plantation as the locus of the space-place influence in the life of the South, and have called it a spacious place. A few words should be said in this connection about the far more numerous farms. Since the places that were farms were less extensive and usually less developed than the places that were plantations, it is safe to say that they were influenced by the space surrounding them much more than the plantations were. The plantation had more of the settled, more of the order and assurance of the settled, and less of the disorder of the wild. The farm was closer to the wild, more subject to it, in more danger from it. With fewer resources, it collapsed more easily, passing perhaps into the hands of a neighboring plantation owner or lapsing back into native forest.

Yet if the farm was in more danger from the surrounding natural world than the plantation was—because the farm was more closely limited by that world—the farmer himself generally received more strength from that world than did the neighboring

planter. Nature, the farmer's more immediate enemy, was also
his more immediate friend. He could be more easily wiped out
by nature, but when he succeeded it was clearer to him that
nature had brought success. The planter was especially unfortunate here, for he had set between himself and the creative earth
another and to a degree always foreign race who suffered the heat
of the sun but gained the strength of the earth. He was too
involved in the settled plantation itself, in maintaining and ex-
tending that settlement, to be as aware as he might have been of
the wild spaces from which he had carved his little kingdom. So,
though holding the most spacious place in the South, it is doubtful that he usually possessed as strong a sense of the power of the
wild as did the yeoman farmers and even the slaves.

It is undoubtedly true that the sectional quarrel that led up
to the Civil War, the long and bitter war itself, and the resultant
defeat deepened to a tremendous degree the white Southerner's
concern both for the Southern region and for the lost social order
destroyed by the war—concern not necessarily for slavery itself,
but for a conservative order, at its strongest for an unchanged
order. As a result of this traumatic experience, the emotion that
had been generated in the defense of the South as a whole flowed
backward to bathe in emotion the most secluded places in the
South. As has been said, the South, which lasted as a nation for
only four short years and which died at Appomattox, was immediately resurrected as a dream. This regional dream then colored
every place within the region.

It is this rootedness of the Southerner, this attachment to
earth, to things, to places, and to a living institution like the
family, that is important. Like the New Englander, the Southerner also was driven by the modern, individualistic thrust into
the future and into the frontier—more into space, however, than
into the future, more into the physical world than into the ideal.
Though by driving westward he changed scenes fairly rapidly, he
changed but slowly the institutions he established within those
scenes. We have noticed that in adopting slavery he had adopted
an institution insusceptible to radical change. So, carrying more
of the past with him, he moved more slowly along the individualistic path of modern man. At the time of the first settlements, the

difference between Northern and Southern settlers may have seemed slight indeed, but within two hundred and fifty years the Southern culture had become the most distinct variant of American culture.

To summarize the main points of this chapter, it appears that Southerners have come to the feeling that they belong to the South through an unusually strong sense of place, both geographical and social, mainly because of the existence of the powerful and prestigious plantation. But since the plantation existed along the unsettled frontiers of both the receding west and the continuing local forests and swamps, this sense of place has been to a degree balanced by a sense of the natural frontier, untamed and strange. However, though the Southerner was bound to a place through the presence of a strong institution, he was bound to space only through fleeting intuitions not clearly localized in any institution. He was bound to a place through a social institution, to space only as an individual. A proper church would have institutionalized this bond. As we shall see, the predominant church, the Protestant, did little more than place him as an individual alone before the immensities.

VII

The Racial Frontier

Not only has the South been more influenced by the physical
frontier than the North; it has also been influenced by the presence of a racial frontier. Of course the term is figurative. You
could see, roughly, where the physical frontier began; the racial
frontier was everywhere, wherever a black man was, or from the
black's point of view, wherever a white man was. For each
thought the other, because of his race, to some degree strange,
unknown, unpredictable. "That's just like a nigger," said the
white, uncomprehending. "White folks is white folks," said the
black, shaking his head.

There was another important racial frontier which the white
settler faced: the Indian. But this was the same, both North and
South, and the effects were the same. Furthermore, the effect of
the Indian frontier upon the American settler was much simpler
than the effect of the Negro frontier upon the Southern settler.
This was due primarily to the fact that the Indian frontier usually
coincided with the physical frontier and was not distributed, as
was the Negro frontier, among settled communities of whites.
Certainly the presence of the Indian along the physical frontiers
of America shaped the thinking and the characters of the white
settlers. The whites adopted a great many articles of food and the
general method of warfare from the Indians. Furthermore, they
were aided in forming a fixed opinion of the red man by two
things. First, the Indian was a fighter and resisted the encroach-
ment of the whites with the same tenacity they showed in their
westward advance. As fighters, therefore, they understood and to
a greater or lesser degree respected one another. In the second
place, at least some whites had a theory about the Indian which
helped to humanize him: the theory of the noble red man.

Granted that the actual settlers didn't think much of this, it was nevertheless a part of the total estimate white Americans and Europeans made of the Indian.

I mention the Indian here because these humanizing influences did not exist along the white-black frontier. For the most part, the black accepted the role of worker, even of enslaved worker, and seldom appeared as fighter. Furthermore, the blacks in Africa had long existed along the borders of European consciousness and were therefore connected in European thought with the corruptions of the Old World. This ill opinion was intensified by the fact that the Moors of North Africa were infidels, and therefore the Negroes to the south of them were regarded with suspicion. The infidels had had Christianity presented to them and had turned against it. Therefore no treatment of them was too harsh.

In brief, the red man was ennobled by European thought, the black demeaned. But though the African blacks were known to Europeans before the American red men were, they were but poorly known, and it was in part their imagined infidelity that permitted Europeans to enslave them, and Americans to justify keeping them in slavery. As an aid to American settlement in the seventeenth century, whites were willing to buy and sell indentured whites and to be bought and sold as indentured whites; they were not willing to buy and sell enslaved whites. Always, of course, men can treat those they do not know, those with whom they find it hard to identify, more harshly than those they do know. To a large degree in white and black relationships in the United States, the whites have been not only ignorant of the blacks but willfully ignorant. The ignorance the exploiter has of the exploited is an important factor in exploitation.

But now let us move to the more complex problem of the effect of the black racial frontier upon the whites who lived along it. I shall largely omit consideration of the white race as a frontier to the black race. It is clear that to some degree whites remained strange to blacks, but several things suggest that they did not remain as strange as blacks did to whites. First, the blacks in their situation simply had to know whites better than the whites had to know them. Second, the culture of the whites, in its superior position, naturally impressed itself more upon the blacks with their divided cultures than did the black culture upon the whites. The blacks were the strangers, the whites the home folks within whose country the blacks had been forcibly settled. This does not deny the general fact that along the racial frontier the white and the black cultures met and mingled in many and often indefinable ways. Whatever weight we give to the contribution of each group, it is my opinion that the present culture of the South can be explained only as a fusion of two very dissimilar cultures. The Southerner is the creation of both groups. But I think the more important and the more complex problem is just how the presence of the black frontier affected the white Southerner.

Even the geographical placing of blacks in Southern communities suggests the frontier. This was true to some degree during slavery; the blacks lived together on the plantation "street." It is even truer if we consider the recent past, when the blacks lived in a certain section of town, usually along the outskirts. The effect of this is especially clear in Southern fiction. The black community is often described as a shadow which surrounds the white community or lies over against one side of it. Sometimes it is seen as merging with the nearby forests or swamps. Lillian Smith, in *Strange Fruit*, even equates the willful ignorance of white women about the relation of their men to black women with the darkness of the surrounding swamps and the coldness of swamp water.

The racial frontier was thus tied to the physical frontier. The strangeness of the blacks, their supposed savagery, their wildness, their dark color, carried extra weight because of the cold, dark woods along whose borders they were seen and into which they sometimes slipped in flight.

To the same degree that blacks formed for whites a racial frontier, whites acted toward blacks as men act toward any frontier: They attempt to bring it under control and keep it so, and finally to settle it and humanize it, to make it a part of the settled, organized country. So, in the early days of black slavery in America, whites kept blacks under control by sheer force. There was little restraint in the use of this force, little limitation upon the freedom of action of the whites except such constraints as any frontier exerts upon the would-be settler: to be wary, to move cautiously, to be continuously aware of the power of the frontier to destroy, either with a sudden blow or with long-continued insidious pressure.

Perhaps this is the place to comment briefly upon the paradoxical presence of freedom and slavery side by side in America. It was often remarked by antebellum visitors to the South that the most passionate defenders of freedom among the Americans were the Southern whites. It has been suggested that this happened because the absence of freedom was clearly evident in the lives of the slaves, and this evidence intensified the determination of the freeman, the white, to remain free. But there is a stronger reason than this.

To some degree the freedom of the white produced the slavery of the black. In the new frontier lands of the Americas, European settlers reverted to the largely outmoded pattern of slavery. First, there was the need for labor to subdue these vast, wild lands, a need unmet by the accepted system of indentured labor. Second, and more important in the present analysis, there was the loss of restraints involved in the movement from the old, settled, and ordered society of Europe to the unordered frontier. Released from these constraints, men became both better and worse. For this is what freedom is: the possibility of becoming better or worse. The Puritans were sure that life was better in the New World than in the Old, closer to the hoped-for kingdom of God; the non-Puritans felt it was better here because of the increased chance of a wider, richer life. But whether it was better or not, and if better, how much better, depended upon the way the settlers used their new freedom. And when freedom from the constraints of Europe resulted in chattel slavery, it was worse—clearly worse for the enslaved blacks, and in the long run worse for whites and blacks together.

So, in the early days of American slavery and along the geographical frontiers of its later days, the racial frontier was distinct, and slaves were treated as men always treat a frontier—with the maximum of force and the minimum of persuasion. But, just as men settle geographical frontiers, so whites "settled," to a degree, the racial frontier. And to the degree that this frontier was settled, blacks were brought into the total community and became a part, though never a completely integrated part, of that community. As this happened persuasion was substituted for sheer force, though force always lay in the background. This was most clearly seen in the establishment of many a yeoman farmer —where there was only one slave or only one slave family, and where the blacks and the whites worked and to a degree lived side by side—and in the house servants and artisans of the plantations.

This softening of the conventions without abolishing the basic fact of slavery, this degree of "settlement" of the racial frontier, is clearly seen in the contrast between the more persuasive race relations that developed along the Atlantic Seaboard and the more direct, forceful relations of the Old Southwest— and indeed, between the race relations of these two regions today. David B. Davis points out a paradox here. For instance, in South Carolina, though the laws regarding slaves became increasingly strict from the settlement of the province to the Civil War, they also showed an increasing concern for the life and welfare of the slave. The growing Northern opposition to slavery was the main factor in increasing the strictness of the laws; the growing humanitarianism of the eighteenth and nineteenth centuries, together with the increasing understanding between whites and blacks, was the main factor in bringing about a greater concern for the life and welfare of the slave. In brief, the passage of time itself, especially the passage of the eighteenth and nineteenth centuries, "settled" to some degree the racial frontier.

The whites also brought the blacks into a more human, though not democratic, relationship by developing the myth of the black as an irresponsible but affectionate child. This myth was developed out of the actual association of blacks and whites upon the plantations (where the blacks were irresponsible mainly because the whites refused them responsibility), upon the rather close association of white and black children, and upon the close association of whites with black house servants and to a lesser degree with black artisans.

This myth of black childlikeness, however, was always balanced by the myth of black savagery. This stressed the wild frontier nature of the black race as opposed to the white. These two myths came into sharp prominence in the decades immediately preceding the Civil War. The fact that white Southerners could hold two such opposing beliefs at the same time indicates how divided the mind of the South really was, even during the period when it was concentrating its strength for conflict with the North.

It may seem that this balancing of the wild against the tame in the white man's estimate of the black man is an illustration of that proper tension between the wild and the tame which should exist in every human being. This is not so. In the individual, the proper tension rests upon a balancing of freedom of impulse against social order, social constraint, and rationality. In a sense, of course, the depths of a man's nature are a frontier even to himself, the abode of possibilities, creative and destructive, as we are well aware since Freud. If this is true of the white man, it is also true of the black. But this was by no means the frontier the whites saw within the blacks. The frontier they saw was simply an animal or savage frontier, comparable in its dangers to the physical frontier. They did not value the blacks because they too possessed within themselves untold, uncharted wilds; they feared them because of their superficial strangeness, a strangeness which the whites often refused to understand in order that they might hide from their own eyes their exploitative activity.

Yet for all the evils that the continuance of the racial frontier produced, it is almost certainly true that some good resulted. It is the good produced by the presence of any frontier. This is the ever renewed sense of the strangeness, the wildness, the incompleteness of life, a sense which the modern industrial world has almost eliminated. For the modern industrial world is based upon at least a superficial rationality, upon order, upon everything and everybody being shaped to fit into its or his appointed slot. There can be no room for strangeness, for uncertainty. Such attitudes would upset the machine. It is true that we still have strangeness and uncertainty in astronautical explorations, but only a few can actually participate in these, and because of the expense involved, no room can be allowed for chance. A few men adventure to the moon, but the adventure is computerized for every foot and second. The extreme interest of the man in the street in the first adventure along this new frontier suggests that he is bored with the dull sameness, the entirely settled condition of his daily life.

The racial frontier in the South, ever present everywhere, has helped to maintain in Southerners a sense of the strangeness of life. It has been an abiding element of disorder in the South, and its presence has continually pricked the consciousness of the South with the faint persistent question: What gives?

As the chief laboring group of the South, the blacks were most important in driving back the physical frontier, and, of equal importance, they became to the whites, as we have said, a sort of buffer between themselves and the earth, shielding the whites from the harshness of earth—"the heat o' the sun" and "the winter's furious rages"—but also cutting them off from the strength of the earth. Of course there was no such immediate effect upon the great majority of non-slave-owning Southerners. Actually, they were not cut off from the earth; ideally, to some degree they were. For, since slaves were the chief manual workers, manual work itself gained a bad name; and since most work had to do with the earth, there arose a kind of mental bar between the worker and the earth. This was intensified by the fact that most yeoman farmers looked forward to becoming plantation owners and so getting rid of the manual work.

Making the necessary allowances, then, it does seem that one unfortunate effect of slavery upon the white has been to cut him off, more or less, from the earth. But to the degree that the black cut the white off from earth, the black himself took on some of the attributes of earth—its mystery, its tenderness, its fierceness, even its darkness. This strengthened the myth of the combined childlikeness and savagery of the black. Thus taking on the mystery of deep forests and dark earth, the black began to symbolize the mystery of life itself, at its worst a bottomless abyss bridged only by faith.

For just as the black was for the white a buffer against the earth, so he was more fundamentally a buffer against the Abyss. Whenever the white looks down, says James Baldwin, he sees the black. This helps him to forget the Abyss underlying all. It is for this reason that the white fights so desperately to keep the black in his place. If ever he should stand beside the white, the white looking down would see only the Abyss.

But since he is, by both the white's experience and the white myth, also gentle, so to the Abyss itself there accrues at times some quality of tenderness. So the black, forced by the white into a racial frontier, has in this situation prevented the white from facing honestly the Abyss, yet has kept him from ever forgetting it. He has blurred the white man's mind but kept his spirit troubled.

VIII

The Inner Frontier

To think of the frontier is to think of freedom. Even the shallow frontiers of woods and swamps which have typically separated Southern farms and plantations have given a degree of freedom to the inhabitants: freedom from routine work through hunting and fishing and, occasionally in antebellum days, freedom for the slaves to escape. As for the western frontier, the freedom it offered drew men westward for two entire centuries.

When men move to a frontier, they shake off many of the restraints of a settled society, carrying with them only such as have become habitual. For a while, then, they act largely under the physical restraints which the frontier itself imposes, until the new land has been settled and they have been settled in it.

Throughout most of its history the South—indeed, the American nation—has had an open frontier, that is, a frontier on the far side of which lie generally open lands waiting to be taken, not another nation matching in power the one on the near side. It is true that the Indian "nations" lay along our western frontier, but they only slowed down the advance of the far more numerous and better equipped settlers. This suggests the nature of frontier freedom. It tends to be a freedom to take, an individualistic freedom, and in the westward advance of the European settlers in America, a nationalistic freedom. However, this freedom to take—from the Indians and to a degree from other settlers—was in part balanced by the need for considerable cooperation among the new settlers in an untamed land.

The numerous local frontiers that lay along the farms and plantations of the South—the woods shallow or deep and the deep swamps—had little effect in creating an undue individualism, a freedom from social restraint for selfish advancement.

Their expanses, their shadowy strange places, simply lessened for a while in those who explored them the weariness and boredom of work. Their presence has added to the playfulness of the Southerner, his inability to take work entirely seriously, and his tendency to be easily diverted from the basic issues—especially when the basic issue, race, seems to lie beyond solution.

Throughout its history the South has had frontiers of both kinds. It has been a land with a free western frontier—like the rest of the country—and with semi-free local frontiers. Has the effect of these frontiers been liberalizing upon the people? Are Southerners a liberal people?

Politically, no. Though we have certain liberal tendencies, we are predominantly conservative. But there have been times of great liberalism, the most striking of which was during the founding of the Republic. However strange it may seem, and however limited it was with the Negro still a slave, it existed among the great Southerners who helped found the nation. Clement Eaton traces its career in his book *Freedom of Thought in the Old South.* It also existed among certain slave owners who, long before the Revolution had identified freedom with patriotism, freed their slaves because of their eighteenth-century sense of human dignity. This liberalism began to fade with the revolt of Nat Turner in 1831 and received its last formal antebellum defense in the debates of the Virginia House of Delegates in 1831–32. Following that, with the sharpened attacks on slavery and its more passionate defense, it disappeared. It reappeared, however, a hundred years later in the handling of international problems incident to World War II but was again eclipsed, this time by the rise of the race issue to national prominence.

I am less concerned with the presence of political liberalism in the South than with an inner liberalism, a freedom of the spirit, an expansive inner landscape which might resemble somewhat the outer landscape of the South. The people who built the expansive plantation houses and gardens of the region must have had such a sense. For these homes do match the quiet rivers on whose banks they often stand or the rolling landscape which often stretches away from their doors. It isn't possible, of course, to distinguish in the minds of the builders the interest in beauty from the desire for "conspicuous consumption." But if conspicuous consumption was present—as doubtless it often was—even this indicates public approval of architectural spaciousness.

Most of the spacious homes of the Southeast were built during the eighteenth century, the century of liberalism. The lines tightened in the more materialistic nineteenth century, in the South as elsewhere. The invention of the cotton gin helped to turn men's minds away from present enjoyment toward future attainment. This statement seems to be contradicted by the fact that the great houses along the Mississippi River were built during the nineteenth century, but they couldn't have been built earlier since the region hadn't been settled yet. When they were built, it was out of tremendous wealth newly won and insecurely held. This accounts in part for their showiness, in contrast with the usually more sedate beauty of the earlier Atlantic Seaboard houses.

It is probably significant that, showy or not, these homes continued to be built as long as they were. Paul Zweig, in discussing the decline in private architecture since the eighteenth century, points out that "the growth of the state and the increasing centralization of power since that time have been accompanied by a marked decline in the standards of private architecture, as if the wealthy had begun to sense the public irrelevance of their fortunes when faced with the hugeness of national politics."[1]

The centralization of the state was slowed down in America by the federal principle, and the South was the chief proponent of this principle. Therefore the sense of private strength vis-à-vis the state lingered longer in America, especially in the South, and this sense expressed itself naturally in great private houses.

However spacious or narrow the minds of the men who built these houses, there is still truth in the remark once made to me by a Southerner of only slight education: "I think Southerners are a tolerant people." I would agree—outside the race issue. But then, it's almost impossible to get outside that. As I understood my acquaintance, he meant that Southerners are fairly easygoing; they put up with all kinds of people and conditions, accepting even uncongeniality as part of the whole of life. There are many grotesques in the South, many "characters." Maybe the strain of life here has produced them, but the liberal spirit of the South accepts them.

Yet, even while making this defense, I feel there is a great lack of inner freedom, of liberalism, of broad inner landscapes in the South. Perhaps the outer landscape is not the essential thing. Though the inner landscape is affected by the outer—a too limited physical environment resulting in increased aggression or a spacious physical environment giving some sense of freedom to those who inhabit it—the inner landscape is not controlled by the physical landscape. "The heart alone makes nature live." There is a beautiful illustration of this in Maupassant's "Two Little Soldiers." Luc and Jean, on their regular Sunday walk, become friendly with a peasant girl who passes by their picnic spot to milk and feed her cow. At first, when the three were just friends, upon parting, "as long as they could see her at all, they followed with their eyes her tall silhouette, which faded, growing smaller and smaller, seeming to sink into the verdure of the fields." Later, when Luc and the girl had become lovers and had gone into the woods, "Jean saw nothing but the wall of leaves where they had entered." When they had all been one, she had seemed "to sink into the verdure of the fields"; when passionate love had disrupted the friendship, the woods seemed to the rejected Jean "a wall of leaves." With the social landscape altered, the physical landscape altered to match it.

The character of the inner landscape, harsh or bland, tends to repeat the quality of the social landscape. For it is the spirit of those who live there that creates the social world and is then shaped by the world it has created. If there are chasms, faults, obstructions in the social world, there will be similar chasms, faults, obstructions in the inner world. To the degree that freedom is absent from the outer world, freedom will be absent from the inner world. In brief, social and personal landscapes are mirror images of each other.

There was certainly a great lack of freedom in the outer world of the South. This affected the Negro primarily but everybody secondarily. Booker T. Washington summed it up: "You can't keep a man down in a ditch without staying there with him." The master, in order to remain so, becomes the slave of the slave.

He has a physical freedom the slave lacks, a freedom to move at will and the social freedom to advance in position. He is bound mentally, however, by the necessity to move always with caution and only after careful consideration of the effect of such a move upon the slave. He cannot move freely and adventurously even in the world of thought, for thought may lead to action, and even before action it may result in a loss of confidence in the social order and the crumbling of that order from inner weakness. The South feared the abolitionist not so much because he might arouse the slave as because he might subvert the slave owner.

The Civil War and the Emancipation Proclamation freed neither the Negro nor the white from this inner slavery. Emerson said—and he was speaking in general, not about the South—"if there is one thing you can't think about, you can't really think about anything." Thought is like this. It passes rapidly across frontiers and quickly finds itself in strange, prohibited regions. Eudora Welty seems to be saying that the white Southerner cannot think deeply because he soon runs head-on into the problem of the black, a problem which, in order to avoid thinking about it, he has usually told himself is insoluble. It was practically insoluble even to an objective thinker like Jefferson, and the more the slave system was woven into the fabric of Southern life, the more insoluble it appeared. Faulkner has one of his characters, V. K. Ratliff, remark, "Thank God men have done learned how to forget quick what they ain't brave enough to try to cure."

The truth is, there has been little of the frontier in Southern thinking, little of the adventure of the mind, little of the excitement that comes with pursuing ideas wherever they may lead, across what frontiers, into what strange lands. The South produced no Jonathan Edwards, no great poets except Poe—who was Southern mainly in being a romantic. It has, however, produced in the last generation a group of imaginative writers in poetry and prose, all poets in spirit, who can compete with other Americans, but this has come when the South is in rapid change, racially and economically, when the physical frontier is in one sense gone and the racial frontier, at least the frontier the whites made, is rapidly going. The blacks are now making their own racial frontier, and we have yet to see what this will do to us.

Neither has the South produced any great prophetic preachers, men who explored fearlessly man's relation to God. It has produced some great defenders of the Southern way of life, but these men were priests rather than prophets, their church the South and their religion the Southern way of life. They were essentially politicians, not preachers.

We have produced great politicians and some great statesmen, and this is significant. For their function has been not to probe the inner landscape of the mind—reaching out to the frontier of the inscape, seeking new meanings—but to defend as best they could the outer world, its institutions and its people.

To say there has been little depth in the Southern mind, little sense of far frontiers (or, as Frost said, of "a further range," beyond even the snowcapped Himalayas), is another way of saying there is a lack of a sense of distance. And this is a little strange since the South itself has always been actually spacious, always marked by its near and far frontiers. What is the reason for this?

Antoine de Saint-Exupéry, the famous French flyer, who was lost in the last days of World War II, puts his finger on the trouble. Love, he says, creates the sense of distance, of danger, depth, perspective. Consider the parent and the child. The child may still be safe at home, but the parent in his love often imagines him as already out in the world, far from home, subject to all the chances and the dangers of life, where even well-intentioned friends may destroy, and innocence is no sure protection. Was not the Norse hero Balder killed by a sprig of mistletoe? "A pity beyond all telling," says Yeats, "is hid in the heart of love"; even the clouds, the winds, the shadowy hazel grove "threaten the head that I love." To love, said Unamuno, is to pity.

The world of love is a world in depth with perspectives, a three-dimensional world with powers and forces of its own, into which the loved one goes and where he may be saved or destroyed by these forces. The world without love is flat, without depth, as is the inner life of the person who sees it without love.

Spaciousness comes with love. It is the love of the tame and known that creates the love of the unknown and wild, the love of the near that creates the love of the far. How can one be indeed far unless he be near? This is but the other side of Kahlil Gibran's question, "How can one be indeed near unless he be far?" Within the microscope lie the mirror images of distant constellations. At its nearest as at its farthest, everything is strange, and it is love that makes it so.

Of course no one sees the world without any love or with complete love. At any moment, in any situation, there is more or less love. All we can say here is that the South needed more love than it had (which would have meant less fear), and that this is proved by the fact that its inner world was shallow and but slightly touched by the lure of frontiers.

This is ironic because the South has talked more about love than any other American region—to some degree illustrated it more. Love of family, love of place, love of land. The talk, of course, was motivated in part by the lack of justice in race relations and indicated an attempt to substitute love for justice, an attempt which inevitably produced a vast sentimentality. But what shall we say of the honest love for family, for place, for land? Why did it not produce its proper sense of distance, of depth, of inner perspective?

The answer seems to be that it was not enough. The complete explanation of this cannot be attempted here. Briefly, the South was too fearful because of the racial frontier it faced with primary intent to expand, because of the exploitative lure of its physical frontiers, and, in the last hundred and fifty years, because of national interference, to develop freely the ties with people and places it was naturally disposed to develop. The exploitative thrust outward and forward, and, more recently, the defensive clinging to what we had, was not balanced by a true and loving knowledge of ourselves, our people, and our land.

The Southerner, at least the white Southerner, has gained the reputation of being a free individual, caring little for others, adventurous, even roistering. This is more an appearance than a reality. In reality he tends to be highly social and conventional. As we have been saying, he is distinctly not a frontiersman in his inner life, and one reason is that he has generally accepted the racial frontier. Having accepted this, he cannot plunge deep inward to ask what it means. Partly, then, because his inward adventure is so limited, he may engage in forms of outward adventure to compensate for the loss, developing his own likes and dislikes, apparently without regard to his neighbors. But this is in part to help him forget that he has sold his inner freedom to the neighbors.

Only in part, however. There is, as we have said, a looseness of social structure in the South and a basic interest in people that supports a rather large tolerance of differences. The Southerner is an individualist partly because he wants to be, partly because he has to be to let off the steam built up within his highly directed inner life. The lack of inner frontiers may drive men to probe outer frontiers.

I have gone along with my own argument so far, but with increasing uneasiness. For I have argued myself into the position of at least implying that there was a deeper inner landscape outside the South than within it and that this was the product of the deeper, truer love of non-Southerners. I can't quite swallow this. For it is the typical American—and modern—thrust of the non-Southerner which has put men on the moon—of which I do not disapprove—and has also killed hundreds of thousands of men in South Vietnam—of which I do disapprove. I can see little of love either in the situation in Vietnam or in the ghettos.

But if the sense of distance is essentially the creation of love, what shall we say of the infinite distance conceived by modern astronomers and now in the process of being conquered by modern explorers, or of the opposing infinitesimal distances imagined in the structure of the atom and our command of those distances, to compress or explode them?

Let us admit that the scientists were, with considerable wholeheartedness, pursuing objective truth, following "knowledge like a sinking star/ Beyond the utmost bounds of human thought." Let us admit that at least the greatest of them were primarily concerned to understand the world, not to manipulate it. But within the last twenty years many of them, recognizing what pain and fear the knowledge of atomic fission and fusion has brought upon the world, have regretted that they were not more completely human in the explorations, more widely concerned with men and women and their hopes and fears, less purely concerned with simple physical facts.

With accelerating speed we are approaching infinite and infinitesimal distances because we have deliberately jettisoned the human cargo—man with his hopes and fears—and carry with us only our computerized brains. And this is the result of free, untrammeled, unrestrained thought. We have now reached infinite and infinitesimal distances and depths, and our hearts cry out to our brains, like Shakespeare's Capulet to his wife, "Take me with you, take me with you, wife," but in vain; our computerized brains make no reply.

If the brain is freed from the burden of the heart, it may take us beyond the farthest physical horizons, but these will not be the distances created by love. For the brain analyzes, abstracts, separates things from one another and man from man. This is mainly what the modern, the liberal brain has done, so that now men tend to be atoms united only in masses and by the law of averages. The freedom the brain brings is chiefly freedom *from,* the loosening of old bonds, and this is what the modern world has been most concerned with. Only the heart can bring freedom *in* —in synthesis, in union, in a social order. The brain primarily knows disentanglement, the heart entanglement—at worst destructive, at best life-bringing. The brain knows freedom in the usual sense; the heart knows belonging, another and an almost forgotten kind of freedom.

If we are going to understand the South, we shall have to assume that in spite of the relative lack of critical thought in the South, there has been a kind of thinking here, a thinking more of the heart, a grammar of sentiments expressed better by the term *meditating* or *musing* or even *brooding.*

In this connection Allen Tate remarks, "If I may bring to bear upon [the Southern mind] an up-to-date and un-Southern adjective, it was an extroverted mind not much given to introspection. (I do not say meditation, which is something quite different.)"[2] Tate doesn't say what he thinks meditation is. Whatever it is, I think it is close to the best action of the Southern mind.

There's the story of the farmer—he must have been a Southerner—seated on a rail fence, gazing off into the distance. When asked what he was thinking about, he replied that he didn't know;

his mind was "way over in Jehovy." It is possible that even without knowing it he was musing, feeling his way into the total
scheme of things.

A man thinks *about* things. One of his main purposes is to
shift these things into a more satisfactory arrangement. He muses
or meditates, certainly he broods *over* things, not primarily to
shift them about, but rather to get the total feel of them and let
them change somewhat as they wish, even though the changing
may change him who observes it. The term *brood* suggests it best.
The intention, seldom clearly realized, is to let things hatch out,
take on added meaning in themselves and in the heart of the
brooder.

To the typical thinker this is a poor sort of mental exercise.
It doesn't seem to get you anywhere, and it seems lazy. It probably is lazy—the most fundamental form of Southern laziness. But
by and large it holds the world together instead of splitting it into
fragments. Fragmented modern man has thought too much
about and brooded too little over the world he is fragmenting.

This musing upon things, this meditation, this brooding is
a form of love; as we know things better, we love them more, and
as we love them more, we know them better. We said earlier that
there has not been enough love in the South; we say this again.
A part of the trouble was the relative strength of the individualistic, competitive, materialistic spirit that marked the South as it
did the rest of the nation—though far less the South than the
North.

There was a part of the South, one aspect of its spirit, that
found it more important to belong to society than to be freed
from it, that exercised itself in meditation, in musing, in brooding. In so doing, it grew to understand and value increasingly the
order to which it belonged.

The South was not as stripped down as the North for
spiritual and material achievement. The South still encumbered
itself with relatively non-utilitarian attitudes and institutions. The
physical was not stripped of its spiritual meaning nor the spiritual
of its physical support. The world still had a body with meaning.
The modern focus upon abstraction has split the body into fragments and shattered the meaning, until now at last we have

reached a technological power beyond imagination—about which our hearts are bemused and anxious because it is beyond imagination, out of the reach of the human heart.

This division between the material and the spiritual, this abstractionism, was first developed and has been carried to its greatest extremes in the industrialized and urbanized North. The Puritan settlers made a sharp distinction between this world and another, with the intention of cherishing the spiritual world and despising the material. This left them free to use the material world in any way they desired. They desired, so they said, to use it for the glory of God, but using it while fearing and despising it, they used it with increasing material effectiveness and decreasing spiritual meaning. It was their slave; therefore they became slaves to it. It yielded them tremendous material riches but at the same time kept them from really belonging to the world, for they had abstracted its meaning from it and therefore from themselves. They had made of it a shadow and of themselves corresponding shadows, doing a dance of shadows in a senseless world.

The world of the South was not as dense as the world of Europe, nor was it as thin as the world of the North. The South stood between Europe and the North, between the more structured medieval world and the less structured modern world, between the density, almost certainly too great, of Europe, and the thinness, almost certainly too great, of the North. This intermediate position between past and future makes any discussion of the South difficult. The institutions of the South revealed both the solidity and density of the older European institutions and the thinness of the newer Northern institutions which, with the success of the North in the Civil War, became the typical American institutions.

The plantation united the denser, more completely human feeling of kinship with the thinner, more abstract will for material gain. It was in part a relatively dense institution expressive of the past, in part a relatively thin institution aimed at the future. For a while it had such success as the South had. It has now failed. The present so-called plantations of the Mississippi Delta have become mainly productive machines geared for profit. Fewer and fewer laborers "belong" to them in any sense of the word. They belong to fewer and fewer people.

Of the three main institutions of the South, the family has been the one that has done most to give to the region its quality of density. For just as blood is thicker than water, so kinship is thicker than interest. In a kinship-oriented society like that of the South, a man will unhesitatingly defend a kinsman against his own interest. This is solid life set alongside solid life, in contrast to the more abstract manner of setting a particular interest alongside another particular interest. It is a contrast between the sense of depth in a society and the sense of shallowness; a contrast, at the extremes, between belonging to a society and being free of it—separated, "alienated" from it.

At the other extreme from the dense institution of the family is the thin institution of race—thin because it was basically a method of abstracting labor from the total man, of making "hands" out of people, thus separating the physical aspect from the total human being.

Yet though the white South tried to do this to the blacks, it did not try wholeheartedly. It could not, because it still remembered, though vaguely, the ordered society of the Middle Ages in which each man had a place, a place determined by God and culminating in God. In the South there wasn't too much conviction in this belief in divine order. It had been seriously undermined by a faith in every man for himself, but it was still there, and when in the nineteenth century the slave economy of the South came under increasing pressure, it was revived in order to legitimize that order. But always there was, and even today is, some of this sense of an overarching order.

So, in brief, the institution of the family in the South and the institution of that spacious place, the plantation, working together did the most that was done to prevent the institution of race from throwing its pall of abstraction over the entire South. And it gave to the South such density as it had. As we have said already, it is this density, this emphasis upon the solid—the complete thing, place, person—that, though it has limited the freedom of the Southerner, has given him a sense of belonging that is unusual in the nation.

Doubtless this sense of belonging has often been too strong, or rather, has not itself been permeated with sufficient freedom, and has therefore caused some Southerners, indeed many black Southerners, to rebel against it and reach for more freedom. Even the family, perhaps the primary institution for the development of a solid, dense society to which one may most deeply belong, can become too strong and erase by its power the inner freedom its existence makes possible. This is the overpowering sense that Walker Percy describes as prevailing at the Southern university in *The Last Gentleman.* Everybody was a cousin or acted as a cousin to everybody else. "Here for God's sake the air fairly crackled with kinship radiations. That was it. These beautiful little flatfooted girls greeted you like your own sister!"[3] He felt smothered by this ever present family.

No wonder the University of Mississippi objected so strenuously to the introduction of James Meredith. By enrolling there he would become a member of the white "family" in a much more intimate way than Negroes had ever been simply by being "our people" or "our family."

So the South overdid belonging. The glaring proof was slavery, wherein one man belonged legally to another. Yet the fact remains that in its attempt to keep a culture oriented strongly toward things and people—the solid, living world as contrasted with the shadowy world of abstractions—the South provided a world of density, of actual shock, of great joys and bruising hurts, wherein a man might love. For love at its best is between wholes: whole men for whole men, whole men for whole things. "Only the complete outer," said Hocking, "can interest the complete inner." A man may be concerned with abstractions, either from material interest or intellectual curiosity, but he cannot really love them. Being shadows themselves, they can demand from him only a partial, shadowy attention. The South in its main institutions made considerable effort to attain wholeness and to avoid partiality. It did this basically out of love—love in its most general sense—and this general love was conserved by the institutions it created.

Again, let us be careful. As I said earlier, there wasn't enough love, and the South finally collapsed. But the strongest factor in this collapse was that critical, abstracting force, that modern drive for free, analytical thought, that individualistic, Lockean thrust which the South, along with the rest of the nation, bore within itself. This force beyond its borders combined with the same force within its borders to break the South. What this same force—running wild now and hardly challenged any longer by the South—may do to the nation remains to be seen. Too much freedom, said Plato, leads to dictatorship. It has to. When people split up too much, they have to be forced together or human life is done.

To conclude this discussion of the South's inner frontier, we can say that such a frontier, with its usual implications of freedom and discovery, has been rather shallow and ineffective. But we can also say that Southerners, in their quiet, brooding concern for people and things in place, have increased their humanity and have pushed inward the frontiers, not of knowledge, but of life.

IX

The Temporal South

It is clear from what we have said about the importance of place (both geographical and social) in the South that time is also important. For it took time to create these places, especially the most solid and imposing of them, the plantation, an institution which, though now in its twilight, still exerts a strong influence upon Southerners. We have already noted that the Southerner's sense of time, especially of the past, is probably the first thing the stranger notices about him. Was this sense created entirely by the presence of the plantation—and the subsidiary farms—or did the Southern settlers bring with them attitudes that helped to form the plantation and therefore to establish the importance of place in the South?

Here we need only refer to arguments we have already presented. Though the Southern plantation was in part the creation of European commercial interests transmitted to America through the desires and ambitions of Southern settlers, it was in part a hierarchical structure wherein each man had his place, the whole order being subsumed under the order of heaven. It is true that the heavenly order was deeply compromised in America by earthly ambition, but it remained in the early picture of the estate of the English gentleman now living in Virginia or Carolina, and in the much later picture, a result of the Romantic movement in the South, of the feudal lord with his ranked retainers.

But the important point is this: The Southern settlers, as we have already said, brought more of the past with them than did the New England settlers, or at least brought it in a different form —more in the form of images depending heavily upon the past than in moral and material drives aimed chiefly at the future. During the Colonial and early National periods, they moved westward as fast as the Northern settlers, and since the frontier was their form of the future, they moved as fast into the future. But still they carried more of the past with them. For before the end of the Colonial period—that is, before the westward rush really began—the plantation had become the dominant economic unit in the South, and this, or its ideal, was what Southerners carried with them as they pushed toward the Mississippi.

The plantation was the great conservative institution of the South. Supported as it was by slave labor, it was doubly conservative, for though different masters treated their slaves differently, there was no room for radical change short of emancipation. Northern settlers, on the contrary, carried forward not so much one form of production as the attitude and training to find the best tools for whatever form of production seemed most profitable. For like all settlers in the New World, they were short of labor from the beginning, and finding themselves unable to use slave labor profitably, they turned to the invention of laborsaving devices. It is significant that though Cyrus McCormick was born in Virginia and invented the first reaper-binder there, the headquarters of what was to become an industrial empire was finally established in Chicago.

Furthermore, the tendency of the South to carry with it more of the past then the North did was strengthened by its growing tendency to linger over the present. The growing ideal of the South—frequently, of course, not the actuality—was to take life easy. Time moved more slowly in the South; men moved more slowly through it. There were several reasons for this. First was the summer heat; second, the fact of slavery, where a few had time for pleasure and many had time only for work. This work, however, was motivated mainly by the fear of punishment; few workers under such conditions would work more or faster than they had to. Also, in such a society, leisure, being available only to the upper classes who set the tone, became an ideal for all. Undoubtedly, also, as Cash says, there was an element of simple hedonism: the desire to enjoy life. The average Southerner would hardly have agreed with Henry David Thoreau in many things, yet like Thoreau, he may have felt that life was more to be enjoyed than used. And a part of his enjoyment was the love of place. This is significant in our discussion of time, because such love came only through time and was the product of moments, days, and years of working in the same place and coming to know it in all its details. The Southerner was not primarily an artist; his "pause for contemplation" was neither to create beauty nor consciously to appreciate it, but the effect was essentially aesthetic. He did pause, he did contemplate, he did come to know in its details and to love the place where he lived.

Underlying all of this was a stronger tendency to accept the world than his New England brethren had, a greater faith in the world. If we admit that history revealed he had too much faith, we also suggest that the typical American, predominantly the descendant of the early New Englander, has had too little. He has improved the world almost beyond acceptance. In regard to time, the Southerner tended to accept its passage; he rode with it, trying to make something of the moments as they passed and of the places wherein those moments found him.

But let us go back to the plantation. Though it was basically conservative, when the westward movement really began after the Revolution it moved westward with the frontiersmen themselves. This was especially true after the invention in 1793 of the gin for delinting upland cotton. This set the South on fire. Prior to this time, and succeeding the Revolution, there had been much foreboding in the South. Virginia, the first home of tobacco, was losing out to the richer lands of Kentucky; the production of indigo was falling because of the loss of the bounty formerly paid by the British government; rice and sea island cotton, though great wealth producers, could not be widely cultivated. But with Whitney's invention cotton ran like wildfire across the plains and valleys of the South, even to the very foot of the Blue Ridge. The mind of the South was turned to the future. Plantation owners became rich almost overnight. But the Seaboard planters could not compete for long with the planters on the fabulous "black lands" of Alabama and Mississippi. In *Flush Times of Alabama and Mississippi*, Joseph G. Baldwin, Alabama-born humorist, tells of those impossible days.

The great success of these frontier planters worked against the planters on the old lands of the Atlantic Seaboard, and together they planted too much cotton and sent the price steadily downward. Then, especially in the East, there were cries almost of despair. "Grass will be growing in the streets," they said in South Carolina during the 1820's; and during the 1830's William Gilmore Simms, South Carolina planter and writer, was so oppressed by the dark clouds along the horizon that he wrote several essays on Hamlet and claimed to see, certainly in South Carolina if not along the Old Southwest frontier, a growing number of men of the Hamlet type. They would hesitate and hesitate, he said, seeing all sides of the question, and finally in desperation might be swept by the hotheads into fatal action. And this is what really happened.

The self-doubt of the South—its premonitions about the future—was not continuous. Depending mainly upon the price of cotton, the future seemed brighter or darker. The price was good during the 1850's, and though the war clouds were rising, even Simms felt sure of the future, embattled though it might be. He was swept into the dominant mood, thus fulfilling his own prophecy.

With all the rise and fall of moods in the South during the thirty years preceding the Civil War, the general deep current flowed less and less rapidly into the future. Increasingly the South became defensive, trying, especially under Calhoun, to solidify itself so that it might protect its values against the rising national tide of criticism. The extreme idea of a Southern nation including Mexico and Cuba and circling the waters of the Gulf of Mexico and the Caribbean was as much a reaction to the growing political power of the North as it was the direct expression of plantation expansionism. The end was to protect the Southern way of life against the Northern challengers. The focus was increasingly upon holding on rather than advancing.

The loss of the Civil War, the unshackling of its main labor force, the bitter wounds suffered by the whites in Reconstruction and later by the blacks in redemption, together with the long-continued and extreme poverty of most of its people—all this weakened the South tremendously. Indeed, it almost broke the drive of the South into the future and turned its mind, especially the mind of the whites, unhappily toward the past.

As late as 1961, in *The Legacy of the Civil War,* Robert Penn Warren said that the most unhappy effect of the Civil War upon the South was the Great Alibi. The defeat gave white Southerners the chance to excuse all their failures by saying, in effect, that their fathers had lost the war and they hadn't had a chance since. But not only did white Southerners excuse their failures by recalling a doomed defeat; they created an impossible, romantic image of the antebellum South and in a way worshiped their creation. They also continued as completely as they could the slave status of the black. Through segregation he was relegated to "his place," a static position at the foot of the economic and social ladder. Having done this, the whites necessarily stayed "in the ditch" with him, thus slowing to an imperceptible pace the advance of the South into the new industrial world.

In brief, the South, which began with considerable regard for the past and a reasonable confidence in the future, spent much of the century following the Civil War in an unhealthy contemplation of the past: past glory and past defeat. Indeed, the Civil War itself stamped an abiding image of glory and defeat upon the general mind of at least the white South: the image of Pickett's charge at Gettysburg, one of the great charges of military history, broken the very moment of success on the top of Cemetery Ridge. The effect of such an image upon the military-minded people was disastrous. If, in the century following the Civil War, failure was the lot of the South, what difference did it make? The heroes are always defeated. Defeat puts us in the great tradition.

This defeatist attitude was countered somewhat during the last quarter of the nineteenth century by the overoptimistic prophets of the New South. These men were as wildly romantic about the future as their opponents were about the past. The complete story is told in Paul Gaston's *The New South Creed.*

By World War I this defeatist attitude was disappearing. That war brought the South back toward the mainstream of American life, a mainstream under the impetus of war rushing even more rapidly into the future. And one of the powerful forces for change that the war touched off in the South—a force really released twenty-five years later by World War II—was the black man breaking, at first hesitantly, then impetuously, out of his place and driving toward a future imagined as radically different from the past. This is where we are today, with a decreasing number of blacks driving hard toward a new and better future.

Just as the whites after the defeat of the Civil War romanticized the past, remembering glories which never existed, so now the blacks, excited by victory, also romanticize their past, filling it with insurrectionary heroes and the general mood of rebellion. J. H. Plumb, in a review of several books on slavery, says: "No amount of black protest or black re-writing of history can overcome [the fact that the] American Negro slave protested less in his society than the free peasant class of Europe, or of England for that matter."[1] Why, he does not know.

But this can be said for the blacks: If they misread the past, they do so in the attempt to gain courage and faith for a better future. The whites misread the past because they lacked faith in the future and sought comfort in nostalgic memories of earlier times.

One might risk here a general statement, expressed in figurative form, of the relation of past and future in the mind of an individual or of society. The image is Perseus overcoming the deadly Gorgon by looking not directly at her horrible face but at its reflection in his polished shield. The Gorgon's head is the past; the reflection of that head in the mirror of the shield is the imagined and desired future. To look directly at the past is to be turned to stone, for the past is in a sense—and in spite of Faulkner—dead, and he who contemplates it too long is corrupted or turned to stone. Only he who is going into the future can safely contemplate the past, and he is safe because what he sees there is seen by the light of that future into which he is going. The ideals which we pursue are products of the past as the reflection in the shield is of an actual head. Pursuing these ideals, we can observe safely their roots in the past, their strengths and weaknesses, their directions. Unlike Perseus, however, we do not have to destroy the past; we merely leave it behind, taking with us its living forces which themselves are driving us forward. But if we are not going anywhere, the past is dead in us, and its contemplation will corrupt us.

During the past fifteen years the segregationists of the South have admitted, either vocally or tacitly, that they weren't going anywhere. They were simply trying to hold a weakening position.

Enshrouding themselves with the ghosts of the past, they could still resist, but they could not use that past positively, because no ray of living hope illumined it.

Black separatism is rooted in the old white-controlled segregation. Whether it is illumined by real hope remains to be seen.

X

Individual and Community

Thus far we have described the three main institutions that have shaped the South—plantation, family, and race—and have shown in addition how they related the Southerner to space and to time. We shall now try to reach nearer the heart of the matter and ask how they related the Southerner to himself and to society. Men are related to space and time, both individually and as a group, but more basic is the question: How are they related to one another? Space and time are important because only in space and through time are human relations established, and also because infinite space and everlasting time always challenge men to transcend the here and the now.

To return to our key word *belonging*, we have said that the Southerner belongs to, is attached to the South mainly through the institutions of plantation, family, and race. These are the chief structures that have formed him. They and other unstructured influences have made him the kind of man he is. We have already suggested generally how he has responded and to a degree still responds to space and time—how he belongs to the Southern region and to the history of that region. Now we shall try to show how he belongs to himself and to his fellows, how he is a part of them and they of him, and to indicate wherever possible how these traits are related to the basic institutions of the South.

The structure and history of the South have produced in the Southerner a character that is on the surface deceptively simple, at bottom highly complex. Perhaps the simplest thing about him is that he prefers things and people to ideas. But when we pass beyond this simplicity, we find a character who is *both-and*: both a rugged individualist and a role player; both extremely direct and extremely indirect; both committed and humorous; both highly mannered and strongly moralistic. Let us take him first at his simplest, in his interest in things and people.

The Concrete

This interest of the Southerner in things and people has been stressed repeatedly in the last generation. An early expression appeared in the pages of the Southern manifesto *I'll Take My Stand* in 1930. It was especially stressed by one of the most notable contributors to that book, Allen Tate, and appeared as a plea for the solid life of the South as opposed to the shallow and shadowy, the abstract existence of urban manufacturing centers. Robert Penn Warren, another famous contributor, said as late as 1956, in the book *Segregation,* that the Southerner fears nothing more than abstractions. They seem to him, with their massive inclusiveness, to roll over and wipe out all the dear realities of the world. In 1970 another knowledgeable Southerner, Pat Watters, said: "Some day the rest of the nation will realize that it has been by this keen sense of the specific—the refusal ever to get embroiled in generalities, in dangerous abstraction, principle, ideals,—that the Southerner has ever out-tricked them; out-traded them: losing the war but winning the peace."[1]

This fear of abstractions, the obverse of a keen interest in things themselves, may have arisen within the last hundred and fifty years, but the positive interest in things goes back much further than that. It appears in the Southerner's attachment to particular places, about which we have already spoken. It appears in his greater concern for solid images out of the past than for abstract plans for the future. It appeared very early in a greater love than the New England Puritans showed for the world as it is, and therefore a weaker will to make it into something else. It is realistic rather than idealistic.

Around this core of interest in things as they are, there gathered in time the fear that these things might be forcibly changed. The basic fear here was aroused a century and a third ago by the threat of abolition. Because this fear was so great, it brought with it the fear of all the other *isms* that were common in the North in that period: feminism, communitarianism, reformism of various kinds. No real reform might be considered in the South because it might ultimately bring into question the fact of slavery. Since the Civil War and the forcible changing of Southern life to conform to a non-Southern plan, this basic fear has continued in the South; its most recent appearance has been integrationism—if we may use such a term.

If Southern concern for the concrete, the thing, the person, had no deeper rootage than the fear that abolitionism might destroy the detailed life of the South, then blacks would hardly have feared abstractions, since abolition was in their favor. But, though doubtless they longed for freedom, they also, like the whites, have always been deeply concerned with particular places, with actual life now rather than with a possible life in some abstract future.

Though suffering from present actuality, they learned to extract value from it. Since the future could mean so little, they learned to make the most of the present. It is true that in the revolutionary movement of the past few years, blacks have begun to lay great stress upon the unformed and abstract future defined only as being radically different from the present and the past. But they are struggling against a tendency not only of the white South but of the black South as well.

I recall a meeting I attended several years ago of the Advisory Committee of the Southern Project, an effort of the National Student Association located in and directed toward the South. Two of the NSA officials were present—Northern, intelligent, and indeed remarkably sympathetic. The rest of us were Southerners. Invariably the blueprints, the social plans, were suggested by the Northerners. Invariably the Southerners, without regard to age or race, had their doubts. They couldn't really see anything wrong with the blueprints, but after all, would they work in Columbus, Georgia—or elsewhere in the South? Always they focused on the local, the particular, the concrete, in preference to the abstract. This may be in part an effect of the history of failure in the South and the consequent sense that one should be cautious about all plans; but it is also, I am sure, an expression of the Southerner's strong interest in the thing, the place, the situation itself, and his weak interest in abstractions.

Yet, though we have stressed this trait of a strong interest in things and people as an indication of the Southerner's surface simplicity, even in this matter he is not really simple. Of course he could not be, for, like other Americans though less so, he was from the beginning concerned with hopes and plans for the future, a future different from the past, an individualistic future to be constructed by critical analysis and abstraction out of the ordered and authorized past. As we have already said, the most individualistic thing he did was to turn away from the late feudal nature of his immediate past and to reinstate the largely outmoded system of chattel slavery. This was a form of that capitalism which was to capture the modern world, an agrarian capitalism in distinction from the industrial capitalism of the North, less radical and rational than that, less individualistic, attempting to maintain still a place for every worker, but for the black worker a place highly dehumanized and permanent, fixed by law at the bottom of the ladder—which in this case was no ladder at all. In setting up this system—and the system of segregation which later took its place—he depended upon a large use of those abstractions which generally he seemed to fear so much. For the general effect of both of these systems was to prevent the black from being seen as an individual, the abstraction of race having been substituted for the total man. This suggests that the white Southerner did not really fear abstractions in themselves but only such abstractions as might endanger the continuation of that particular abstraction upon which he had built his social order.

Yet even here something in him made him attempt to blur what he was doing or to do it much less thoroughly than he might have done it. As we have already pointed out, even the slaves on the plantation belonged to it in a richer though more absolute sense than the early mill employees of the North belonged to their mills. As a part of this, the plantation owner claimed a personal relationship with at least a certain number of slaves, for instance, with house servants and artisans, and later, following emancipation, with house servants and certain tenants and wage hands. The landlords probably found it easier to indulge in this escape from reality under segregation than under slavery, for whereas slavery was clearly undergirded by strict and limiting laws, segregation was enforced by a much vaguer structure of law —custom and simple opinion—and the whites could more easily see their personal ties with blacks as being the essential thing. These so-called personal ties were in fact highly limited by the total pattern of segregation. However, the fact that whites did try to establish such personal ties suggests that they did not feel easy with the slavery-segregation patterns within which, by a process of abstraction, they had enclosed all blacks.

Perhaps a word of caution is needed about what we have called the typical Southern concern with concrete things as opposed to abstractions. This should be carefully distinguished from the modern American interest in a plethora of things— more bathtubs, cars, boats, etc.—held one after the other. The typical modern uses these things mainly for two purposes: for simple pleasure or, more importantly, for prestige. A successful man is supposed to possess such things. We have admitted that prestige was probably one of the motives for building the great houses of the South. There were, however, a mere handful of these. Far exceeding them in number were the many homes and homeplaces—and the dear objects connected with these places— that Southerners developed. As we have already suggested, it took time to develop these, and through time and use these objects came to stand for more than themselves. They were touched with an aura of sentiment; they carried suggestions of the past; they were proofs of continuity in a changing world.

John Crowe Ransom has pointed out the great similarity between values of sentiment—or, to speak without derogation, sentimental values—and aesthetic values. Both grow out of the same kind of loving attention to the object. The artist may see at a glance the deeper values in, for instance, a home scene; the man who lives there may have taken years to store up this detailed knowledge and the accompanying values, but both value the object not only for itself but also for its symbolic, expressive value. There is the moon, for instance, seen year after year above the corner of the barn, or Arcturus riding high above a particular pine.

Insofar as the Southerner developed such ties of sentiment for things, places, and people, it was out of his complete nature

that he developed them. He was responding with both understanding and feeling to the world around him. In so doing he was
being incompletely modern. For the typical modern—as the rec-
ord proves—has not made any complete response, but rather has
reacted to certain possibilities within objects and people, possibilities actualized by abstracting certain aspects of people and
things and by building out of these abstractions a different and,
it is thought, more desirable world. For instance, the complete
man is seen as a "hand," the complete tree as lumber. I am not
forgetting how the white Southerner, a modern in this, made
"hands" out of black men. But part of the time the Southerner
was not the abstracting modern; he was the more complete man,
responding both intellectually and emotionally to the surrounding world.

In a sense, typical modern man has run away from reality
more than the Southerner has, for he has taken one aspect of the
complex world and followed it toward its farthest limits. This was
a relatively simple thing to do, and one reason the whole effort
has succeeded—at least physically—almost beyond our dreams is
that the effort was so simple. We put men on the moon by focusing upon the properties of matter. At the same time our reporters
questioning the wives of the astronauts act like incompetents and
asses. They are handling human nature with the same objectivity
that astronauts use in handling the moon landing craft.

Granted, of course, that to be human is to be abstractive. By
a process of abstraction I translate the towering form beyond my
window into the meaning *live oak*. But then what do I do with the
live oak? (At this point the live oak becomes a poor illustration,
since now that its curved limbs are no longer of use in shipbuild-
ing, there isn't much I can do with it except observe its towering
spread, sit in its shade, or, if a child, climb it and swing from its
limbs. The pine, also visible out there, is a better illustration.) I
am told that my uncle, the former owner of this place, almost lost
the plantation to his creditors because he loved the great pines
too much to let them go for lumber. In contrast, the buyer of the
adjoining Coldstream Plantation cared so little for its beautiful
boxwood gardens that he sold the boxwood and planted cotton
in its place. Wisdom lies somewhere between the attitude of my

over-responsive uncle and that of the highly practical buyer of Coldstream Plantation. My uncle was, of course, more Southern, the buyer of the neighboring place more modern.

The Southerner's concern for the concrete, the particular, the local, appears also in his concept of justice. Justice is mainly a local matter. There may or may not be an abstract justice, but anyway it isn't important now. Justice is not only local; it also tends to be personal: it is the public activity of a just man. The South has always praised its leaders as being just. When we consider the rank social injustice underlying the life of the South, we are puzzled. But then we learn that the just man is the solid man, the unchanging man, the man of integrity who if necessary will swear to his own hurt. Justice is what this man does. As for abstract justice, even during the period of slavery—except in its most intransigent latest form—slave owners would often agree that slavery was unjust in the abstract—they too knew the eighteenth-century doctrine of the rights of man—but they were also apt to insist that in its actuality slavery was as just as they could make it. Justice, therefore, especially racial justice, varied from community to community, even from slave owner to slave owner. It was essentially the order laid down by the leading man. He was, especially on the frontier or in newly settled areas, the "outlaw" leader, as Thompson calls him, the man who lived where the usual forces of law were still nonexistent or at least weak, and who was therefore the law beyond or outside the usual law. It was of course the massiveness of the plantation and the existence of the widespread plantation system that supported this power.

But, as Thompson also suggests, it is useless to look for any clear concept of justice on the plantation. "The institution was and to some extent continues to be characteristically one of those aggregations of persons which, like the family, exists in the fact that people are reckoned as belonging to each other. It was this 'reckoning together' that made the plantation, again much like the family, a unit of collective expectation and obligation, where social relations are so primary and personal that people do not talk of rights and duties; this kind of talk is reserved for the more formal relationships of the city and the larger state."[2]

There is an interesting comment on justice in the memoirs

of the English actress Fanny Kemble, who became the wife of the Georgia plantation owner Pierce Butler and spent ten years on his plantation. Once she strongly criticized Butler for having a female slave whipped. It was unjust, she said. It was not, he replied; the woman knew the rule and the punishment for breaking the rule. She had broken the rule and had been justly punished. Pierce Butler was upholding order; he had no intention of submitting the existing order to the criterion of universal order —supposing that such a thing existed.

The Southern stress upon the concrete present was a stress upon the order of the immediate situation in contrast to the possible disorder of the surrounding or impending frontier and the unordered future. It was also an order defined by particular men, not by universal man. Finally, the stress was upon order, not upon freedom, whether for good or for ill.

Individualism and Role

We have noted the individualism of the Southern settler from the beginning as it appeared in his refusal to follow the wishes of the London Company and later of the Virginia Assembly to settle towns, and in his insistence upon making his own way as a tobacco planter along the creeks and rivers. This early individualism has been supported throughout the history of the South by the continuation of farming as the chief occupation and by the continuation of the frontier along the west, as elsewhere in America, but also in minor form around the farms and plantations scattered throughout the forests and along the vast swamps, and finally by the presence, after 1865, of the "frontier the Yankee made."

This, of course, is W. J. Cash's phrase. But Cash meant only the unsettlement and devastation caused by the Civil War. Beyond this settled frontier there is another frontier that the Yankee as the typical modern individualist has made: the frontier of the forever changing, the forever unsettled, the still accelerating in both physical and social matters. Frontiers increase individualism, and individualism continues frontiers. The stronger the influence of the Yankees became in the South, both preceding and following the Civil War, the weaker became the ordered, hierarchical structure of the South; the less men had the sense of playing roles, the more they felt it was every man for himself.

W. B. Yeats has remarked that always in great periods men have felt they were playing roles. This comes from the fact that during its great period a culture is on the make, is creative, and its members therefore are both constrained and proud to feel that they belong to it, that each has a place, a role, therein. The alienation of modern man, his feeling that he has no place, is a correct indicator of the lack of national or regional greatness today, in spite of the fact that our technological achievements far surpass anything ever before attained.

So there were many things both to keep alive and to increase the modern sense of individualism which the Southerner, like other Americans, though less than they, felt: the original temper of the people, the continuing geographical frontier, and the tightening social frontier of the ever new tomorrow.

All this has been deeply modified by the sense of role, of place, which develops in a settled, conservative society. For though, as we have seen, this society expanded westward in the American fashion, it changed little in the expansion. Its style was set by the presence of slave labor organized mainly through the plantation system. The only difference as the society expanded was a greater freedom among the whites—the natural effect of any frontier—and among the blacks, generally though not always, harsher slavery as they suffered the greater freedom or license of the whites.

But the same basic relationships remained. The slave had his fixed place at the bottom, and because in a free land always touched by the frontier it was necessary for the whites to organize to keep the blacks in bondage, every white too had his strict role to play, his duty toward the community, primarily toward the whites, secondarily toward the blacks.

During the first half of the nineteenth century, two opposing forces affected this sense of obligation to the community. The first, which weakened it, was the spread of "Jacksonian democracy." This showed a growing belief in the common man and a growing tendency to throw off the yoke of the aristocracy, a yoke which the common man had generally accepted as natural during the eighteenth century. With this development there was a widening split between the common man and "quality folks" and a growing lack of concern in protecting the economic status of the "quality," which depended of course upon slavery.

At the same time attacks upon slavery from the North and from western Europe were growing stronger and the threat to the "peculiar institution" of the South greater; as a result, the whites of the South were drawn closer and closer together in defense of slavery. For though the poorer whites envied the slave owner, they surely did not want to be brought into more complete competition with the blacks through the abolition of slavery. The white South, therefore, was united in the years just before the Civil War as it has never been before or since.

Yet even then the South was not united. In 1857 Hinton Rowan Helper, a Southerner, published a book entitled *The Impending Crisis of the South, and How to Meet It,* a fierce attack upon slavery as an institution sapping the economic life of the South. The appearance of this highly critical book can be taken as symbolic of the South. The South has never been as united as it has seemed to be. The race question, both under slavery and under segregation, has been so important both in its moral and in its economic aspect that white Southerners had to insist that they agreed, though often they disagreed radically.

After the Civil War the blacks, having been freed from their legal place as slaves, had to be put into some other unfree place—I speak now as the average white Southerner of that time felt—and as one means of keeping them there, there was popularized the phrase "the Negro in his place." Now that black slavery no longer existed with a legal code to maintain it, it became increasingly the responsibility of every Southern white to see that the new status of the black was maintained. Of course after Reconstruction segregation laws were passed fairly rapidly to replace the slave code, but until the *Plessy v. Ferguson* decision of 1896 gave the South the green light on the race problem, the region had to move cautiously in the realm of law. Therefore custom became increasingly important, and it became increasingly the role of the white to keep the Negro in his place. Doubtless this was accepted by the quieter sort of whites as a moral obligation; the rougher sort took it also as a personal privilege.

This role of white over black was a poor defensive one, offering practically no part to the role players in the creation of a great society. Unfortunately, this was the only role allowed the poorer whites and the primary role for all whites.

This has meant for the white Southerner a purely negative role during the last one hundred years. His job has been to keep something from happening. But he has been cemented into the community in a still more negative fashion. The Civil War was fought almost exclusively on Southern soil. It was lost. Out of this futile defense of the homeland, and out of its destruction, there arose in the mind of the white South the shining image of the Lost Cause. This was a highly romanticized concept, but the image, though slowly fading, has influenced the South for a hundred years. There arose a memory of a unified South which had in fact never existed. It became the role of the white Southerner to remember and honor this imagined past and as far as possible to keep it unchanged. Furthermore, since the South at large had been the place he had defended with considerable glory but finally to no effect, the tiny place that he owned or where he lived took a quality of dearness from the dearness of the land as a whole. Glory splashed from the whole on to the parts, and it became the function of the white Southerner to cherish and defend both his social and his geographical place as he had tried fruitlessly to defend the whole.

It is clearly evident that the basic weakness of all this cherishing of place, whether social or physical—though it does serve as a balance to frontier and farming individualism—is that it is too defensive. Instead of being a true opposing pole of such individualism, it was largely a defense of Southern forces against outside force—insiders against outsiders—or a defense of the inner ruling group against the inner subservient group. In other words, it was group against group along either a national frontier or a racial frontier. Wisdom may lie in the proper balance between individual and group, between the free frontier and the settled place, but there the settled place was also a frontier, toward the North a national frontier, within the South a racial frontier. In brief, the history of the South has been shaped by frontiers, and the true softening spirit of the settlement has had too small a part.

Yet, to repeat what has been said, there was always an attempt on the part of both the white and the black South to bring increasing agreement along the racial frontier and increasing settlement of it. For one thing, whites and blacks often lived as neighbors in the South, responding to each other's physical and sometimes even spiritual needs, as neighbors do. This was especially true where circumstances permitted the white and the black to meet alone; in such a situation each could sometimes afford to drop the accepted white or black role and adopt the common neighbor role. When other whites or blacks were present, this dropping of racial roles was usually not attempted.

This is to say that in certain relations, such as neighbor and neighbor or in the often intimate relations of mistress and servant, humanity itself, with all its complexity, came to the fore. But in most relations theory ruled. Men reacted to one another as black and white, servant and master, inferior and superior. They reacted to roles, to places, rather than responding to men.

How does it happen that the South, responding so strongly to roles, has so often boasted of its personal relationships? For to most of us a role seems impersonal, something the person doffs and dons like a garment. This was not the situation in the older South. Consider that excellent drawing of the Southern plantation owner Major Buchan, in Allen Tate's story *The Fathers*. Major Buchan was deeply embarrassed if anyone asked him a "personal" question. Apparently he thought of himself as playing certain roles: he was "Major" Buchan, a "landowner," from the "place" Pleasant Hill, son of certain parents, father of certain children, holder now or in the past of certain offices. He defined himself by this complex of roles. Beyond such definition he didn't think anyone needed to go. It is questionable how much he went beyond it himself.[3]

When a man accustomed to such public definition says he knows personally other people, white or black, he means he knows them in the roles they are supposed to play. He does not mean to overlook what we call their personal lives; he simply does not consider such lives of primary importance, as he does not consider his own personal life of primary importance. What he overlooks is the relative completeness of his own roles contrasted with the meagerness of the role assigned to his own poor white neighbors and Negro dependents. Unable like him to find satisfaction in their own meager public role, these people are not only driven inward toward a sheer personal life only slightly attached to public life, but may also be driven to root out such attachments as they have.

We may say that the South was too highly organized in its social relations, or rather, organized without understanding the transcendent meaning of such relations. It saw its settlements, its places, its roles mainly as defenses along physical and racial frontiers. As we said, it paid too little attention to the frontiers of the spirit.

Every place, if we consider it long enough, every person, if we consider him lovingly enough, is touched with hints of strangeness, of the faraway and the unknown, and the known place and person can become also unknown frontiers. The South developed a high regard for places, and, strange as it sounds, for persons, but always for places occupied by certain persons and for persons in places and in place.

This is a true human regard, since our deepest concern for space is as a home—a place—for people, and our deepest concern for persons relates them somehow to places on earth. But it is an incomplete regard, for man transcends his immediate surroundings. Any place seen completely reveals the world, perhaps the cosmos, and any person seen completely reveals mankind. The South was enriched by its common concern for places and people, but it feared to follow this concern into its final meaning, to plunge beyond home into final frontiers. It failed in this primarily because it had created and continued to maintain a racial frontier which crisscrossed even its quietest settlements and prevented these settlements from thinking quietly about themselves.

The South did try in a formal way to generalize its social order, including slavery. It saw the universe as a hierarchy exhibiting order, and slavery as the base of this order; to remove slavery would be to weaken the entire order. (This philosophical argument was even more common in Europe than in the South.) The basic trouble in the South was that the hierarchical order never received the theological justification it had had in medieval

Europe. For the Southerner—an offbeat American, but still on the make as an individual—did not really believe in the hierarchical order. First, the actual order upon which the imagined order had to rest was too changeable; second, the non-hierarchical egalitarian thrust of democracy was gaining strength with every passing decade; third and most important, the hierarchy did not really culminate in religion and the church. The whole structure was a pyramid without an apex in God. But more of this when we consider the church and the culture.

Let us return to our present question of the balance in the South between place and space, the settlement and the frontier, the role and the individual. Southern places, Southern roles, were so defensively shaped by the continued presence of geographical and racial frontiers that men could not realize in them their significance for inner frontiers. Life was too embattled for the individual to play freely and creatively his social role. He tended to lose his freedom in the role, or upon rare occasions to become a grotesque, a "character," and thus play the role of the individual.

Manners and Morals

The mannered life of the South, its stress upon the way things are done and said, "the way you hold your mouth," rests upon several bases.

First in time there was, as we have already said, the feeling —stronger than in New England—that life is made for living, that the world as it is—not as we may reform it—deserves some acceptance, that the present therefore is important, not simply the future. This means that the way we relate to people and things is important in itself, not merely as a means to future achievements.

Second, there was the aristocracy, such as it was, and an aristocracy sets standards. It may set different standards for different classes, but it is the key to the general tone of society. There was of course an aristocracy along the length of the Atlantic Seaboard. Its distinction in the South was that it became and remained a landed aristocracy, an aristocracy therefore less mo-

bile than the aristocracy of busy town and urban areas, an aristocracy also more resistant to change.

Furthermore, this aristocracy was based finally upon slave
labor, and this type of labor, as we have seen, became a drag upon
mobility and social change and created a tendency to slow down
the movement of time. As for the development of leisure among
the aristocrats, both the fact and the ideal were relatively late
developments. Though great plantation owners and their families didn't do much physical labor, there is plenty of evidence to
show that there was tremendous work for all in the first building
of the plantations and, indeed, usually in their development
along the westward-moving frontier. It is true that later on, generally in the nineteenth century after the great days of Atlantic
Seaboard development were past, softness set in, there was less
work and more play, and time may have become a burden on the
hands of wealthy people.

Any concern for manners takes time. Men who are trying
desperately to make a living have little time to put on just how
they do it. So, as a leisure class developed in the South, more
attention was given to manners. This class was developed at the
expense mainly of the slaves. It was their work which created the
master's leisure. Yet this very fact made the slaves move slowly,
take more time, engage wherever possible in palaver about how
to do what had to be done. In brief, they had no reason to plan
and sacrifice for the future; the present was sufficient. They were,
in effect, a leisure class whose concern was to waste as much time
as possible.

We approach the most important key to the Southern emphasis upon manners. This is the whole labor system. And even
beyond the fact that this was an exploitative system, it was and
continued to be a system of people, not of machines. It is true
that for a long while the South had as many machines as the
North, but with the swing toward industrialization in the early
nineteenth century, the North turned increasingly to machines,
the South turned far more slowly, at times and in places not at
all. Now machines make no response to manners; you may praise
them or curse them, but they respond only as you actually handle
them. But people respond to manners, and the overall concern

of the South with people in its productive processes has forced it to give considerable attention to manners.

It may be objected that a great number of these people were slaves or, later, peons. Being so, they responded only to force. I would not for a moment deny the presence of force in the background, but most planters soon learned that it was uneconomical (to say the least) to rely upon force alone. Persuasion was usually important. Of course more of this was used with house servants than with field hands, but it was rarely completely absent.

Let us consider for a moment the general purpose of manners. They are an agreed-upon way of acting that will permit people to get along more easily together. Their purpose is to ease the abrasions of life, abrasions that occur even among close acquaintances and friends. They are a generalizing force in personal relations; they keep life from becoming too personal. They are a way of holding people off or at least slowing down their approach to the core of our life. For, though we all want to be known, we are at the same time afraid of being known, since the knowledge others have of us is power over us and may be used against us.

In professions like the military, where men live close together not because they want to but because they have to, manners are so important that there is developed a particular form of manners, an etiquette, in this case military etiquette. So, under the slave system, and later under segregation, there developed a racial etiquette, the purpose of which was to keep some psychological distance between certain people who had to be together.

But any particular etiquette is simply one form of manners, and its general purpose is to keep those who are together from unnecessarily bruising one another. Of course racial etiquette bruises the black by equating him with all blacks. Individually he is considered less important than his blackness set off against whiteness. Racial etiquette is very definitely a method of control.

Yet all manners are a method of control, the difference being that manners in general are used as a method by which individuals control together their relations, while etiquette—certainly racial etiquette—is a method by which one group controls its relations with another.

However, to assume that manners—or even racial etiquette—have been used only by whites to control blacks is to underestimate seriously the capacities of human nature. The same manners whites have used to control blacks have been used, more subtly perhaps, by blacks to control whites. Take the whole Southern manner of being agreeable. When blacks are being agreeable to whites, they are following the accepted Southern pattern, regardless of race. But after they have agreed, what do they do? More or less what they intended anyhow. The speed of work in the South, the quality of work in the South, the actual doing—or not doing—of work in the South rests largely upon the black's following up his agreeableness with action. Generally it's been a poor follow-up. The white may swear and perhaps become physically violent, but meanwhile, by the use of good manners, the black has done the required work poorly or slowly or not at all.

Furthermore, it has to be recognized that, though manners may have found a basic support in the existence of an aristocratic class, they were also strongly supported by the Negroes themselves, some of whom at any given time had recently come from Africa. Granted that the whites went to considerable lengths to erase African memories, it is hardly possible that they could have erased entirely the influence of the highly formal African cultures from which the blacks had come. The formality of these cultures is seen even today. The blacks in America cherished formality not only because it slowed down the actual work but also because of itself. They saw life as a matter of many customary forms. This attitude let them fit easily into the mannered nature of Southern life with its accent on the present and on the way of doing and saying things. Indeed, as in so many other things, it is the fusion of black and white attitudes that gives the South its peculiar flavor.

Racial etiquette was one of the methods of maintaining the racial frontier. In place of the physical distance involved in the actual frontier, it substituted psychological distance. But, as has been said, if you put human beings together, human nature itself, with all its complexities, inevitably comes into play. So the distance implied by racial etiquette was continually being shortened by manners in general. The frontier was continually being penetrated and humanized.

As for the agreeable style of the South, it was a way of dealing with basic disagreement. It is easy to see how this accomplishment was especially valuable here because of these disagreements: between modern and medieval man, between free men and slaves, between great plantation owners and small farmers. It was bought, however, at great cost. The important issues remained hidden, the dirt was swept under the carpet, men hoped for better times while letting times grow worse. Indeed, it was largely through manners that the basic issue of slavery and racial discrimination was hidden and blurred. In place of justice there was the gentle tone, the kindly word, the apparently personal interest. By such gestures the whites tried to make the blacks forget and did make themselves largely forget the injustice of the Negro's lot.

This interest of the South in manners was in part an aesthetic interest. It was a part of the general interest of the South in the physical world and in the human body, its gestures and movements. The ideal was graceful movements and beautiful manners. This emphasis upon grace (among men, controlled strength with grace) is related to the aristocratic tradition in the South. For the true aristocrat this outer control was matched by inner control. The true aristocrat was master of his body, and indeed of others around him, because he was first master of himself. Doubtless this was sometimes proved among the Southern aristocracy, but unfortunately not always.

The question about Southern good manners, as about good manners anywhere, is to what degree they were merely put on and to what degree they expressed the heart. My opinion is that, except in highly cultured circles, they expressed the heart. There has been, as we have seen, a vital need for men to be agreeable with one another in the South, but beyond this there has been, I think, a real desire. Men really wanted to be agreeable. They wanted to get along easily with other men. Furthermore, good manners are like any other learned accomplishment. Men enjoy practicing what they have learned; the skilled carpenter, for instance, enjoys carpentry.

Beneath the question of the sincerity of manners, of how truly they express the heart, is the more basic question of the breadth of vision of the heart. To what degree is it an informed heart? How well do its cherished manners suggest some world wider than their immediate application—not only the particular moment and scene which they shape, but the whole wide world of man and nature? Using the term in its largest sense, Southern manners have done this but poorly.

There are two scenes—one fictional, one actual—which illustrate this. The fictional scene is from Allen Tate's story of antebellum life, *The Fathers,* and represents the funeral of Major Buchan's wife.[4] The actual scene is from Noni Jabavu's *Drawn in Colour,* and represents the funeral of her murdered brother among the Bantus of South Africa.[5] In Tate's account the words, actions, gestures, of the funeral serve to draw together the numerous family and friends of the dead woman and restore their ranks broken by death. The same strength of family appears among the Bantus. There, however, the aim is not to rebuild the human ranks against death, but to restore the broken ties between man and the universe. There it is assumed that the earthly family, with its close relationships, is somehow matched in the universe itself. Death has broken both earthly and heavenly ties, and now they must all be restored. This was the theology of Allen Tate's Southerners; there was also a heavenly family, but they did not really believe it. In heavenly matters it was just the individual against God. All the bereaved could really do was to draw the earthly family together against future inroads of the marauder Death. The manners—the manner—of the two contrasted funerals show these things.

All this is by way of suggesting that, though Southern hearts may have been reasonably sincere in the manners they created and cherished, they were narrow, limited, poorly informed. They did not understand the vastness of the tiny scene wherein they spoke their proper lines, the eternal implications of the present moment. They were well-mannered people, sometimes beautifully mannered people, but for the most part provincial.

The relationship between manners and morals is so close that it is often hard to distinguish one from the other. This is suggested by a phrase that used to be heard fairly often in the South: Christian gentleman. *Christian* suggested the nature of the man's heart, his basic attitude; *gentleman* suggested mainly his manner, though it was assumed that certain manners usually went with a certain social and economic environment. It is probably significant that in the above phrase *Christian* is only the adjective; *gentleman* is the noun. In other words, manners are more important than morals.

The old phrase said "manners maketh man," meaning we become inwardly what we continually appear to be. Furthermore, in the final analysis the goodness of a deed depends upon how it is done. The exact *how* depends upon the inner spirit, but this spirit is only known as it is expressed in words, gestures, tones, hesitations—action in general. There are morally good people, with beautiful spirits, who are awkward; but in this case the awkwardness, the hesitations, the blunders are expressions of the beautifully sensitive spirit.

Insofar as the South put manners first, it was emphasizing beauty and taking the aesthetic approach. We have said before that though the South produced few poets, it produced a poetic-minded people; they were incipient poets. Just as to the poet the important thing is not what you say but how you say it, so, though less extremely, to the Southerner. The main general difference is that the focus of the poet is inward as he approves or disapproves the words he hears himself saying; the focus of the Southerner is outward as he watches for the approval or disapproval of his fellows. Strictly speaking, Southerners were rhetoricians rather than poets. "The poet quarrels with himself," said Yeats, "the rhetorician with others." But both are highly concerned with how the thing is said—and done.

Yet there is also in the South a strong emphasis upon morality. It appears most clearly in certain areas and among certain classes. As for the areas, it is found more in the Piedmont than in the coastal plain, more in the old farm area than in the old plantation area, most of all in the Appalachians, foothills and mountains. As for class, morality is found most among the poor and deprived, especially among poor and deprived whites. For certain reasons blacks have taken moral concerns less seriously than their poor counterparts among the whites. First there was their inheritance of manners from Africa, a fragment, perhaps, but still effective. Second, there was their focus, intensified by their circumstances, upon the present and its sensuous aspects. Third, partly as a consequence of these two, there was their lack of Puritan preoccupation with goodness, with work, and with the individual.

The strongest Puritan influence came into the South during the eighteenth century with the advent of the Scotch-Irish, who were strong Calvinists. They settled mainly in the Piedmont; it was there, as we have just said, that the stress on morality was strongest. But for various reasons which we shall need to discuss under religion, by the time of the Civil War, Puritanism had swept across the South. New England, liberalized by then from its strict Puritan beginnings, was aware of this; the roles of the two sections had been reversed. It appeared even in the Southern universities. Thomas Cooper, a freethinker, a deist—they called him an atheist—was president of the University of South Carolina in the 1820's and 30's; by the end of 1851 this office had been assumed by James Thornwell, one of the great leaders of the conservative Presbyterian Church.

This whole matter may be clarified somewhat if we consider the sanctions by which manners and morals were maintained in the South. Generally speaking, the sanction of the plantation belt was shame, that of the Piedmont was guilt. I remember noting with surprise the (to me) strange insistence upon duty in Ben Robertson's *Red Hills and Cotton,* a personal account of life in the Piedmont of South Carolina, a hundred and fifty miles from where I live, in the old plantation belt. (For a while, of course, all South Carolina was plantation, even into the foothills of the Blue Ridge.) On the farm, part plantation, where I was brought up, we did our duty; we did our duty—or else. But there was little talk about it, as apparently there was in Robertson's locality. What was really hammered home with us was the avoidance of shame. "Honey, ain't you shamed?" was the cry of many a nurse-maid or other servant. We avoided forbidden things to keep from being shamed, not to keep from feeling guilty.

My wife remembers that when she was a child her father made her feel guilty, her mother and grandmother made her feel ashamed. Her father was from the Piedmont of South Carolina; her mother's people were from the coast.

The general use of shame as a sanction indicates the strength of the community. Though the sanctions of guilt rest finally upon the community, they have been far more deeply internalized and individualized, and seem to the person involved to express some perhaps universal force speaking from deep within himself. The sense of shame, therefore, would be a natural expression of the corporate life of the plantation, especially with the strong sense of status, of place, that belonged to that life. The sense of guilt would belong rather to the more individualistic life of the farms and the towns, where place was less fixed, and being out of place was therefore less easily determined.

The sense of shame would also be strongest on the plantations because of the presence there of so many blacks, some of them only recently from Africa. In Africa even today shame is one of the most powerful forces used to keep the members of a society in line. Social deviants are laughed back into line; public efforts are made to make them feel shame for what they have done. It is unrealistic to think that this strong African trait was wiped out by the transfer of Africans to the New World slave environment. They not only maintained it but were able to transmit much of it to the whites.

The whites with whom they were most closely associated, the plantation people, were already sympathetic to such an attitude. For the whole plantation depended upon people being in place, and the system was justified, insofar as it could be, by the philosophy that it was an expression of the universal order. But, as we have said, the Southerner, who was medieval man rapidly becoming modern, did not really believe in a universal order; he believed in a human order, especially the order of the plantation, and the easiest way to keep people in their places within this order was to shame them when they departed from it.

Of course the plantation owners themselves, with the passage of time and the development of the plantation system, became more concerned with the obverse of shame, which is honor. To the degree that the South was a society built upon shame, it was also a society built upon honor. In such a society men try to avoid shame and to gain honor. We have been saying much about the importance of place or role in such a society. The words of Alexander Pope are applicable:

> Honor and shame from no condition rise;
> Act well your part, there all the honor lies.

The fact that I heard little about honor and much about shame when I was growing up probably indicates that the great days were then in the past, and the South was merely trying to hold on to something old, not to achieve something new.

Just as to avoid shame a man tries to avoid public condemnation, so to gain honor he tries to win public approbation. The South certainly didn't carry its code of honor and shame to the extreme that certain medieval European societies did; this code was modified by the equalitarian influence of Christianity expressing itself mainly through the development of modern democracy, and by the individualistic, utilitarian thrust of modern man. Nevertheless, within limits, the code of honor and shame was the code especially of the Old South in its greatest days. It is a remnant of that old European individualism which was a natural accompaniment of relatively lawless, unorganized society. In a society of honor and shame, each individual is supposed to protect himself. Gentlemen were supposed to settle disputes among themselves, not to go to law about them. It was the killing of the gifted Hamilton by the notorious Burr in 1804 that caused most of the Northern states to outlaw dueling; nearly three-quarters of a century later, the killing of Shannon by Cash resulted in a law against dueling in South Carolina. The South held on to this practice and to this concept of honor because it was an old society of status, and, as Jean Péristiany says, "Honour is the aspiration to status and the validation of status."[6]

The South also held on to the concept of honor because of its military nature. Says Péristiany: "This morality of 'prestige' through individual force is always the morality of the soldier, which is acceptable and desirable so long as there are danger and good luck."[7] The military nature itself was related to the danger of slave insurrections and to the Southerner's liking for the outdoors, outdoor sports, and the spit and polish of the military. Even today the South furnishes more than its quota to the armed forces and is hawkish rather than dovish in regard to the present crisis in Vietnam. Furthermore, the military world, putting such great stress upon appearances, is a world where honor and shame are clearly visible—more so in the past than at present. You put on honor with the uniform, the epaulettes, the shining sword; you may be stripped of it in shame, as is the dishonored officer whose epaulettes and insignia are torn off, his sword broken. He is thus left uncovered and, in a sense, naked. In the military world honor is clearly visible, as is dishonor. The Southern concern with the look of life, its desire for the shining and the splendid, was satisfied by the military life.

Indeed, even in general, honor is dress, dishonor is nakedness. Shame reveals our nakedness, but usually before men, not God. When Adam and Eve were ashamed of their nakedness before God, it was before God walking like a man in his garden, taking the cool of the day.

The thrust of the modern world has been, until recently, to replace danger, uncertainty, and irrationality by a rational industrial order. Even in Spain, still a backward country by the end of the eighteenth century, the old ideas of prestige, affronts, and duels were being replaced by the modern glorification of virtue, efficiency in work, utility, and the general good. Strangely, at about the same time our South was strengthening its own ideals of honor. The duel was imported to America during the Revolution. We know that the Romantic movement of the late eighteenth and early nineteenth centuries was both a playing up of the individual and a turning backward across the rational eighteenth century to the less rational Middle Ages. The South had its own individualism which it wished to protect against the impending more rational and industrial order. For this and other reasons it was strongly influenced by the Romantic movement. Mark Twain even made the extreme comment that Sir Walter Scott, the South's favorite author during the first half of the nineteenth century, had brought on the Civil War by filling the minds of Southerners with pictures of knights in armor, ladies in distress, the knightly tournament—the whole picture of chivalry.

There is something to what Twain says. At the time of the Civil War, the gentlemen of the South sometimes referred to themselves as "the Chivalry."

But with all this individualistic thrust, it must be recalled what kind of individualism it was—how different from the atomic individualism of modern man. Under the code of honor, the individual always sees himself as he is seen by others. He must be well-thought-of; most of all he must be well spoken of. Without these others he does not exist; in his relations with them he finds his meaning. And just as he finds his place in their eyes, so he sees them in their places, each one in his own place.

So, in the Old South, honor had to do with personal, that is, social relationships. Whenever possible, men met one another in their places, or roles, and treated each other according to the demands of the code. If the stranger could not be placed, then he was under deep suspicion, and almost any measure might be appropriate. The Southerner tried to get around this unhappy condition by incorporating the stranger as a guest. The Southern ideal of generosity—by no means always observed—was a part of this effort to give strangers a place, and so to make persons out of these anonymous beings.

The importance of the family in the South and the importance of the plantation system bound together by the family— that is, the importance of primary as against secondary institutions in the South—made it a natural home for the expression of honor. In such societies "the relationship with others, through its intensity, intimacy and continuity, takes precedence over the relationship one has with himself." Here the individual learns the truth about himself through the intermediary of others.[8]

I recall a personal incident that illustrates the weakening of family ties and of honor in the South. About 1907 my father got into a quarrel with an in-law, an uncle of mine. He asked me and my older brother, boys of eleven and thirteen, to have nothing further to do with this in-law. Politely we refused. We told him we were sorry he and Uncle Jimmy had quarreled, but it wasn't our quarrel, and we didn't intend to carry it on. He did not insist. He could not. He was too much an individualist in the modern style, driving toward an atomistic world, to represent with any strength this old pattern of family and honor. If my family-oriented mother had made the same request of us, we might have complied. Though Father didn't admit it, I think he was proud of what his example had taught us.

In the highly personal society, especially of the late antebellum South, the leaders avoided dishonor and sought honor; at the highest they sought that shining honor we call glory. This was what belonged to their place, a place which could be held only as long as it was not tarnished. For the leaders of the South—in this sense again like the medieval knights—did not hold their position merely by birth. The South tried to establish a universal and unchanging order. We have already indicated its lack of universality, and it was certainly never unchanging. Some families persisted a long time, but the usual picture across the South was of commoners rising rapidly into positions of aristocratic leadership and leaders losing out or becoming commoners again. In such a society, where place was so important but at the same time so insecure, the leaders needed most of all to be well spoken of. Therefore they were continuously concerned with that honor and even that glory which only the goodwill of their neighbors and fellows could confer upon them. And the honor of each member of the group was the honor of the entire group.

All this sounds rather strange today, for we have become so deeply involved in getting and spending that we have almost forgotten the need for honor, certainly the need for glory. This is the opinion of Hannah Arendt; it is also the opinion of the Southern poet Robert Penn Warren.

The man who seeks honor seeks to stand out among, indeed above, his fellows, and yet not to exploit them, though he may at times do this. He is encouraged by his fellows to rise to this position of leadership because his achievement satisfies a deep need of society. The need for honor, for a visible glory, is the need to keep alive within society at large the ideal of the wild, the free, the adventurous. The attribution of honor to a leader is the tribute of the average man, a highly social, accommodating person, to the one who stands alone, who is willing to go on an adventure. This is the sense of the wild within the tame, the looking upward of the barnyard fowl to the honk of the passerby.

This is the call of the horizon, the frontier, of which a whisper still lingers in the heart of every man.

The importance of shame and honor in the South is a part of its highly public life. Southerners are by training citizens—in the largest sense *public* people. At its best the South is splendid; it has a shining quality, appealing to the eye. It was for the eye that the great houses and gardens and the long avenues were built. The reward of the kind of people who built them is honor; the punishment is dishonor or shame. Shame also has to do primarily with what is seen, with the body, the surface of life. It is shameful to wear—especially not to wear—certain things. Glory has to do with display; but to display what should not be displayed is shameful.

Perhaps we touch here upon Southern reserve, upon a private inner life. Living so much of his life in public, the Southerner has to maintain inviolate some small inner life. Here, perhaps, is his religion, so hidden away, so much his very own, that he would feel ashamed to reveal it. And if you try to uncover this inner, personal life, the Southerner may feel ashamed and dishonored, and in the old days, if he was a gentleman, feel obligated to reestablish his honor by means of a duel.

What we have in the South is a tension between the strong poles of public and private life. Because the Southerner is so strongly a public figure, he has to be equally strongly a private figure. On the surface he is frank and easygoing, but this is matched by an inner silence and reserve. In this inner world he faces silently the sacred images: God, Honor, Courage, Lady, and others. In the outer world he talks, dickers, compromises. But I sense a split between these two worlds. Do they really stand in polar relation to each other, each drawn to and repulsed from the other, or are they simply separate? It seems to me the outer world is too public, the inner world too private. It has been said in praise of the old Southerner that his private word was as good as his public bond, that he backed up his public life with his private life, that he was the same man. And indeed, this is what Southerners have praised their fellows most for: their integrity—though they usually called it justice. This, then, was the ideal of the South, and we can say at least that the Southerner did more than most Americans to attain it; he attempted to humanize all his activity. But he failed, as I see it now, mainly because he did not push his inner horizons deep enough—home to God. He attempted to unify his public and his private life about God, or, if about God, then about two gods: his inner life about the individualistic God of the Protestants, his outer about society itself.

We have already suggested that the use of shame and guilt as sanctions probably varies in different areas of the South and among different classes. We may add several pertinent comments here. The Southern writers Robert Penn Warren, William Faulkner, and C. Vann Woodward have emphasized in their poetry, fiction, and historical writing the belief that the South—especially the white South—is burdened by a sense of guilt. Woodward gives this as one of the several characteristics that distinguish the Southerner from other Americans.

Robert Coles is a New Englander, a psychiatrist who has spent half a dozen or more years in the South studying its children and their families, especially during the ordeal of desegregation. He came South, he says, with the feeling that Southerners were just like other Americans. His experience here has caused him to revise that feeling. Now he feels that the Southerner, white or black, consciously or unconsciously, feels a sense of shame. Things ought not to be as they are; something is wrong in society. The segregationist is ashamed that the South has come to this pass of open racial confrontation; the Negro is ashamed that he has permitted himself to remain a part of a society that is nominally democratic and Christian but actually so racially prejudiced. I raised with Dr. Coles the question as to the difference between the shame he perceived in the Southerner and the guilt Warren and others perceived. He did not make a complete reply, but he did say, "I think shame is more personal than guilt."

It has often been said that shame is the primary sanction of early societies, where the individual is still relatively unconscious of his separate self and strongly conscious of society, while guilt is the primary sanction of more advanced, individualistic societies, where, because of the individualism of the members, each carries deep within himself a sanction against certain attitudes and deeds. This is his conscience, which the individualistic modern is apt to think of as a highly personal thing.

In a sense the guilt-pronouncing conscience is built far more deeply into the person than the shame-pronouncing conscience. In this sense it is more personal. On the contrary, shame is more personal in that it is more clearly related to other persons. One is pronounced guilty by some shadowy, unknown, and inner court, and the pronouncement often does not say guilty of *what*. One is made ashamed by the court of his fellows, particularly selected ones of his fellows; the words are often pronounced, and the shameful deed specified.

In brief, guilt is a more individual thing, shame a more social and therefore more personal thing. The South, having held on longer to the social sense of the Middle Ages, would generally be more susceptible than the North to the sanction of shame; the North, having advanced further into the individualistic modern world, would be more susceptible to the sanction of guilt. Within the South itself, shame or guilt would predominate according to the social or individualistic character of the area or group in question. It must not be forgotten that every Southerner carries within himself strong ties to the more social medieval world, strong tendencies toward the more individualistic modern world. Therefore every Southerner knows something of the sanction of guilt.

The sense of guilt, being more deeply built into the individual than the sense of shame, is probably a greater driving force. More specifically, it is a driving force rather than a maintaining force, a force highly important in the modern, changing world. It is interesting to conjecture what would have happened to Negro slavery in North America if the Puritans had settled the South and if they had continued to be Puritans or developed only as they developed in the North. They freed their slaves in the North partly because they found them unprofitable, but they continued to trade in slaves with the South. If they had been plantation owners themselves, they probably would have driven their slaves harder to make them pay, and, this failing, might have freed them sooner because they did not pay.

We have seen that the manners and morals of the South are

the natural expression of a society by intention aristocratic and based upon slave labor, especially when both aristocrats and slaves carried in their minds, however vaguely, images of an earlier and highly mannered life. We have also seen that both guilt and shame were used as sanctions for conduct—in certain groups and places more of shame, in others more of guilt. But because of the fact that all white Southerners combined within themselves a strong medieval sense of society and a strong modern sense of the individual, all white Southerners had some sense both of shame and of guilt. The black Southerners, who had had long experience of the use of shame as a sanction and who had to learn from the whites all they knew of modern individualism —which was the last thing in the world the whites intended to teach them—felt mainly the sanction of shame. The strength of this sanction within them indicates the community within which they live, both the community of blacks and the more inclusive community of the plantation.

Humor and Commitment

There has developed in the Southerner a curious combination of humor and commitment. I say curious because the humorous person isn't apt to commit himself and the committed person isn't apt to be humorous. Humor is relaxed, commitment intense. Humor sees with a bifocal gaze, the eye of commitment is single.

Yet this dual attitude has developed generally among Southern whites and blacks. As for the humor, I have a friend who has spent his life in the Army and has consequently lived all over the world. "You know," he says, "it's dangerous to be a Southerner away from home. People generally are serious, and they take what I say seriously. I doubt that I mean more than half of what I say. Partly, I'm having fun."

Such an attitude is pervasive and continuing. Commitment is more concentrated and temporary, though there is a milder form known as loyalty, which may be lifelong. The interesting question is how the two attitudes are related and how they developed.

It would be pretty brash simply to say that the Southern settlers were more humorous than the New England settlers. Yet, as we have already argued, they seem to have been less intense, less determined to make a wholesale radical change in their old patterns of life, more acceptive both of their past and of their present. They adjusted themselves easily to their new conditions, careless of towns, concerned with rich land for tobacco. They accepted the infinite variety of the world, yielding themselves to its suggestions. This would not necessarily have made them humorous in their outlook, but it indicated less inner intensity than was so frequent in New England, where men were passionately carving out the kingdom of God according to a model they carried within their minds.

So much for the beginnings. The development of slavery, partly to combat the unusually relaxing climate, made possible a greater degree of relaxation among some of the whites—the fashion setters—and established the ideal of relaxation among most whites, and indeed among the blacks, who had plenty of other reasons not to be intense in their attitudes and efforts.

But slavery, by putting the blacks in an almost defenseless position, made them develop from the beginning the double vision of humor: holding on to the way they saw things while seeing things also as the whites saw them. Verbally they agreed with the whites—at times over-agreed with them. They laughed at all the stories the whites told, even though they themselves were often the butt of the stories. At other times they remained silent, with but the faintest trace of a smile—not enough to permit the whites to become angry, just enough to make them wonder and worry. It has been remarked that the black man either had or developed in his American situation the ability to seem to bend to the will of the whites but at the same time to remain unbending inside. Not that all blacks were able to support this dual attitude; some were terribly corrupted by it. But certainly they succeeded better at the game than did forthright, knock-down-and-drag-out Caucasians. The blacks trained themselves to be diplomatic, to recognize in every situation at least two meanings: one for the whites, the other for themselves.

As for the white South, though it began in relative tolerance, the nineteenth century found it growing less tolerant, more intense. This resulted from the increasing pressure being brought against the South from the outside and the increasing poor man-rich man struggle within the South. For, from about 1830 the emancipationist forces were growing, and from about the same time so were the democratic forces in the South, the latter a part of the Jacksonian revolution. It is true that the pressure from the outside against a key Southern institution tended to solidify the South, but in the growing spirit of white democracy, the yeoman farmers came increasingly to feel that they were being exploited by the slave owners, as Hinton Helper so bitterly said in 1857.

The black slave yielded honor but survived. Interestingly, that honor which was stolen from the black ended up as a talisman for the white, especially the aristocratic white. Every white man, in the individualistic spirit of the frontier, was ready to fight if his name, his worth, or his person was reflected upon, but only the aristocrats developed a code of honor and went through the punctilio of the duel. As we have already suggested, this stress upon personal freedom for the white was a normal accompaniment of the growth of slavery for the black. The extreme of this, the duel, which apparently came to America from Europe following the Revolution, was a part of the military and romantic feudalism adopted by the Southern aristocracy as befitting the growing image they had of themselves. It indicated a growing intolerance of others, a sort of sophisticated frontier violence. It developed in part because its exponents felt the growing opposition, from both outside and inside, and therefore drew ever more sharply and punctiliously about themselves the lines of *noli me tangere*. Perhaps the paradox is inevitable: A land of dishonor for some is a land of honor for others. (We have changed all that now: A land of great wealth for some is a land of great poverty for others.)

In the matter of white tolerance, the loss of the Civil War brought a change, in some sense returning the South to the tolerance of its earlier days. This time, however, the tolerance was more complete. It was a tolerance even of defeat and frustration, and it expressed itself in a complex defensive humor. Through this humor the white protects himself against what he feels are the inevitable disappointments of life by imagining those disappointments even before they come. When they do come, he is not so much distressed as reassured that he had sized life up correctly. A part of this humor takes the form of anecdotes about the Negro and the Yankee, the two groups who have formed a kind of human frontier along which the white Southerner has lived. For instance, there is the story about General Lee, who during the last days of the War looked up from his worktable to see what appeared to be a common soldier entering his tent, assumed he was an orderly, and pushed his sword across to be polished. But the supposed orderly was General Grant. When Grant accepted the sword, Lee had symbolically surrendered, and being a gentleman, he could not request it back. So the South lost the war.

The present presiding bishop of the Episcopal Church of the Upper Diocese of South Carolina, the Right Reverend John A. Pinckney, himself a Southerner, once remarked to me somewhat sadly that when the quarrels with the Negro and with the Yankee have finally been settled, the South will be hard put for humor. But this applies only to the funny stories. The basic attitude of always looking beneath the surface for another meaning, a hidden danger to be guarded against—this humorous attitude, having been won through hard generations, may continue for a long time. It is a cautious, sophisticated attitude, with little of naïveté or simple optimism.

Such humor is the product of frustration and defeat: the Negroes defeated by the whites, the whites in turn (though less clearly) defeated by the blacks and also by the North during the last hundred years. A part of this is the strange reserve of the white and the black South—strange because of the high social nature of both groups—a reserve that holds others at a distance, the double and conflicting attitude of sociability and reserve acting as a kind of irony which permits one to live with some enjoyment but without too much danger.

It is significant that humor is largely absent from the lives of the more radical contemporary blacks. They have some power; they feel they will have much more. They no longer have time to be playful, nor do they feel the need for protective humor.

Yet these same Southerners, whites and blacks, tellers of tall tales and humorous stories, at the same time continually aware of the absurdity of life and meeting it with a sly or sardonic smile, can also commit themselves to the hilt in a hopeless venture or maintain a lifelong loyalty to a lost cause. There is a certain gallantry in this refusal to accept defeat, whatever the cause for which the action is taken. It is doubtless connected with the military interest of Southerners, first white, now whites and blacks together. It is also connected with the influence of feudalism in the South. It is essentially an imprudent, unbusinesslike attitude rather rare among modern men. It is hardly a criticism of the South that it has been gallant; not always, however, has it exercised its gallantry in worthy causes.

Basically, the commitment of the Southerner—the whites certainly, the blacks probably—is the commitment of a man used to acting upon impulse, not generally introspective or trained in self-analysis, a man who through most of his history has been able to get along with little formal education. There isn't too much division, therefore, between the head and the heart—that most modern ailment. He finds it hard to agree to disagree. Either he agrees with you or he disagrees with you. He is your friend or your enemy. He would prefer to agree, and he is inclined to assume that you agree with him until you have made it clear that you do not; this is a part of his tolerance. Of course if you are a known outsider, he begins with the assumption that you disagree.

As for the historic commitment of the white South, it came at the end of a long period of increasing pressure both against and within the South, and therefore of decreasing tolerance and humor. Under pressure and stress the South lost its bifocal vision and became narrow, intolerant, and intense. Its social order was increasingly under attack, and it drew together to defend that order, the slave owners because (for one thing) they had too much involved in its continuance, the yeoman farmers because (for one thing) they couldn't imagine an order in which the blacks would be free.

Then came defeat. The old order was gone. But the white South still had the strength to set up a similar order—with the blacks as peons—and the North no longer had the will to prevent this. Therefore the South set up such an order, and in part to support it created over the years a splendid image of the Lost

Cause and of the magnolia-starred South that had—so they be-lieved—preceded the War.

During the postbellum period, at least among the whites, the quieter virtue of loyalty took the place of the fiercer virtue of commitment. And it should be noted that in all conservative societies—and the South was certainly conservative relative to the rest of the nation—loyalty is the prime virtue. If things are to continue as they are, no one has to question and plan, everyone has simply to be true to the status quo. I do not mean there were no voices for reform, change, and progress in the South, but these spoke out against a strong tendency to hold on to the past and to keep things—especially the Negro—in their places.

Yet, though white Southerners were almost a single voice in defending the old throughout the political defeats and economic frustrations of the better part of the past century, in their quiet moments, in their daily lives, they carried a deep sense of the general absurdity of life, its ability to mislead, to obstruct, to overthrow. In the beginning they had shown some tolerance toward the great variety of life and of people; now they became tolerant, perhaps too tolerant, of life's apparent trick of mislead-ing men and frustrating them. Their pervasive humor was a shield against this danger. They had two faces. With one they faced together the great imagined past and the economically and racially difficult present; with the other they faced individually the daily hardships and disappointments of life and protected them-selves against these disappointments by humorously imagining them before they happened.

In this duality of attitude they were not too far from their black neighbors who, it will be remembered, also had two faces, one of which they showed to the white man, the other only to themselves. But the whites, having the predominance of power, were more damaged by this than were the blacks.

We have been showing how difficult it is for humor and commitment to exist in the same person at the same time—difficult, but not impossible. In general we might say: great com-mitment, little humor, or vice versa. But there is a story—perhaps apocryphal, but deeply suggestive—that illustrates the presence of humor and commitment together. During one of the forced

marches of Stonewall Jackson's famous "foot cavalry," the General rode back along the column to encourage his men. Near the
end he came upon a soldier, too old to be in any man's army,
probably hungry, certainly weak, staggering back and forth
across the track. "Well, Soldier," said the General, "I hope you
make it." "Yes, General, yes, I'll make it. But General, I hopes
to God I never loves another country." He was committed to the
hilt, for life and death, but he realized somehow the absurdity of
it all and hoped he wouldn't do it again. Yet, even at that, he knew
he might commit himself absurdly to love another country.

In all this the Southerner, especially the white Southerner,
was an existentialist long before the recent popularity of the
term. He did not understand his life. Indeed, he too had been
infected, however mildly, by the modern disease of abstraction
and was losing contact with a complete life. Nevertheless, there
was more body in him, more completeness of life surrounding
him, than in the more abstracted lives of typical Americans. So
he had more to hold on to and stronger fingers for holding on
with. But even what he had was incomplete. It had the prime
advantage of being earthy, but it was too earthy; it was earth-
bound. Whereas the spirit of the typical American had abstracted
itself from the body in order better to control and manipulate
that body—both the individual body and the body of the world
—the spirit of the Southerner, though sustained by the body (his
own and the world's), was also constrained by it and often lost
in it.

Therefore, though he had the feeling that that to which he
committed himself was worthy of commitment, he knew somehow deep down that something was wrong. And it was. He had
loved too much a too limited country. Only the complete world
can command the commitment of the complete man. The Southerner had this world clearly embodied for him in the institution
of the family, somewhat less clearly in the institution of the plantation, but all this was weakened by the abstraction of race. And
probably most of all because of this abstraction, he felt the gap,
the lack, in his world. Even such a rich embodiment of the world
as he found in the family and to a lesser degree in the plantation
could not bear its proper spiritual bloom; he could not really

transcend the world of kinsman, friend, and leader. He was still caught in this world.

Vaguely he sensed this, and the humorous twist in his commitment indicated his realization. He was committed, but it was absurd. He was, as I said, our first existentialist.

The blacks have had far less to commit themselves to than the whites. It was only in a poor sort of way "their country." The whites have made a great thing of the loyalty of the blacks to their "white folks." The idea has been overdone. Undoubtedly there were loyal slaves, after emancipation loyal servants, people who were more conscious of the human ties than of the legal and customary bonds. This was inevitable when one considers the variety of whites involved with the blacks and the complexity of human nature. A human being does not cease to be human without a struggle. Nevertheless, it is only within recent years that blacks have envisaged clearly something worthy of their commitment. This is "Freedom Now," and they have committed themselves with typically Southern wholeheartedness—indeed, I think, with a wholeness of which the white South has seldom been capable. For they brought to the struggle, especially in its innocent sit-in days, a dual quality of this-worldliness and otherworldliness, of manners and morals, of Southern culture and Christianity, that the white South, though it dreamed of it, could seldom attain, certainly not in masses like this. They were the best of the South, for they were the South closest to its basic ideal: that a man should live in this world and another at the same time.

But the white South generally did not recognize the South in them. So, though the blacks moved to some successes, they moved too slowly, and slowly, therefore, the Southern kindliness and good manners of their approach—in the broadest sense, its humor—faded, and its place was taken by the dark glasses, the hard stare, the threat of violence, and the actual violence of the revolutionary. They have no time now for humor; their commitment is too narrow.

The white South recovered some of its early humorous tolerance in defeat; the black South has lost some of its age-old humor in a limited success. The question is: Would they have kept it if success had come more truly and completely?

In summary, Southerners, white and black, have been a people involved for so long in such situations—geographical, social, and political—that they have developed, for Americans, an unusual attitude of commitment and humor. At times in each group commitment has been clearer, at times humor; at rare moments they have been combined. Perhaps, though I am not sure, they are basically a tolerant people—as befits the tolerant nature of the physical world they live in. Even during those periods when they have faced a harsh human world—at times the creation of themselves, at times of others—they have defended themselves against it with considerable humor, seldom, and then but briefly, by the passionate, single-minded commitment of the typically tragic personage.

Directness and Indirection

There has developed also in the Southerner a curious combination of directness and indirection. This is common to both blacks and whites and is due considerably but not entirely to their life here together. Even beyond the strains of that interracial life, however, sometimes prior to them, sometimes apart from them, there is a quality of indirection both in the Southern white and in the black. In the black, certainly in his African experience (though how much of this he kept here no one is sure) there was the whole stress upon manners: how you do and say a thing, the subjection of all details to an enclosing pattern. From the point of view of the less mannered person, the person more concerned with ends, this is wasteful. To those who stress manners—and manner—it is not, for the end is in part the living moment; you are always at the end. We have already noticed how the blacks made life more livable in a slave economy by playing up this interest in manners.

Melville Herskovits points out that in Africa even today blacks have a great store of reserve, of hesitancy, of indirection. This appears especially in their political life: their taxes are usually indirect and hidden. As for the value of these traits in the New World, he says that "diplomacy, tact, and mature reserve are not necessarily hypocrisy; and while the situation of the Negro in all the New World, past and present, has been such as to force discretion upon him as a survival technique, it is also true that he came on to the scene equipped with the technique rather than with other procedures that had to be unlearned before this one could be worked out."[9]

As for the Southern whites, even without association with the blacks they would have developed their own form of indirection. Contrast them with the typical Puritan. The Puritan was moving into the future on a straight line, cutting through this corrupt world toward the glorious city of God. The Southerner paused and looked around him, built homes in the wilderness, came to love them with all their imperfections (perhaps even *for* their imperfections), and brooded upon them. It is too much to say he thought about them. He was never very good at thinking, which demands that one move from one point to another. In his more digressive path into the future, his eye was occupied with the things he saw about him and his mind was filled with images of these things. If he thought, he thought in images. So his inner world was a counterpart of that outer world where he was preoccupied with particular people and things. His thinking, such as it was, was circular, moving around and around things and people. So he tended to see things and people as three-dimensional, to give them value in themselves, not to take them simply as means to the next station in his advancement.

I am aware that the white man's treatment of the Negro seems to give the lie to these last remarks. Certainly it strains them. Undoubtedly this supposedly slow, indirect turning of the white man's mind around the present was usually sharply modified when he was dealing with the black; he saw the black much more simply as a means to a better future for himself. Yet I would maintain that even in black and white relationships there remains something of this playing of the game for the sake of the game, this pleasure in the immediate present.

I am aware also that by no means all Southern whites, even among themselves, have shown this indirectness, this circling around the present fact and image. One of the most striking characters in Southern fiction is Sutpen, of Faulkner's *Absalom, Absalom!* Sutpen spends his life driving inexorably into the future, to his own doom and the doom of those near him. This is

straight-line, tragic thinking. There are and have always been in
the South many men of whom Sutpen is the ideal type. The main
group out of which these men come is the Calvinist Scotch-Irish,
the most Puritan group ever to settle here. They came mainly
between 1717 and 1775 and undoubtedly changed the temper of
the earlier South. Undoubtedly, also, they were changed by that
more permissive, more tolerant temper. Some of them were seduced, or if you wish, merely softened, or, perhaps, made more
human. As a result, by no means every Southerner broods over
images of present charm or past splendor; many of them are
horse traders who will outtrade the sharpest Yankee. Nevertheless, the fact remains that there is a distinctive quality of indirectness in the Southern approach, a circularity of thought which,
though it has been intensified by race relations, is not finally
dependent upon race relations.

This is clearly evident when two Southerners, strangers to
each other, meet. It's like two dogs meeting. Figuratively speaking, they walk round and round each other. The dogs are more
direct in their attentions; each is trying to get the smell of the
other. The Southerner, however, is trying to learn how the other
is related to the world—geographical, social, familial. The inevitable first question is, "Where're you from?" It has been said that
if the answer to the first question indicates that the stranger is a
non-Southerner, the questioner, losing interest, says, "Oh," and
soon drifts away. If, however, the stranger turns out to be a fellow
Southerner—say, a Texan—the questioner is apt to remark,
"You know, I had some kin people moved to Texas a hundred
years ago, named so-and-so. Wonder if you ever met any of
them?" So the Southerner has moved from geographical placement to family placement. The point here is that every Southerner—and this even cuts across racial lines—feels somehow kin
to every other Southerner, and family being so important, perhaps blood kin—but this is not supposed to cross racial lines.

To put the matter generally, the Southerner tends to see a
man as having a role in the world, a role determined by his
various physical and human relationships. If he knows these relationships he will know the man. He does not see the man simply
as an individual—cut off, separate, alone—but as belonging, as
he himself belongs, to some kind of community.

It must be said immediately that this is the old picture of how strangers met in the South; it's fast fading now. Even naïve Southerners begin to show some hesitancy in asking a soldier where he's from—he's from so many places. And beyond the soldiers, there is the whole increasingly mobile population of the South: newcomers from the East, North, West, and tourists passing through. So it makes less and less sense to ask them where they're from. But what then do you ask them? If you cannot relate them to some place, some job, somebody, how do you understand them? You can't ask them how they stand on current issues, what they think: it's too dangerous. As a result, the sociable Southerner, just curious about people, eager to walk around them and look at them, to know in this indirect way something about them, is stopped in his tracks. Since he cannot confront them, he remains unknown and unknowing. It's a curious unease in such a friendly land.

So much then for the natural indirection of the Southerner, white or black. This has been strongly augmented by the racial situation in the South. Much can be said for the natural indirection. It shows a strong social feeling, a strong sense of the value of the present and of present relationships. Less can be said for the augmentation of indirectness resulting from race relations. Certainly the black has seldom replied truthfully to the questions or remarks of the white; it has been too unhealthy. Rather, he made the reply he was supposed to make, a reply tending to increase the self-concern of the white. What effect has this had upon the white?

One clearly unhappy effect is that it has often led the white to make brutally direct remarks and ask brutally direct questions simply because he could. His humanity has been corrupted by the power he held. A contrary effect has been the same kind of circuitous reply to the black that he got from him. Now both sides were playing the parts of partial strangers, each keeping his distance, each aware of the situation, and each more or less amused, though always discreetly, by the game being played. It becomes a form of diversion. The white diverts himself from any clear realization of the basic injustice of the situation, the black permits the white to do this and even aids him in doing so, because he himself cannot bear the thought of the explosion that might follow straightforward questions and answers. We may call this lack of courage on both sides, but in addition to this, it is also the attempt to soften somewhat a structurally harsh relationship, to add at least some human understanding to a situation in which the participants cannot afford to understand each other.

We live now in a period of confrontation, and most of the above goes by the board, but I am speaking of the long past and its effect upon us; and one of the most striking effects is the habit of indirection, augmented as it has been by white and black relations in the South.

This indirection appears not only between whites and blacks but also, I would suppose, among blacks and certainly among whites. It may be less strong when blacks are dealing with one another; but even here the carry-over from frequent association with whites must be strong, especially when one remembers how dependent blacks have been upon whites, how these degrees of dependency have varied, and how, therefore, no black can be absolutely sure that his too-direct conversation with another black may not be reported to some white. Therefore he relies heavily upon silence or upon circumambient words.

White Southerners have always discussed among themselves the race problem, but usually in anecdotal form dealing only with its superficial aspects. For the most part it has simply been bad form to take up the basic issues. Especially in critical times like the decade preceding the Civil War, slavery was simply not discussed, and everyone remembers how in the critical years from about 1950 to 1960 segregation was not discussed. The white South assumed only one basic position: pro-segregation. There were many who disagreed, but they were usually careful to keep their thoughts to themselves.

In brief, the presence of the Negro has helped to make the white Southerner talkative and to keep him from really talking about anything. But the paradox is that this indirection can move swiftly into even violent directness. How do we explain this?

The violence of the South is, first of all, American violence, the violence of a new country separated from the accustomed ways of Europe by three thousand miles. This is a form of frontier violence. The South suffers particularly from this violence because it remained frontier longer than any other part of America. Officially the American frontier was closed in the early 1890's; yet Howard Odum has said that even as late as 1920 the South was, according to sociological indices, a frontier land. I remember my father, as late as 1910, going to the county seat on Saturday with his revolver in his hip pocket. On the frontier every man looks out for himself.

Again, the generally impulsive nature of the Southerner, white and black, permits him to fall easily into violence. When he is moved, he acts. He is not trained to stop and think. Historically this is probably due in part to the poor education Southerners have received, but it is also due in part to the Southerner's interest in the present moment, his relative unconcern for the future. He can fill the present with nothingness, or he can fill it with sudden, extreme action. This is the kind of picture you find in Faulkner: the sleepy crossroads store, the lounging countrymen, and the entire scene suddenly galvanized into action. Oftentimes this action has been related to the following basic source.

The South has been prone to violence because it rested its economic life upon violence. No matter how kindly particular masters handled their slaves, they always had recourse to violence, and from the beginning the very order was based upon violence. The situation affected the Southern white in two opposing ways. It made him more prone to violence toward blacks because he could get away with it—the undue power corrupted him. But it also made him cautious about the use of violence, because the potential counter-violence against himself was too great; there was always the possibility of a slave insurrection. Therefore the more responsible whites have always stressed humaneness, agreeableness, getting along with people.

As for the less responsible whites, especially the poorer whites who were given little responsibility, and the blacks, who were given practically none, the high degree of violence among these two groups is in part the result of the long and harsh pressures under which they have lived. Pressed too long to the wall, they fight among themselves. The poor whites also fight against the blacks. In Lillian Smith's interpretation this is part of the tacit understanding since the Civil War between the leading, responsible whites and the poorer whites: the poorer whites left economic and political control largely to the wealthy whites upon condition that control of the blacks should be left largely to them. I'm afraid this is generally what has happened. The old paternalistic leaders of the South, unable to control both the freed blacks and the poverty-stricken and embittered poor white farmers, yielded their milder control of the blacks to the harsher control of the poorer whites, with the understanding that the poor whites would continue under the economic and political control of the wealthy whites. This suggests the degree of corruption that slavery and segregation had brought to the whites.

To summarize, the indirection of the Southerner, white and black, is in part the result of his own indirect nature, circling the present, moving tangentially into the future, and in part the result of the ever present racial frontier along which he moves in indirect, devious ways. His directness, his violent directness, is based on his native impulsiveness, but is also related to the long continuance of the physical frontier, with the hardships incident thereto, and to the fears and hatreds incident to the racial frontier. Basically a tolerant man, and still tolerant in matters unrelated to race, the Southerner has developed through his unhappy history a strong intolerance in this matter.

PART
TWO

Spiritual Values

XI

By God's Grace, the South

We have concluded now a broad sketch of the culture of the South. Our next question is: What is the religious significance of this culture? More specifically, since I write out of a Christian background and express at least generally Christian ideas, it is: What is the Christian significance of this culture? How does it relate to Christianity? At what points does it support or oppose Christianity?

There are Christians who feel that these questions are meaningless. They believe that culture is one thing and Christianity another and "never the twain shall meet." I do not agree. I do agree that until the kingdom of God shall come, wherever or whenever that may be, there can be no completely Christian culture; but some cultures, I maintain, are more favorable to the coming of that kingdom than others, else why strive in this world for its coming? There are indeed certain sects that do not strive for its coming. This is an honest attitude. But generally Christians have striven to make the world better and must therefore have believed that it could be made better.

But what gives any man authority to think he can see things from the point of view of the kingdom of God? The great prophets of Israel, whom we still respect and praise, said they got their authority from God. It was an astounding claim, and even they realized that there were prophets who made the claim falsely. Of course the false prophets thought they were the true ones, and sometimes even the true prophets were mistaken. It is not well to be too sure of God. It takes time to separate the true from the false, and men can still argue about the degree of truth stated by any prophet, false or true.

The main point is that any man who believes in God would

like to know what God is doing in the world, what kind of action he upholds, what kind he lets fall. Such a man, therefore, listens to those who claim to describe the work of God, and if he believes what he hears, he tries to act upon it.

Of course God has been reported dead, but the report is vastly exaggerated. So long as mystery surrounds us and inhibits us, so long shall we need some explanation, and that may very well be God. To return to today, even those who are not concerned to know what God is doing, believing that he isn't doing anything, are, if serious, concerned to know what works in the world for good and for ill. We have honored the prophets, regardless of whether they have spoken for God or just for themselves, because they have at least tried to give an answer to the basic human question: What is the meaning of life?

All men have a point of view, a basic belief about the world. Every so-called objective historian has. He sees history as largely determined by economic forces or political forces or religious forces or maybe ideas. I see all of these forces as operative and as interacting with one another. But I am finally concerned to understand history as an expression, direct or indirect, of the will of God. The main events recorded in the preceding section are reported in the secular histories, but I am interested in how the human actors have responded to the events, and how, through their responses, they have become a certain kind of people and as such have fallen heir to both these and other events.

My concern with history is largely pragmatic. I want to know what has been done in order to know better what can be done, to use better the resources, and to avoid the dangers. God, I believe, is our greatest resource and our greatest danger. Do I wish then to use him? A simple affirmative answer could be given only by a foolhardy man with a small god. But our most palpable resources are the world God has given us and the human race itself. We are enjoined by the Christian Scriptures to use these for his glory; the Presbyterian catechism declares, "Man's chief end is to glorify God." Thus, to use these resources is to accept them in their totality, that is, to accept God. In this sense he is our greatest resource and our greatest danger.

The South, perhaps the most religious part of the country,

has been saying this over and over, but it has said it individualistically. Individually we are saved by God's grace; without that grace
we sink under his just judgment. I am going to apply this doctrine
regionally and say that insofar as the South has been saved, it has
been saved by the grace of God.

For the most part, such goodness as exists in the South was
not planned or intended. I repeat, for the most part. The intentions of men, for good or for ill, do make a difference. But
including these and often overriding them, "There is a destiny
that shapes our ends, rough hew them how we will." So it happened in the South as elsewhere, not that men had nothing to do
with it. They expressed this goodness; they maintained it. And
not automatically but because they wanted to. But on the whole,
they didn't plan it the way it came out.

Such goodness as the South reveals, therefore, may be as-
cribed to the grace of God. The South is evidence of what God
can do when given a chance. Men give him a chance either by not
being too assuredly busy or by failing so disastrously that they
have to pause and ask what went wrong.

I know how all this sounds. Many critics of the South will say
that if the South is evidence of God at work, then the sooner he
quits work the better. I can only hope that these critics will read
on, lured, perhaps, by the desire to understand an as yet unex-
plained region. Perhaps the mystery lies in the fact that God is
working here, and, as men have long realized, he works in mysterious ways.

If he works, he works everywhere. There are certain times
and places, however, where his work may be more easily seen. It
may be that he finds it easier to work in such places. I once
remarked to a Northern audience that God had a better chance
in the South because Southerners were prone to rest between
jobs or even on jobs, and that while they rested God had a chance
to modify the work. I wouldn't insist upon this, though it appeals
to my easygoing temperament. God can also hold back his hand
while men make fools of themselves, and then bring down the
whole structure, as he is said to have done with the tower of
Babel.

When this happens we call it the judgment of God. But the

same event may also be the grace of God. "Whom the Lord loveth he chasteneth." Whether the event is grace or judgment depends upon us. Both grace and judgment describe the effects upon us of God's underlying and overarching providence. It is God who has provided this universe we live in, this green planet —so startlingly blue from the moon—that we inhabit. Our young daughter once thanked God for the world, that he made it "and we didn't have to do it." It is true that we are remaking it— whether for better or worse remains to be seen. But we are remaking it according to the physical laws that control it and according to our wishes. If some of these wishes are evil, did God give them to us? I don't propose to tackle this problem. I would say only that he made us with some capacity for freedom, and if in expressing that freedom we do evil, this is not to say that God wishes evil but that God will risk the chances associated with human freedom.

So God has created the universe, the world, and human beings with a degree of freedom. This is what is given. All this is God's providence. From the beginning and moment by moment the world is his world. So far as we are concerned, all depends upon how we take it. Do we take it as coming from him, to test us perhaps, but always to bless us? Or do we take it as coming from nowhere, to be used up and thrown aside, as each of us may wish? Or perhaps we feel it comes from some great evil spirit who is to be outwitted as long as possible. To accept the world, its totality and its moments, as from God is to know his grace; to take it as something else is to feel his judgment.

"All things work together for good to them that love God," or to them that love the whole, whether they call it God or not. Hocking once remarked, "Only the complete outer can interest the complete inner." If a man is concerned with the whole, he is wholly concerned, and God's grace rests upon him whether he realizes it or not. In the parable of the last judgment, Jesus told the surprised redeemed that their lives had been proof that they loved him, even though they had not consciously known him.

Thus, because they loved wholeness, all things had worked in them toward wholeness, toward God. For those who have within themselves the love of God—if they have enough of it—

life will increase this love. Aware already of the whole, they will find all things, both good and bad, increasing this awareness. No harm, said Socrates in true Christian spirit, can befall a good man. "To him who has will more be given," the Scriptures say, and this confounds our human ethics. Perhaps we may say again: God does the best he can with what he has. Just as Jesus wept over Jerusalem because its inhabitants would not receive him, so perhaps God weeps over the world because it will not be reconciled to him. But always he is attempting the work of reconciliation. "God was in Christ reconciling the world to himself." Something of his Spirit is in every man, longing to accept this reconciliation, to pass beyond the divisions of life, outer and inner, and to be at one with the world, or, more exactly, with the inner creative spirit of the world, with God. "Thou hast made us for thyself," said Augustine, "and our hearts are restless till they find rest in thee."

So to be divided within oneself, from the world, from God, is to be under his judgment; to be at one with oneself, with the world, with God, is to receive his grace. As we study the life of the South, we shall be continually estimating these opposing forces within ourselves: God's grace working for reconciliation and wholeness and God's judgment indicating fragmentariness. In a sense God's judgment is simply the absence of his grace, the relative absence of God himself.

Those who refer to God's grace and judgment often use the terms carelessly. A man out in a storm, barely missed by a stroke of lightning, may say, "By God's grace the lightning missed me." But on the same day, down the road, somebody else was struck. Do we say that the second man suffered God's judgment? Some moralistic people do, but Jesus disposed of this question by asking another, "Do you think the men on whom the tower of Siloam fell were more guilty than all the others?"—implying that they were not.

No, the lightning stroke comes in the providence of God. He has provided a natural world which under certain conditions flashes in lightning. If a man gets caught in such a situation, this says nothing about God's grace or judgment. It merely says that there is chance as well as human freedom in the world. If the man whom the lightning has missed should, because of this event, become more aware of God's continuing presence and care, this effect upon him might be called the grace of God in his life. If, however, the opposite effect should occur, if his close escape should increase his own sense of pride and untouchability, then he would reveal in himself the judgment of God. The image of his own weakness and dependence had appeared for a moment, and he had not seen it. The light had shone in the darkness, and the darkness comprehended it not. Now there is a deeper darkness.

It is clear that what I am concerned with is what is sometimes called natural grace—not that special grace which appeared in the life of Jesus Christ, but that general grace which is a part of every moment, more visible in some moments and places than in others, but always a possibility. When I say judgment, I am referring not to any final judgment but to the continuing judgment that befalls us as we fail to respond in love, with grace. The strange thing about the South is that both its social structure and its history would lead one to believe that it had lain most of the time under God's judgment; yet it reveals many evidences of God's grace. This does not mean that Southerners generally have been filled with grace; perhaps it does mean that they show more evidences of grace than other Americans.

I hasten to say that one of the marks of the presence of grace is the sense of sin. St. Paul, who preached grace if any man ever did, said—perhaps boasted—that he was the greatest of sinners. This simply means that the sense of wholeness, of completeness, sharpens the sense of incompleteness. Those who have found God are most aware of his absence and seek him most earnestly.

It may be appropriate to remark at this point that Southerners generally have been more graceful than other Americans. Certainly they have tried to be more graceful: they have emphasized the body and the use of the body more. This raises the whole question of the relation between physical grace and the grace of God. For all I know, they may oppose each other— though I hope not.

Now let us see if we can establish any criteria for the recognition of God's grace and judgment in the world. Does he leave any footprints to mark his passage?

XII

The Footprints of God

There have been times when I saw the Christian position as an absolute one: one was either aware of an eternal morning flooding one's heart and the world and shining from the up-turned faces of others, or one was not aware. So few men, it seemed to me, were aware. But there were other times, more frequent now, when, looking about me, I could see men reaching in tiny ways toward God—a fleeting smile, a compassionate tear, an inclusive gesture—or, if you will, I could see in these homely, common things the Spirit of God himself.

If the Spirit of God within men reaches toward God, more strongly here, more weakly there, then there are some groups of men, some cultures, some societies in which this urge is stronger than in others. Just as man is more human now than he was half a million years ago, so now certain cultures foster his humanity more than others do.

And while I'm making clear my own attitude, let me add this: I'm not concerned that men should be Christians; I'm concerned that they should be men. Jesus said almost the same thing: If you do my will you are my followers, whether you know me or not. This is what life is about—that men should become human. I'm not an existentialist at this point. There is a human ideal, and men are reaching for it. As we become human we become divine. We are indeed called to be sons of God.

It is appropriate that men should most easily see God in the quiet of the evening, when the fever of the day is done and the pause in action permits some contemplation. But men have also felt his presence at other times, even in the fury of action. As I have already suggested, I believe that at all times God is walking and working in his world, sustaining it and continuously creating it in grace and in judgment. Certain times and situations marked by completeness, by reconciliation, or by spiritual freedom reveal his presence more clearly than others. As men realize completeness or reconciliation or spiritual freedom, they are near to God. He is passing by; these are his footprints.

Man is a social being; he does not exist humanly outside society. What is not always realized, however, is that man's search for himself in other men transcends humanity and includes the total world, even the universe. It is within this infinite and eternal universe that he searches for the meaning of life, and, as Augustine said, he is restless until he finds rest there.

But it is doubtful that ever in this world he finds complete rest and is absolutely and continuously sure. He remembers the perfect moments, and he hopes; he lives by faith. The rare moments in which this faith becomes reality are called mystic. In such moments a man feels that he is one with the Whole, and the Whole is one with him. Though in a sense he has lost himself, he has really found himself at last in God. He belongs to the Whole and the Whole belongs to him. His need for belonging, of which we spoke earlier, is at last though briefly satisfied.

To few men are such moments of utter completeness granted, and then only by God's grace; we cannot command them. Yet they are the climax of numerous generally unrecognized moments of relative completeness that touch the lives of all men. No society can ensure to its members either the ineffable moments or the tiny flashes of glory, yet a living culture has the power of making its members feel that they belong to it. This sense of belonging is by no means the same as the sense of belonging to the Whole, but it is a step in that direction.

A man will be both aided and hindered by the society of which he is a part. If that society is strongly individualistic, he will be continually thrown back upon himself and will tend to see himself and others as separated individuals. This may include a deep sense of separation from nature, as it has in the modern world. A strongly social order, on the contrary, if it is still growing and has not become crystallized, will tend to encourage in him the sense of belonging to the social and perhaps also to the natural world about him. In such a social order he will at least be on the way to finding a completeness similar to that which he lost at birth. In such a society the footprints of God are clearly visible.

God may be recognized in the world, then, as grace—by completeness or the search for completeness—or as judgment—by the shattering effect of extreme incompleteness, of human fragmentation. He may also be recognized in moments of reconciliation if the reconciliation is to life itself, not merely to some superficial aspect of life. Men do not naturally like the way the world is put together. Much of their animal nature would prefer a world without human tensions, a world simply of eating and sleeping and mating. But there is that in man which demands more than this, and it is this extra demand that makes him unhappy. The contemporary situation has made many men so unhappy that life begins to seem to them absurd. They have a radical quarrel with life. But practically all men at times, and especially when they love life, are apt to echo the sentiment of Omar Khayyám:

> Ah, Love! could you and I with him conspire
> To grasp this sorry scheme of things entire,
> Would we not shatter it to bits—and then
> Remold it nearer to the heart's desire?

Most men who face life seriously have to quarrel with it and, if fortunate, come to be reconciled to it. If they do, it is because the great Reconciler has passed by, the Spirit of wholeness, whose effect is to move men to accept the whole, even though this includes the entire structure of human imperfection and striving and anguish, forever constrained by the powers of time and space.

How can one be reconciled to imperfections, to incompleteness, and yet strive for perfection, for completeness? Jesus clearly enjoined us to do the latter: "Be ye therefore perfect, even as your Father which is in heaven is perfect." We can be reconciled not to our imperfections themselves, but to the fact that we are imperfect and that therefore we should strive for perfection, or, if you wish, strive to permit the Spirit of God within us to lead us toward perfection. We do not naturally like the tension, the absurdity, even the cross at the heart of life. But this is a part of being human. "Man," said Yeats, "has created death." Out of our loves, out of our hopes and our fears, we have created that dark end, an end the animal is unconscious of except in the moment of its coming. By our humanity we have created death and find it hard to be reconciled to it.

But death is only the end of human time and is prefigured in every moment of our lives. Momently we die, momently the present slips into the past and is in a sense no more. The terrible moments pass, but what we find hard to forgive is that the beautiful moments also pass, no matter how passionately we cry, "Ah, stay, thou art so fair!" We can remember them, of course; in a sense we can bring them back; but the body of the world, the strong and tender flesh, is gone, and our hands touch only shadows. If we had made the world, we would not have made it like this.

Nor would we have fixed ourselves so firmly in space. It is true that today we are loosening the grip of space upon us. We move more freely through space, yet we know of no way to be here and there at the same time. In a sense our lives are fragmentary, made up of flying moments and changing places. We do not like it this way, but we must be reconciled to it. When we are willing to admit and accept the incompleteness within ourselves, we may find completeness in God. This is what the mystic vision tells us. In God there is no here or there, no now or then, only the eternal present.

If in a given group men tend to recognize the imperfections of life, both in the world and in the human heart, to recognize them without deifying them, to be reconciled to them without worshiping them, in that group the footprints of God are clear. There is no doubt that societies and times differ in their opinions of the imperfections of man and of the world—as regards man, in their opinions of sin.

Finally, as men approach freedom they approach God. Where true freedom exists, there God is. If you read the New Testament straight through, you find its pages rustling in the wind of freedom. The new men who walk these pages have been freed of their old fears—of the universality of death, of the meaninglessness of life, in a sense even of their fellowmen, however powerful. They have become spiritually free.

This is the true freedom. Freedom *in* the world, not *from* it. The principal ties and powers still operate; man is still subject to them. But in his spirit he is free because he knows that they and all things are subject to God. He sees all things as having their places in the whole. Instead of walls he sees depths and distances. In such a view matter is etherealized, spirit materialized.

The wise man is he who, by the power of imagination, sees within the present object and moment universal and eternal significance. He moves freely within the moment, he enters through imagination the natural and human bodies about him, and he moves freely within them.

Nicholas Berdyaev has written most extensively about this in a book entitled *Freedom and the Spirit.* For him the two terms are synonymous. The Spirit is freedom, and as the Spirit lives in man and man in the Spirit, he is free. Free *in* the world, not *from* it.

Though no social order can give to its members spiritual freedom—insure, that is, that through imagination they will live in the Spirit and the Spirit in them, and thus live freely in the world (for this would be the kingdom of God)—one social order can do more than another to this end. However we describe social orders, some, I am sure, take men further toward spiritual freedom than do others. In so doing, they reveal the footprints of God.

Certainly reconciliation occurs only where love is. Just as certainly the individual finds completeness in the whole only through love. Why not, then, simply say, "Where love is, God is," and be done with it? For two reasons: the term *love* is too inclusive and it has often been misused. As to its misuse, there is no need to cite the modern stories, on the one hand of lust, on the other of pure sentimentality, to prove this. As to inclusiveness, it could be made to cover the complex matters of completeness, reconciliation, and spiritual freedom.

It is these three that we shall use as the criteria for determining God's clear presence in the world. He is always present, but he is more clearly present in some times than in others. And he is present in both grace and judgment. Indeed, as we have said, the judgment falls upon those who cannot recognize the grace and itself becomes grace for those who recognize it as judgment.

This is put too strongly. Men do not have to recognize God in order to serve him. Jesus said this in the parable of the last judgment. As men seek completeness, reconciliation, and spiritual freedom, they indicate the Spirit of God within themselves, and the grace of that complete, reconciling, and free Spirit falls upon their lives. It is those who do the will of God, not those who merely call upon his name, who are his servants.

We shall now examine the culture of the South to determine, as well as we can, where God's grace and judgment have been present within it.

But before we do this, it might be good to ask what experiences and thoughts have brought me to the conclusion that the presence of completeness, reconciliation, and freedom indicates the footprints of God, and also how I relate my findings to the South at large. To what degree did I distill them from the culture, to what degree from the church? Such a question is naturally of interest to me, but whether it is significant in this study depends upon how representative of the South I am. If I am not representative, then the question of the relative influence of the culture and of the church in the formation of my ideals is unimportant. If I am representative, it is important.

XIII

Where First I Saw Them

Since I began writing about the South, I have assumed that, with whatever variations, I am basically Southern. Without this assumption I couldn't have written *The Southern Heritage* or *Who Speaks for the South?* or the present book. Right or wrong, then, this is the assumption I act upon, and, granted this assumption, it is important whence I got the ideals I am using to test the essential values of the South.

It may be helpful to note at this point what Flannery O'Connor has to say about Southern identity. It is "not really connected with mocking-birds and beaten biscuits and white columns," she says, "any more than it is with hookworm and bare feet and muddy clay roads. . . . It is not made from what passes, but from those qualities that endure . . . because they are related to truth. It lies very deep. In its entirety, it is known only to God, but of those who look for it, none gets so close as the artist."[1]

I am not an artist, but I use as much as I can the artist's main tool, the imagination. It was through the imagination that I found in completeness and reconciliation and freedom the footprints of God. It is through the imagination that I now relate these basic attitudes to the culture and the church which produced me.

If anyone wishes to find in Jesus the original and chief exemplar of the ideals I state here, I have no objection; indeed, I approve. But I am clearly aware that many of the Jesus-worshipers of the South find in him something entirely different from what I find.

Let me point out that this attempt to see the South as a generalization of myself and myself as a specification of the South is itself typically Southern. For Southerners have always stressed personal, not abstract knowledge. In fact, as Robert Penn Warren says, there's nothing the Southerner fears more than an abstraction. We are Hebraic in this, not Greek. To the Greek, knowledge was thought; to the Hebrew, knowledge was experience. The strong Southern sense of knowledge as experience bears witness to the importance of the Bible to the South in its reliance both upon concrete images and upon total experience.

I am sure that for me it was the culture which was primarily responsible for the ideal of completeness. I shall cite only one experience, from my thirteenth year, though there are others. It was a coldish morning in September 1908, before sunrise. My older brother and I stood with our mother on the back piazza of our home, drinking hot coffee which Mother, as a special favor that first day of school, had made for us before we went out to do the farm chores. We stood together there, looking out to the east through the great pines in the yard to the distant barn, beyond it to a field, and farther still to a dark fringe of woods against the reddening sky. I didn't recall this scene till thirty years later, but ever since recalling it I have found it burdened with meaning, with complete meaning, with completeness—aesthetic completeness, of course—the lovely, quiet morning—but more than this, moral completeness. For I wasn't simply looking at the dawn; I was a part of it; I was a part of the occasion. I knew that morning, and I knew it because I had accepted and become a part of the total setting of that occasion.

It was a particularly Southern occasion. Here was the family, perhaps the essential Southern institution, represented at the moment by a mother and two sons, but having in the immediate background a father, brothers and sisters, and a grandmother; here was a family task, celebrated by the steaming cups of coffee drunk standing, a stirrup cup for the road ahead; here was a clearing in the forest, cut out only three years before, with the great trees and the cypress ponds—the frontier—still unconquered; here was a place, loved both because we were making it ours and because it was part of a lovely land, a place spread out beneath the morning sky, the urgent sun just below the horizon. And, finally, at the heart of it all was a woman: the angel, the mother, the mistress, the sexual machine. The romantic feudalism of the South wasn't simply romance; the South has really been a female-oriented culture. When I remember my mother, therefore, as the center of that September scene, I am Southern. You may call it sentimental Southern or Oedipus-complex Southern, I don't care. I am too certain that this scene is close to the heart of my life, a reasonably satisfying life, and that it has an unsentimental abiding meaning and more than sexual implications. I can sum it all up by saying that, as I remember it, there was something of the Lady in the Dawn, something of the Dawn in the Lady.

What does this mean? It means that on that occasion I had bridged, in whatever frail fashion, the fearful gap between man and nature, had sensed in nature something of the kindliness of man, in man something of the brute strength of nature. If I should ever come to feel that God was both the beginning and the end of our endeavors—out of stardust into the kingdom— that conclusion would rest most heavily upon this moment.

I have come to that conclusion, and the whole matter illustrates the dictum of W. B. Yeats: "Wisdom comes first in images." Long before we know clearly what we know, deep down our bodies—our hearts, as we say—already know it. We believe before we can know. He who comes to God, say the Scriptures, must believe that he *is* and that he is the rewarder of those who diligently seek him; and Augustine said, "Unless ye believe, ye shall not understand." This means that life is always a gamble: momently we take our lives in our hands.

It is worth remarking that in the moment of finding the Lady in the Dawn and the Dawn in the Lady, I had taken a step which Southerners generally and maybe Americans have usually been unable to take. This is particularly significant for Southerners, for we understand at least the first part of the image, the importance of the Lady or, more generally, the human being. But even the Lady was of supreme importance in a very limited world. She was complete mistress of the home, but apparently upon condition that she not interfere with the plantation, thus to avoid in one minority group, women, too much sympathy for another minority group, slaves.

In stopping with the Lady alone, the separate human being, the individual, we both overvalued and undervalued that individual. The South has always depended heavily upon individuals, upon "The Man"—in whatever sense—upon whose integrity (or "justice," as we usually called it) the health of the community depended. But we undervalued that individual, or better, hamstrung him by not imagining a social structure that would express objectively his individual integrity and thus make of justice not only an individual but also a social matter. We have generally failed to see the individual in the community—of both man and nature—and the community in the individual, or, to return to our image, to see the Lady in the Dawn and the Dawn in the Lady.

The paradox of this is that we are perhaps the most community-minded region of our nation. We are, in other words, haunted by God or, more aptly, by the Holy Ghost.

Later on, indeed much later on, I connected that long-past September morning, especially as regards its quality of completeness, with Christianity. By that time I had passed beyond personal tragedy and beyond the ideal of the tragic life into the view that the tragic hero, however admirable, is isolated and incomplete, and that the ideal of completeness is expressed best of all by Jesus. In an essay entitled "Beyond Tragedy," written in 1936, I described Jesus as the complete man, the God-Man.[2] "Truly," said the centurion, "this was the Son of God!" In him was the eternal Dawn. He divinized for me at last that cultural occasion of my thirteenth year. He put the stamp of his approval upon the world I had imagined.

Though I credit Christianity and the Christian Scriptures with this insight, I'm afraid I can't give much credit to the formal church. Of course it was the existence of the church in the South that caused me to read and later to ponder the Scriptures and to take seriously many positions in the world. But the church illustrated and even taught rather poorly what I read in the Scriptures. The church talked about the incarnation but didn't really believe it; I had seen the Lady in the Dawn and did. The church talked about the infinite, eternal, and unchangeable God, but he was mainly an idea or maybe a ghost haunting bright Sunday mornings or deepening the shadow of wintry days. The church said there was an order behind the changing world, but it did not connect this order with the order of my life. It was something apart; it was not the final meaning of that urgent September dawn. It did not explain for me the changeless quality of that passing moment, "some eternal greatness incarnate in the passage of temporal fact." It was only a bodiless idea, an admirable skeleton of good Presbyterianism, but unmuscled and unfleshed.

I went out from the church of my boyhood persuaded that the preachers were talking about *something*—they did impress me as sincere men—but they weren't really talking to me. They hinted at a meaning which they did not grasp. It may be that, given the relative completeness of my early life, this hint of a possible meaning did combine with the meaningful scenes of my life, which by their completeness suggested a religious answer and did direct and intensify my search for religious answers. I certainly went away to college determined above all to get the final answers; ironically, it had never occurred to me to ask the preacher. I was going to ask the philosophers. I did. The answer was rather dusty. I do know that much later, during a time when any large meaning had vanished from my life, I continued what was for a while a futile search because I could not believe that life was without meaning. From the beginning it had meant too much, and the church had backed this up—only with words, however, which for years did little more than echo down the corridors of my mind.

This suggests the enveloping mystery of the whole thing. It may be that the Calvinistic theology I heard with little attention and less concern did touch, however faintly, my Sundays with mystery. I am rather sure, however, that a stronger influence was the gray Spanish moss beyond the tall windows, swaying slowly in a summer dream or whipped by wintry winds. If Calvinistic theology never hurt me, it may have been partly due to the swaying of the Spanish moss.

In regard to reconciliation, the South taught me less, but it taught me something. If I came, as once I did, to the ideal of the tragic hero pitted against gods and men, it was out of a Southern background of frustration and defeat and the necessity (says Faulkner) to resist even though it isn't clear what one is resisting. But even when I was too young to sense this opposition, I was aware, I think, of the potential sadness of life. When I was a child

I occasionally overheard my parents speak of someone's having lost a child. The natural place to be lost was the endless woods back of our house, a fragment of the frontier still left within our old community, and so I imagined (without real sadness) these children as being lost there. The woods were starred with lost, wandering children; they wore their lostness like halos. I was as yet far from being lost myself, but somehow I knew that there was lostness in the world. Was not this knowledge connected with the battle flags of the Lost Cause adorning the schoolhouse walls and the songs of the Lost Cause sung on Friday afternoons? Was it not connected with the pathetic remark of the Negro nurse, "Honey child, in this life you's got to learn to want and not git"? And when, some years later, within twenty minutes of leaving home for the first year of preparatory school, I had to choose whether to go or stay because my grandmother was worried about who would take care of the cows (I stayed and thus subjected my will to the wish of the larger family), was I not learning a kind of reconciliation? You may say that I was simply being submissive, even supine, but when I remember how passionately I tried later to follow my will and came to admire most the tragic hero because he above all was passionate, I cannot believe that at fourteen I simply didn't care. No, at that moment I made a step, however small, toward being reconciled to those thwartings of desire which were so common in the general life of the South.

By its reliance on custom and ceremony, the South did something to bear these thwartings, to be reconciled to them. Restrained and supported by the groups he loved, the Southerner received some preparation for the restraints that would come later from the larger groups he didn't love and from the constraints of time and space. "The South," says Flannery O'Connor, "has survived in the past because its manners, however lopsided or inadequate they may have been, provided enough social discipline to hold us together and give us an identity."[3]

So the mannered restraints of the South offered some support in the problem of reconciliation—some, but not enough. Long years after these childhood and boyhood experiences, the thwarting became so bitter that I quarreled with God about it. The question was not whether he would be reconciled to me, but whether I would be reconciled to him. When Margaret Fuller, the stormy New England petrel, remarked late in life that she had accepted the universe, the crusty Thomas Carlyle said, "Egad, she'd better!" But Unamuno, the author of *The Tragic Sense of Life*, added the footnote that Carlyle spoke like an Englishman; a Spaniard would not have felt himself obliged to accept the universe. So at the moment I was Spanish, doubting whether I would be reconciled to God. I was, finally. I passed beyond tragedy, perhaps into Christianity, but it was my realization of human incompleteness that carried me past. Not only was my own life incomplete; *all* life was. I was only a man. In the joy of realizing my humanity, I was reconciled to human failure, even to my own.

The main point here is that—along with the rest of the South, white and black—I had been getting used to failure since those lost children wandered in the woods. And even when I became aware of salvation through failure, though I am perfectly willing to call this a striking evidence of God's grace, I did not forget that it was simply an extension of that early experience of completeness, itself so Southern in its stress upon the family, the work, and the living world. The family had now become mankind, and in spite of all failure, day was still dawning over that wider scene.

About freedom, that final test of God's presence in the culture, perhaps the South taught me least of all, and this is understandable. Again, what I have learned has been chiefly the result of the Southern ideal of completeness. As for freedom, the South, resting upon black slavery and racial discrimination, by contrast necessarily emphasized the individualistic freedom of the master and then of the whites in general. This, though somewhat restrained by the ideal of completeness, was freedom to exploit. If I had not been deeply impressed by the ideal of completeness, I might have gone along with the nineteenth-century religious ideal of spiritual freedom: freedom from the world, of which the Christian gets a foretaste here on Sunday but must wait for its fruition in another, an eternal world. But such incompleteness, such a division of life, didn't make sense to me. I was too Southern. And so I sought freedom in the world, in belonging to the world, in being a part of it, in acting that part. The South knows about this freedom, but its world is too limited, its community too narrow. Furthermore, the Southerner's need to belong to something larger than himself, to some community, is often outweighed by his individualistic desire to have the world belong to him.

When, being constrained and bound by life, I was thrown back upon the Scriptures, which I had read faithfully as a boy but had been careless of for a long time, I realized for the first time what a wind of freedom blew through the New Testament. But though the church recommended the Scriptures, it had lost any large sense of the freedom there revealed. It was legalistic and moralistic, far removed from the rich immediacies of Southern life.

XIV

In Space and Time

There are of course no actual footprints of God to be found in space or in time, though religious men have often felt his presence. The real footprints are in the hearts of men. We have just said that insofar as men are complete, reconciled, and free, they are near to God and God is near to them. But these human moods sometimes occur in fairly direct relationship to space and time and may be discussed in this relationship.

For the purpose of clarity we shall discuss space and place separately. Any place is in space. The difference is that a place is humanized through man's association with it in time; space itself is not, or if so, only slightly. In *The Burning Fountain*, Philip Wheelwright makes the distinction as follows: What primitive man "perceives and understands is not space but place, and one place is distinguished from another by its qualities and potencies quite as much as by position. Concrete place, unless abstract space, is not homogeneous. Space exists by postulation; place is known experientially and responsively."[1]

Thomas Traherne makes a slightly different contrast. "Infinity is the first thing which is naturally known. [A man] thinks not of walls and limits till he feels them and is stopped by them. That things are finite, therefore, we learn by our senses. But infinity we know and feel in our souls."

Whether we know infinity—space—in our souls or our minds or both, Wheelwright and Traherne agree that we know places, with their limits and sometimes their limitless implications, through our daily experience. Place is the governing factor and as such might well be considered first, along with its cofactor time.

But to do so would be to reverse the order in which space

and place influenced the Southern settlers. As we have seen, one of the first things that impressed them was the vastness of the space in which they were to find their places. For though place is space humanized, space itself, uninhabited space, has varied qualities of its own, some more valuable than others for the making of a human place. For instance, oceans and deserts, whatever they may become in the future, have been until now large spaces to be crossed; forests have been excellent portions of space for hunters. Flat or lightly rolling grounds, either prairie or forest, with plenty of rainfall and a mild climate, have been excellent space for farmers.

This last was the kind of landscape which met and held the eye of the Southern settler. Even before he outgrew his foolish search for gold, he began to see the landscape of the South as admirably suited for planting, for hunting and trapping, and for herding cattle. To vary Robert Frost a little, "He was the land's before the land was his." He only guessed how extensive it was, but he could see its richness and beauty.

He called it the New World. Since this is what he began with, we shall begin with it too. We shall seek first in the expanses of this New World for the footprints of God.

The importance of man's relation to the physical world is suggested by a great image from Rilke: "Could we but find a pure, reserved, narrow humanity; a strip of fertile fruitland of our own between the rock and the river." Here Rilke is using the natural world to communicate to others the nature of man himself, contrasting the moderation of average humanity with the wild and often untamed powers which appear both in great men —heroes, poets, prophets—and in the natural world. There is a wildness circumscribing the life of men to match the wildness of rock and river bordering the narrow strip of fruitland. In a simpler image, but still from the natural world, Melville has the wild Captain Ahab, afloat in the vast Pacific, remind his first mate with longing that on this sunny morning, "they are making hay somewhere under the slopes of the Andes, Starbuck, and the mowers are sleeping amid the new-mown hay." But men always make hay under the slopes of the Andes; our lives, however quiet, move against a backdrop of terror.

It is probable that almost the first thing the Southern settler saw was the most important. The basic appeal of the South—the basic appeal of all southern regions in the northern hemisphere —is rich and sunny land. This, says James Sellers, was God's unique gift to the South, the prime evidence of his grace. The basic fault of the South has been that it has misused God's gift, thereby turning his grace into judgment. But the gift was not entirely misused, and so some of the original grace continued. Then also, more subtly, some of the judgment was accepted and became another means of grace. But this is what this book is about.

Since God walks in freedom, and since freedom is incident to all frontiers, and since the South has been a land bordered by a western frontier and crisscrossed by local frontiers, we shall now ask of this spatial freedom of the South: To what degree was it merely freedom *from*, lack of attachment to, which could easily give rise to exploitation, to what degree freedom *in*, the freedom to belong to, to become a part of?

It was undoubtedly both of these things. Southerners, like other Americans, ran through frontier after frontier almost like wildfire, raping the land and burning out the soil. But always there was land not fit for clearing, suited mainly for hunting and fishing, and the mild seasons encouraged these sports. Such sports are a curious intermixture of freedom to exploit nature and freedom to become a part of it. It is probably true that even the original trappers, whose very living depended upon an exploitation of the wild animal population, were in many moods a very real part of the forest world they inhabited. They knew the ways of that world, accepted them, became to a degree a part of them. They may have left the settled world because, like the typical frontiersmen, they wished to be free of human restraints —ready to move on when they heard a neighbor's dog bark—yet they learned and accepted the restraints of the forest, and in accepting them doubtless found some real freedom in them.

Leaving aside early trappers, whose business it was to exploit animal life, the later hunters and fishermen show clearly this combined freedom from and freedom in the forest world. Some of Faulkner's stories reveal this: the almost mystic participation of the hunter with the great bear and with the forest to which he and the bear belong combines at moments with anger at the wholesale reduction of the wild bottomlands of the Mississippi to ordered rows of cotton. The hunter is both using and defending the wild world. He values, as did Thoreau, the wild within the tame or the tame surrounded by the wild—man's order forever impinged upon by the order (or is it the chaos?) of nature. This is the question we are forever trying to answer to prove if possible that nature is our home, to find a home there, to bridge again the gap which opened in our lives when we became self-conscious. The hunter too faces this question. He too seeks to be at home in nature, but he admits, within both nature and himself, a quality of wildness that the usual workingman, busy at taming nature, is prone to deny.

Let it be clearly said that insofar as the frontiers of the South encouraged in men the desire to be free from others in order to exploit them, they encouraged an evil tendency and may represent the judgment of God in the South. To some degree this is evident. We have already seen that slavery appeared in America partly because America was an unsettled, unstructured world, and within the South slavery was harsher along the western edges of settlement than along the long-settled Atlantic Seaboard. But while admitting this exploitative effect of the frontier, we should not forget that the frontier (western, but especially local) has touched the Southerner with a sense of freedom in the natural world, a sense of belonging somehow to this world. This is the grace of God.

Though any place, any scene, may strike the observer at first glance—as beautiful, for instance—the sentiment for place, which is so strong in the South, is the product of time. As John Crowe Ransom points out, sentimental attachments grow slowly and usually bind the individual to the place where he makes his living. These attachments are more than emotional, says Ransom; they are also a kind of knowledge closely related to aesthetic knowledge. Aesthetic knowledge, instead of separating the knower from the object known, binds him to it. He finds himself in the object, the object in himself. So sentimental knowledge, or the knowledge of things that underlie sentiment, binds the knower to the known, bridges the gap between him and at least a detail of the physical world, a limited place set in limitless space. It is therefore a step toward completeness, an indication of the grace of God.

This is not to say that men do not also find God in sheer space. In a sense it is true that "where nothing is God is." But the kind of God men find there, the character they give to space, is based upon what they have found in place or in places. The primary importance of place as distinct from space is indicated by Philip Wheelwright in the passage quoted above. We may add here his comment that "each place—so far as it is known and accepted as a place—comes laden with intimations of universality. A boyhood scene revisited will reveal something of this character, although the what of it can hardly be spoken without breaking the spell."[2]

I recall two scenes from my boyhood that carry in memory this strange sense of universality. Both are of buggy trips I took: one, only five miles perhaps, along a winding woods-road, by intermittent clearings and cabins, through endless backwoods to a friend's house in the next community; the other, to the far end of the county to another friend's house, across branches and swamps and alongside larger fields. In neither case was I ever quite sure we would find the way; every fork of the road had to be considered. It was a journey into an unknown world, doubly strange because so near to home. In a sense these wandering roads became all wandering roads, these fields and woods the landscape of the world. Years later I found this universal quality of particular places strikingly expressed in *The Wanderer.*

From the beginning the Southern settler had a stronger sense of place, certainly of social place, than did the New England Puritan. As for his sense of physical place, this grew with the development of the plantation in the agreeable climate of the South. With this concern for place came a resurgent sense of time. The Southern settler was less concerned to change radically the social structure than to accept it and enlarge his holdings in it. I doubt that in the beginning the new leveling spirit of democracy was any stronger in New England than in the South—aristocratic privilege existed in both regions—but the individualistic thrust of Puritanism was, and given time, this would bear its proper fruit in a democratic society.

In such a land, where land itself was the main productive capital, the Southern settler naturally associated social place with physical place. A man's place became not only his social status but also his physical location, his house, his home. So he had a place both among men and in nature and was at home with both. How quickly the Southern settler associated social place with physical place is suggested by the rapid rise of the plantations, where the importance of a man was indicated primarily by the breadth of his acres.

The settler was at home, but how much? To what degree did the physical place belong to the owner, to be exploited, even pilfered for his further advancement, and to what degree did he also belong to it, bound by his love of it to maintain and develop it? This was also true of his social place. To what degree did its power over other men belong simply to him, to what degree did individual social position also belong to the community as a whole, obligating a person to exercise responsibly the power which his place bestowed upon him? To the degree that men belonged to physical—and social—places and felt themselves a part of them, to that degree they were moving from the lone individual toward completeness, and the grace of God was with them.

Let us admit that Southerners, like other Americans, often raped the land; let us admit the uglier fact that white Southern males often raped black females. To the extent that these things happened, the land was not their home nor the blacks their "family." But having admitted all this, we have to face the fact that Southerners are more concerned with place, physical and social, than other Americans, and that at least in earlier times a man was known by the plantation he belonged to, whether he was master or slave.

Two things helped to make Southerners more conscious of place, less conscious of time than non-Southerners. First, they were predominantly farmers who depended directly upon a place set in rhythmic, seasonal time—a fact we shall discuss shortly— not tradesmen, mechanics, entrepreneurs only slightly aware of space, keenly aware of the fleeting minutes. Second, the slave-operated plantation, the center of the South, was a massive, or-derly thing which could be moved from one place to another only with great difficulty.

Since it is through time that sentiment grows, the object of sentiment binds one also to time, to the past especially, more slightly to the future. The live oak outside my study window was planted over a hundred years ago, probably by a great-uncle. Draped in Spanish moss, it is also draped in memories, or more exactly, in a sense of the past. It unites me with the past; it bridges, together with this house, even the trauma of the Civil War. It helps that lost past to be a part of me and me of it. I belong to time; time does not simply pass me by; I am part of the flowing stream.

Memoried places also offer sound grounds for hope. I walk the bounding lines of this place and am conscious that my great-grandfather walked them a hundred and fifty years ago. If I have problems, he had problems. He lived, and I live, and my children will live too. Life is not just now; just now is merely the crest of the wave. We move from the past into the future. Men have had moments of success, and these have faded; moments of failure have been endured, and so may we endure them.

The strength of this attitude is evident. Through places— and through persons—we are rooted in the physical world and in time. We have ceased to be lonely individualists. We are mov-ing toward completeness. The animal's instincts and his sense of territory have become the human being's memory and his devo-tion to loved places.

The danger is that we may stop at this point and linger too long. Whitehead calls beauty the pause for contemplation, the moment in which we realize that now, for the moment at least, the great tensions and even agonies of the past have resolved themselves and fallen into a picture, as Miss Millay so beautifully describes it:

> Clear and diminished like a scene cut in cameo
> . . . .
> Are the words that passed, and the pain,—discarded, cut away
> From the stone, as from the memory the heat of tears escapes.
> —From "The Cameo"

But we may pause too long. Instead of inspiring us, the past may suffocate us. "Life only avails," said Emerson, "not the having lived." Thoreau expressed a similar idea. Never learn from experience, he warned, for what we mean by learning from experience is learning from failure not to try again. We should live, rather, in "eternal expectation of the dawn."

And the dawn may come at any moment. As our thoughts and hopes and fears transcend space and time, so more rarely do our experiences. For a brief moment, then, we live in a timeless universe, not foreign to this but only this illuminated. I am not speaking of the rare mystic experience; I am speaking of far more earthly moments: when our dogs leap around us and suddenly we are so struck by their vital love that this seems the only important thing; or when in the middle of a bright afternoon, we come out of a darkened movie theater into the glare and realize with a shock that we have been living in another world; or when we become so absorbed in any game that only its time matters—its quarters, its moves, its rhythms—and the world's time is forgotten.

All such moments are moments of relative completeness. For at least a moment the limitations of space are forgotten, the burden of time eased. We are still in space and in time, but space is now healed of its limitations and time of its burdens. It is by the grace of God that this can happen to us.

We must be bound to a place before we can be free. But we must be bound in love, never in hate. This is the mystery of life: that we find freedom in being bound. Jesus urged men to take his yoke upon them, for his yoke is easy and his burden light. The unlimited will of man leads him to self-destruction. What we most deeply want is to move within a field of self-imposed limits, about objects and people we love. If we love sufficiently, the scene may burst its limits of time and space and become universal and eternal. But these rare moments of limitless freedom are merely the proof that we belong to life and life to us.

A society like that of the South, where concern for places has slowed and made rhythmic the movement of time, is a society whose very structure has aided men to pass from individual loneliness into some completeness. The completeness, however, was too this-worldly. Though Southerners tended to be solid men living in solid places, not abstract shadows flitting through time, the solidity, the density of their lives was too little lightened and illumined by the spark of imagination. More than other Americans we loved our little world, but the love was too much of sentiment which merely clung to that world, too little of insight and imagination which might have revealed in our grain of sand the whole world itself.

When God's footprints appear in space, they necessarily appear in time. In the Christian view they appeared uniquely in the life of Jesus of Nazareth, who appeared in Judea in the days of Herod the king. But also from the Christian point of view, this Jesus was from eternity and was a part of the universal Spirit of God, so that in the days of Herod the king the eternal Spirit of the universe took form in Judea.

Something like this is always happening. Moments of eternity—so to speak—infiltrate time, and an aura of the universal crowns the local place. A man is always in both space and time. The question is: How deeply in? I once heard John Cowper Powys, speaking of the writings of Joseph Conrad, say, "He takes us down, down, down into the very bottom of the earth, and out again into God knows where." I should say, into that mystery that lies at the heart of every moment and place, into God.

God is where fullness, completeness of life is, whether we recognize him or not. In the fullness of time Christ came. God is where the present moment is so filled with the past and the future that it breaks the delicate membrane enclosing it, passes beyond time, and becomes eternal. The question for one who seeks in the world the footprints of God is: In a given society, how much of the past inheres in the present and projects that present into the future? In other words, how much of the past is living now? At any moment a man may be absorbed into the remembered body of a dead past or thrust naked into a bodiless future. Both extremes are foolish, and both extremes are illustrated here in America. We are concerned mainly with the wisdom—and the foolishness—of the South.

A part of the wisdom of the South lies in its sense of time. Time has been and to a degree still is organic, not mechanical. By organic time I mean time related to the processes of nature and of the human body; by mechanical time I mean the time of the clock. Organic time is the time suggested by the sun, the moon, and the stars, by the length of the shadows across the fields, by the color of the leaves, and by the response of the human body to these natural processes. In mechanical time, periods of equal length are equal; in organic time, periods of equal length vary greatly, each taking its color from the action proper to it and from the place where this occurs. There is a natural fullness to organic time, a fullness dependent not only upon man's will but also upon nature's interplay with that will. In mechanical time any moment can be filled with anything man the mechanic desires; if his desires should slacken, the moments would be empty. In organic time there is a place for this and a place for that, a time for planting and a time for reaping, a time for work, a time for play, and a time for rest.

In this matter, of course, as in all others, Southerners are also Americans, and as such are concerned with the clock. More than other Americans, however, they are subject to organic time, carrying within themselves the clock of nature, less subject than others to the clock on the wall or the watch on the wrist. The typical American is continually straining to be *in time.* This is because he has largely forgotten organic time, so neither the body of the world nor his own body reminds him of time, and he is forced to keep his mind always on the time of the clock. The typical Southerner, however—decreasingly now of course—carries time in himself and therefore is less concerned to be in time.

This is another way of saying that the Southerner is less rational, more a part of the world than the non-Southerner. Even before the New Englanders led off in manufacturing, they had observed the peculiar sense of time the Southerner, whether white or black, had, and they described it accurately as irrational. Long before the Revolution the South had become to the North "the lazy South," not because Southerners did not work, but because they apparently did not work to any social purpose or at any particular pace. There were always a good many Southerners just sitting around apparently enjoying it. They weren't making rational use of their time. These same men could work as fiercely as any when the place and the time demanded it, but when the

time suggested something else—when it was laying-by time—
they laid the crops by and often lay down themselves. Their wills
were in tune with the seasons; they had little desire to break these
flowing scenes into equal and dead minutes; they were willing to
cooperate with time rather than to master it. They would hardly
have understood that great New England Yankee Benjamin
Franklin: "Dost thou love life? Then do not squander time, for
that is the stuff life is made of." They knew that life was more than
minutes and their sum, that there were times and times, and,
though at their best they did not want to squander time, they did
wish to enjoy it. And they enjoyed it partly by letting it tell them
what to do.

The South has always been noted for its varied diversions,
all indicating a desire to play. Whatever else this is, it is related
to the sense of organic time, for nature suggests both work and
play.

The sense of time as organic is connected with the agrarian
experience of the South. But the Middle West certainly has been
equally agrarian. Why should it not have developed as strong an
organic sense of time as the South did? The answer is in part the
earlier mechanization of Midwestern farms. This was related to
the ability of the farm laborers and, more importantly, to their
basic puritan philosophy: that man should whip the world into
shape, theoretically for the glory of God, actually for greater
profits to man. The main part of the answer, however, is the
African slave labor of the South.

When the American settlers brought in African slaves, they
brought in a people from a culture where time was still organic,
indicated mainly by the sun's position in the sky, not the pointer's
position on the clock. We try, but in vain, to make the clock
human by calling that pointer a hand. Since the Africans were
agriculturists, the times for planting and for reaping followed the
slow changes of the sun and the more rapid changes of the
weather. Living deeply in organic time, always aware of their
dependence upon nature, the Africans developed religious ceremonies to acknowledge this. About these ceremonies their lives
advanced with the passage of the seasons, itself a circular movement. We in modern America retain even today at least one of

these ceremonies, Thanksgiving, but only football and turkey give it a tenuous connection with nature, and the President has to remind us to celebrate it.

So the nature of work and the nature of the African helped to keep time in the South full-bodied. The institution of slavery worked against this—probably worked against it most on the great, well-organized plantations. For as slaves were worked in gangs, they generally worked as "hands," and time tended to be merely a period during which a planned piece of work was done.

Yet the work itself and the nature of the workers tied temporal actions to physical places and to social places of command or obedience, and therefore made of time something more than the bearer of mere sensations. It is easy for us, lured on as we are and should be by the ideals of freedom and justice, to note the evil of slavery; it is difficult to see any possible good in it. It is also difficult to admit that the African's organic sense of time, his formality and manners in expressing this, may have been a most powerful force, in spite of the abstraction connected to the slave's condition, to prevent the South from pursuing—at least quite so rapidly—the typical American flight into a shallow, abstract life. If this is so, it is ironic, for the South adopted slavery basically from the same modern abstractive interest that has dominated the rest of the country. That it got something more than this was due to the people it enslaved, the work they had to do, and its overall picture of an ordered society to which all its members, each in his proper place, belonged.

The Southern settlers were, like their Northern counterparts, modern men on the make, but as we have pointed out, they carried with them a stronger sense of the organic, complete society of the Middle Ages than did the Northern settlers, and they were less devoted to the rational, planning mind. Therefore they were easily and deeply affected by the presence of the more "natural," less rational Africans. As a result of this long association, time moves more rhythmically, less mechanically in the South. There are times of great strain, other times of indolence. Seen from the clock, men are often behind time. Apparently this does not disturb them, since they are still largely in organic time, which is to say that time is in them. Strangely, they are somewhat like Henry David Thoreau in this matter: Time is a stream they go a-fishing in, and as there is a time for planting, there is also a time for fishing.

Taking their cues so often from their natural world, a world which, as we have seen, contains innumerable shallow frontiers, they have remained fairly close to that world, to the whole world of nature, tame and wild. They still have a strong sense of belonging to this world. This is a step, though perhaps only a pagan step, toward belonging to God, for he still walks in his garden in the cool of the day.

The sense of organic time is mainly a sense of the present, a sense of the large surrounding world of nature and of one's place in it, a sense of being part of the tide of that world, flowing and ebbing with it. But there is also a sense of the past and a related sense of the future. Today we tend to forget and even to deny the past. For all of us the twentieth century has been heartbreaking; for the American blacks the past several centuries have been heartbreaking. This is unfortunate, for the depth of the future is related to the depth of the past, and today, with a weakened sense of the past, we plunge toward a shore but dimly seen.

The South was neither stripped of the past nor burdened by it. It easily forgot the towns and villages of Europe when they did not fit the plans of tobacco-growing Virginia; it modified the landed estates of the English gentry into the Southern plantation. Such of the past as it carried lived in its present—with the exception of slavery.

As we have seen, slavery was not a living growth of the immediate past into the colonial present but a transplanting of a form of labor out of a more distant past. It was a dying abstraction dragged forward across the centuries and propped up in the modern world. Even from the beginning it was only half alive in the colonial present, and with the passage of time and the growing democratization incident especially to the American frontier, it increasingly became an anomaly. Adopting slavery, the South was touched with death from the beginning, for slavery could only grow increasingly obsolete as the modern world advanced, and in the throes of death would carry the South down with it.

Yet the South did struggle against the error of slavery by trying to continue in the New World the orderly, complex communities of the Old. Thus that abstraction of slavery, the field "hand," became to some degree—varying from place to place—a person belonging to a community of persons. This was an attempt to incorporate the outdated abstraction of slavery into the communities of the South, to give the lost past some rootage in the present. It was an attempt to weave a living present out of a past in part alive, in part dead. The attempt failed, but at least it made life better than it would otherwise have been.

Insofar as it did succeed, the South became a traditional society, its present happily balanced between the past and the future, with values it could transmit to succeeding generations. This was the dominant mood until the Civil War. The South had little sense of the past as a weight. In spite of the abstraction of slavery, it had pretty well incorporated the past into its own structure. Its leaders kept alive their memories of the past by musing upon the great figures from Roman history, or in the romantic mood, by musing upon the medieval heroes of Scott's novels. As the Civil War approached, however, the South became less sure of itself, less balanced in time. During the 1830's the South Carolinian Simms, brooding upon Hamlet, saw many Hamlets around him, irresolute and uncertain. A dozen years later Calhoun, dying, lamented over "The South! The poor South! God knows what will become of her!" But an upward surge in the price of cotton could set the spirits of Southerners soaring, as they did in the 1850's. Now the future was theirs. They had forgotten the lessons of the past. They would go their way, cut a wide swath, and let the rest of the nation do what it would.

That dream of theirs, the Confederate States of America, they never attained. They established it in war, yes, but they lost it forever at Appomattox. Then, and for almost a hundred years thereafter, the mind of the South—certainly of the white South, which through most of its history had found in its present a relative fullness composed equally of memories and hopes, of the past and the future—became almost hypnotized by the past.

We have discussed three ways, the most important, I think,

in which time has affected the Southerner: as the creator of sentimental values, as the bearer of organic drives, and—as past time —as the home of memories. To the degree that the Southerner has lived in time—and time has been alive in him—to that same degree he has followed, however far off, in the footsteps of God, who also walked and still walks the earth. Insofar as he has been separated, alienated from time, whether from the past or the future—more strictly from a present alive with memories and hopes—to that same degree he has been separated from God, who is the God of the living, not the dead.

It is clear that the Civil War was at least for white Southerners a traumatic event. (Robert Penn Warren says it was traumatic for all Americans.) We remember, often in glorious, or, if black, in inglorious terms, what preceded that event, but we don't know what to make of it. The modern tendency is to forget it, but this is not simple when so much of it still remains in scenes, in human associations, in customs. The will to forget is insidiously undermined by these numerous whispers of the past.

As a result of being cut off from the past by the Civil War, the Southerner, especially the white Southerner, has a past which he cannot use. He is haunted by it. Instead of the past existing within his bloodstream, it stands behind him looking over his shoulder, and turn as he may, he cannot see it whole. But this is his trouble: he is trying to see it because he has lost the feel of it, its organic sense. Or, more exactly, he finds it almost impossible to relate the sense of life he still has—his living present—with that ghostly past.

The Civil War and its long aftermath numbed whatever creative drive there was within Southerners and left them using their energies almost entirely for defense—against the victorious North, against poverty, and whites and blacks against each other. The terrible defeat of the war, unexpected and not prepared for, had weakened tremendously the traditional society and cast doubt upon the values which it had been transmitting. Even the organic drive of the South, the sense of time as the lifeblood of the world, natural and human, was terribly weakened, not necessarily because of the defeat suffered in a four-year war, but because of the continuing economic failures of the next fifty years.

The South was still a farming section, producing, beyond subsistence, for outside markets. Its colonial situation plus the economic crises of farming during the last half of the nineteenth century plus the disordered labor supply, only nominally free and largely untrained, deepened for a long time the sense of failure which resulted first from the loss of the war. If nature also seemed unfriendly, as continued farm failures suggested, what was left to drive a man forward except the bare will to survive?

Even the old sentiments which had grown up around particular places and which had now by the loss of the war been extended to cover that larger place, the South, tended to lose their creative, future-directed drive and became sentimental in the derogatory sense. The Southerner's love of place turned now almost completely backward, and he saw the world around him as but the shadow of an earlier world. Always in danger of being more settled in place than urged forward by time, now that time had nearly ceased its urgings he found himself almost locked into place, sometimes a willing prisoner. The world which to a healthy man is a home to be improved tended to become to the Southerner a home merely to be defended.

But the Southerner's sense of place, however it may have been sentimentalized and (especially for the white) limited to one region, the South, is still strong. The Southerner has always been somewhere. The discouraged reply of the Harlem Negro to the question of how he is, "Man, I'm nowhere," is a negative statement of the importance of place. Interestingly, it is the transplanted Negro who says this, a man who has lost the place, however poor, he once held in the South.

Perhaps this is the place to point out the stabilizing effect of the Negro in the post-Reconstruction South. The basic cause of the war—without his presence it could never have come—the Negro now became the essential factor in recovery from the war. Consider the situation at that time. The antebellum world had almost vanished. The white Southerner, looking about him, found almost everything out of place, and to a man deeply concerned with things and people in place, this was disastrous. Only the Negro remained "in his place." I do not deny that this was a tragedy for the Negro—though not an absolute tragedy, since

he too was a man of place. But to the white South, the controlling
South, it brought reassurance. One remembers Pippa's song:
"God's in his heaven, / All's right with the world!" The satisfaction of the South in having the Negro in his place was akin to this,
for the social order was almost a god in the South, and for it to
be out of order was for God to be slipping from his throne.

This brings us to the problem of summarizing as exactly as
we can the description of the footprints of God in the Southern
sense of space and time. To repeat the general formula: to the
degree that the Southerner has been separated from place and
time, to that degree he has strayed away from God; to the degree
that he has really belonged to space and time, to that degree he
has been following the footprints of God. There are of course
many other ways of being near to or far from God, but the ways
of time and space are significant.

Footprints imply walking, and walking takes time, but it must
also be in space, indeed in places. Perhaps the South has been
relatively unaware that the footprints of God lead somewhere.
But the North—now America—has made the opposite error of
leaping beyond the footprints to a consideration of what it believed to be the blueprints of God—blueprints which unfortunately indicated mainly the unchastened desires of men. The
problem is to see both the footprints and their direction: God
passed this way going where?

In regard to time, Southerners, at least for the last one hundred years, have been caught in an eddy and have spun rather
helplessly on the fringe of the great river. They have thus in this
matter been separated from God, who, as Jesus said, works
through time. In regard to space and place, the situation is more
complex. Southerners generally have been closely tied to place;
they should therefore have been closely tied to God, who works
in the world. Unfortunately, they have been bound to the places
themselves—often in love, but limited love—not bound to the
world through these places with the places themselves the universal reality. If they had been thus bound, they would have been
free in the world. If they had loved the South thus, they would
not have feared and hated the North—or any other outsiders. All

men would have been insiders within that home the world, of which the particular home was the living symbol.

In their love of place and of that inclusive place, the South, Southerners have often been pagans. They worship the god of the place, but they do not see that he is also God of the world. In their devotion to the local god they are separated from the universal God. It is indeed the footprints of a god they follow, but a god who turns and turns within the bounds of Salem, Black River—my own community—and never steps out into the great world beyond.

Thus in the South our best has been our worst because we were neither imaginative enough nor brave enough to see it for what it was.

XV

Among Men

We have been trying to understand the divine influence within the South as it shaped men through the passage of time and the fact of space. We now turn to the more important matter, the divine influence acting upon men through their human relationships. This is the real key. How men take space and time depends primarily upon how they take one another, though of course how they take one another is also related to the quality of space and time in which they live. The Bible is very clear about this. You may find God in any place and time, but you cannot find him outside your love for your neighbor.

Where completeness or reconciliation or freedom is, and to the degree that they are, there God is. It is significant that we can say most of what we have to say under the head of completeness. Freedom has not been a key word in the South, nor has reconciliation. Indeed, it is commonly held against the South that in a free America it knows the least about freedom. Neither has completeness been a key word; it has, however, been a key idea—not verbalized, both because the South was not analytical and because it was living out an old European past. Freedom was verbalized because it was new.

Flannery O'Connor, explaining the Southern writer's penchant for writing about freaks, says: "It is because we are still able to recognize one. To be able to recognize a freak, you have to have some conception of the whole man, and in the South the general conception of man is still, in the main, theological." She admits that this is a large generalization, "for almost anything you say about Southern belief can be denied in the next breath with equal propriety." So she resolves the contradiction in a beautiful phrase: "while the South is hardly Christ-centered, it is

most certainly Christ-haunted.''[1] Haunted by the figure of the
Complete Man, the God-Man, among all the ghosts that haunt
the South the most terrible. We have been far from completeness, but we have never quite been able to forget it. We shall see
in this discussion how the South has continuously moved toward
completeness and has continuously rested upon its achievement
or even moved backward toward the fragmentary life.

Take the matter of the Southerner's concern for things, for
the concrete as opposed to the abstract. In stressing the concrete
detail, Southern writers have simply been Southerners, more
aware than their nonliterary fellows of what Southerners are concerned with. I realize there is a tradition of sentimentality in the
South, in its life and its letters; but sentimentality begins, as did
Miss O'Connor, with the concrete thing, the person, the place,
the actual situation. Southern girls really have been beautiful—
they made a career of it. There really has been an old oaken
bucket. The difference is that whereas Miss O'Connor impreg-
nated the objects she observed with their eternal qualities, Southerners generally have done little more than surround them with
a heavy haze of time-accumulated sentiment. Both began with the
same thing; Flannery O'Connor went further and revealed the
incompleteness of the object against universal completeness.

But in the thing itself—the moment, the person, the human
relationship—lies the mystery of life. (O'Connor's posthumous
book of occasional prose is entitled *Mystery and Manners.*) When
the Southerner started with the thing, he started in the right
direction. He was on the way to the mystery of life in all its
oneness and completeness, but he stopped and rested. It has
been the strength of the Southerner that he has been inclined to
accept things, to let them help him complete his life, even though
they often completed it in failure. For this world, even at its best
—or perhaps most at its best—is a world that only suggests completion. It has at the same time been the weakness of the Southerner that he has accepted things too easily (especially in the
beginning, the gift of this splendid land) and has not realized that
the greater the gifts of God, the greater the demand that they be
used—and their highest use is to enjoy them in God.

The Southerner's relation to the people around him has

been similar to his relation to the things around him, only more complex, since people are more complex than things. More than most other Americans, he has felt himself a part of the human community, but he has both rested in the community as it is, for simple enjoyment, and has exploited a part of that community— primarily the blacks—or if himself black, has been exploited by the whites. And of course exploitation means separation from and therefore lack of completeness in.

However, paradoxical as it may seem, the direct exploitation of man by man in the South was perhaps in the long run less dangerous to the people involved than the indirect exploitation characteristic of the modern world. For the modern world through processes of abstraction has changed simple, obdurate things into complex, controllable things, and we, in the process of controlling them, have lost the old simplicity and become shadowy abstractions ourselves. We did this not because anybody forced us to, but because the material benefits were so great that we could not resist.

The simple, direct Southerner, reaching for immediate power over others, has been foiled by his own directness. At least between white and black the line of separation and exploitation is clear, and this clear division has kept alive in the hearts of those who face each other across the line some sense, however faint and deeply buried, of a common humanity. It is true that neither Southern blacks nor Southern whites know exactly who they are, for they are both keenly aware of race and also less keenly, though insistently aware of a common humanity. The completeness of each community is challenged by the shadowy presence of a total community to which both whites and blacks somehow belong.

In the typical modern world, the loss of identity, of the sense of completeness, is far more serious than this. Twelve years ago I wrote the following passage: "For the typical modern . . . loss of identity occurs in the complex, abstract, unimaginable productive order. The man who enters that dark forest does so largely because of the apparently clear and quick economic gain. The gain is clear and quick. The cost, however, is indirect, devious, and usually unrecognized. . . . modern industrial man, threading the jungle of money and machines, blinded and dazed by both, turns a corner here, enters an alley there, follows a trail until it disappears, and he is left alone in the wood, surrounded by shadowy, lost people like himself but aware only of his uncertainty and the brush whipping his eyelids. He may not even know he is lost, but he wanders in circles just the same.

"I'll say this for the South: there's no such subtlety about being lost down here. We have chosen a simple method, befitting our broad landscapes and expansive natures. We even talk of being lost; sin and salvation have never passed from our vocabulary. In the personal society of the South, in the personal heaven overarching it and in the sight of the personal God withdrawn somewhere within, sin is simple, concrete, and recognizable. We don't alienate ourselves through a thousand apparently inconsequential actions; ruthless and violent, we split our hearts in two.

"The advantage of this is that we can see what we've done." We are continuously reminded of the incompleteness of our communities.[2]

Not only are our communities clearly not what they should be in their sharp exploitative division; they have also failed to become what all human community aims at. Just as our attachment to things has as its highest goal our attachment—our loving attachment—to the whole physical world, so our attachment to a human community has as its final goal our attachment to humanity everywhere, and finally our attachment to the best in the human spirit, which in the eyes of faith exists in God.

The best defense that the Southerner had of his social order was the medieval defense: that order is basic, that life is structured into orders, one above another, and that this all culminates in God. He used this defense, especially during the decades immediately preceding the Civil War, in his attempt to justify slavery, the lowest order of all. The trouble is that he did not really believe what he said. Not only had he lost the strong religious faith of the Middle Ages, but under the increasing pressure of modern egalitarianism he was also losing his sense of an aristocratic society. He still retained the sense of community, but that community culminated here on earth. When he passed beyond earth, he became the lone individual, face to face with God. (He spoke of a kind of family there—Father, Son, and Holy Spirit—but a family overburdened with masculinity: the mother with her warmth was absent.)

The Southern emphasis upon role is an indication of how strong the community is. It also indicates the nature of the community. Each has a role to play in the earthly community; through this role he finds some extension of himself into the community, some greater completion. But what about roles in the heavenly community? Protestantism in its beginnings said (and soon forgot) that every man is a priest. But a priest is a man who stands before God not for himself but for other men. He is playing a role before God. Perhaps contemporary man is returning to a similar concept, but in the individualistic nineteenth century and in the individualistic Protestant churches in the South, men did not play roles before God.

This means that the Southerner did not carry to completion, did not understand in its universal sense, his own concern to play a role in a community. God had passed by, but the Southerner had not seen him. The light had shone in the darkness, but he had not comprehended the light.

We spoke in Part I of the Southerner's ability to commit himself, not absolutely, but usually with a limiting sense of humor. The ability to commit oneself is itself an indication of completeness. There is someone to commit, someone with physical drive, beliefs, ideals. A whole being, not a group of shadowy abstractions.

The Southerner, white or black, laughs mainly to protect himself. And the more he commits himself, the greater danger he is in, and the more therefore he needs protection. He can commit himself because he's still relatively complete. But it is this same relative completeness which reminds him at times of man's actual incompleteness in the world and therefore of his abiding need of laughter as a kind of protection.

Of course there are in the South fanatics who are committed to some cause like white supremacy and who lack any sense of humor about their commitment. Commitment to a cause is always limiting, since all causes are necessarily limited—for instance, abolitionism, white supremacy, black separatism—and therefore limit the people who support them. In their support of the South, Southerners are supporting more than a cause; they are supporting a way of life in all its complexity and variety. As a rule Southerners have been slow to support causes, sensing perhaps their partial and limited nature. "Ideals are a sin," remarked my uncle. "We should love God." Even white supremacy was muted by many contradictory attitudes, slight and usually unspoken, but resulting in a softening of a hard ideological stand.

Finally, beyond the commitment and the prevalent, limiting humor, lies the failure. Somewhere, some time, we reach the limits, and we discover what we are by discovering what we are not—at least not yet. At that point we may discover how completely human we are in our incompleteness.

The white South was limited by defeat and occupation, the black South by a far longer history of chattel slavery and segregation. Therefore both the white and the black South are identified by certain qualities: "a distrust of the abstract, a sense of human dependence on the grace of God, and a knowledge that evil is not simply a problem to be solved, but a mystery to be endured."[3]

But neither the white nor the black South has really taken the next step, which is to recognize clearly that their limitations are human, that

> The troubles of our proud and angry dust
> Are from eternity, and shall not fail,[4]

and that in this common trouble they are not only Southerners but men. The blacks, however, have done far more here than the whites; their tragic sense of life is more developed. By a spiritual standard they are happier men than the whites, more complete men, more clearly aware of man's incompleteness, of his inadequacy.

Here again the Southerner, especially the white Southerner, has failed to generalize his experiences, to read against the sky the rich meaning of the life he has lived. Deeply rooted in place and in time, he has not realized that he stands in the very portico of an eternal universe; in love with the concrete, he has failed to see in it the universal. Member of a worldly community, he has been unable to translate this—for sufficient reason, of course—

into at least the shadow of a heavenly community. The maker and the sufferer of a history rich beyond that of other American regions, he doesn't yet know that among all the Americans he is the most human and therefore nearest to the kingdom of heaven.

As for the modern world, its main thrust has not been toward human completeness, it has been toward human mastery—of nature, of something called human engineering. We build and package and sell ourselves as we build, package, and sell the other products of our civilization. We are hardly even trying to be complete men. The flower children at least sense what's wrong. But it is very hard for them or anyone else to catch a glimpse of human wholeness in a world gone mad among abstractions. Out of its deep past the South still carried such a memory, chastened by frustration and defeat. Whether we can clearly understand what we have and take effective steps to implement it before the whole house of cards blows away in a nuclear storm remains to be seen.

It is this memory of frustration and defeat among both blacks and whites that strengthens the faint nostalgia so common in the South. Unlike the rest of the nation, which seems traditionless and without history because there is a continuity—pioneer, industrialist, capitalist, democratic—between the remembered national past and the living present, the South, where the Civil War defeat broke the continuity of history, is conscious of its past.[5] All human life is pathetic because men have to choose. When a man chooses to enter one door he closes another, and all the possible experiences that lie beyond that door are lost to him forever. The South chose one mode of life, wisely or foolishly, and then had that road barred to it. A part of the pathos—I do not say injustice —here is that the South was not permitted to follow its chosen road long enough to learn for itself exactly what the experience meant—in other words really to become the South—and consequently is still touched by nostalgia for unachieved possibilities. This is strengthened by the fact that the national road offered to it in lieu of the barred road contradicts so deeply the basic desire of the South for human completeness.

There is a curious resemblance here between the situation of the Southerner vis-à-vis the past and vis-à-vis the present world. He is cut off from the past but haunted by it; he cannot use it, but he cannot forget it. As for the world around him today and the ultimate meaning of this world, though he has many hints within his life which carry universal and eternal meanings, he is seldom able to read them. Here again he is touched by the dream of completeness, he is haunted by God. This is his blessing and this his curse.

The Southerner has outdone himself in his desire for reconciliation. He has been too much concerned with having some reconciliation, too little concerned with the quality of what he had. More specifically, he has desired too much to be agreeable, too little really to agree. This seems to make his error intellectual. It is so, but not chiefly so. The error is chiefly a limitation of spirit, of imagination.

Saint Paul says that God was in Christ reconciling the world to himself. To be reconciled to God is to be reconciled to the nature of life: to the passage of time, the ineluctable approach of death, the dependence of man upon the world and other men, and the need of self-sacrificing love (the Cross) as a way of facing these challenges and mitigating the sinfulness accompanying our incompleteness. These are the griefs of life, and it is hard for unredeemed man to be reconciled to them.

Interestingly, the Southerner is more inclined than other Americans to be reconciled to the griefs of life. This is to say that he is more religious, more acceptive of the great surrounding mystery. Indeed, he has been too acceptive, in one sense too religious. He has been too inclined to accept the grievances of life along with its essential griefs. In order to do this, of course, he thought of the grievances as griefs, for a grievance is by definition something that should be corrected, while a grief is irremediable. In his desire to be agreeable, the Southerner has often agreed to the continuation of avoidable evils in the world and of selfishness in himself. The white Southerner at times defended even slavery on the grounds that it was an expression of fallen human nature and therefore unavoidable.

An interesting illustration of how important the South has made agreeableness occurred in Little Rock in 1957. Because of the violence at the opening of the school that year, the ministers of the city called for a day of prayer. Though there were of course variations, the spirit of the prayers may be summarized as follows: "O Lord, we have become very disagreeable to one another; make us agreeable again." Almost entirely absent was the cry of the psalmist, "Against thee, thee only, have I sinned!" Indeed, except for so-called personal religion, this cry has until recently been absent from the South. We haven't admitted that we need to be reconciled to God in our society; we haven't quarreled with him there; we have hardly admitted he is there.

Of course this attitude applied not only to the South, but, with the exception of the social gospel of the last fifty-odd years, to the nation as well. The South was simply more flagrant in its defense of a divided slave society than was the rest of the nation in its defense of an atomistic industrial society. Likewise the South's attempt to heal this breach through agreeable manners was more noticeable. In other words, the South has sinned more boldly than the rest of the nation, and has therefore been more steadily though vaguely aware of its sin. Up to a certain point, the South is the prodigal son who demanded what was his, went into a far country, and squandered it. But because he was in a far country and at last a failure, he could not forget his home. At the critical moment he came to himself, remembered his home and kin people, and headed back. The South has never clearly headed back; it has been stirred more by nostalgia than by the tragic sense of life.

The typical American has been the elder brother. He never left home. He saved his money, put it at interest, became a bank president, a ruling elder, and a Rotarian. But doing this, he wandered unconsciously down the intricate and multitudinous paths of the material world, until without even realizing it he was lost, separated from the inclusive Spirit of his Father. But never having stormed away from home, he had no way of knowing he was lost, and therefore he could not return. This is about where we are now.

More than other American regions the South has been concerned with manners. Manners reach toward completeness in that they consider the present moment as important in itself, not simply as an antecedent to some later moment. The mannered person takes time momently to play the game. At their best, manners are a ritual, a religious game: the moment is important, the participants are important, the action takes place against an abiding backdrop of mystery.

Manners are also a reconciling force between the individual and others, who are both his greatest danger and his greatest need. If he does not find God in them, he does not find God.

Admittedly, racial etiquette—one form of Southern manners —served to keep separate, and in a way incomplete, people who had to be physically close together. Yet, though racial etiquette kept whites and blacks apart, it included them in the same play. The difficulty in understanding this is the same difficulty in understanding how the black community, which usually in the small town fringed the white community like the dark forest, was also a part of the total community. And even racial etiquette, like all manners, was a way of protecting the privacy of the individual. "The uneducated Southern Negro," says Flannery O'Connor, "is not the clown he's made out to be. He's a man of very elaborate manners and great formality, which he uses superbly for his own protection and to insure his own privacy."[6] I realize that the black militants, in the bad manners of confrontation, don't admit this, and certainly I'm not saying that racial etiquette is essentially a good thing. I'm only saying that it made somewhat better a bad situation by providing standards of action and response, and such rules helped incorporate the participants into the play.

Now the ideal of Southern manners—seldom attained of course, and the goal of a too limited few—was gracefulness and graciousness. This applied to men as well as women, though the masculine image stressed easy physical carriage and strength under absolute control. In both men and women, gracefulness suggests rhythmic lightness and playfulness; graciousness, a bountiful spirit. Admittedly, the graciousness was often condescending, the air of the Lady Bountiful, but this was surely not its ideal. At its best it was an outpouring of spiritual and material gifts in humble recognition that the giver had been blessed by life.

Comments here about gracious manners would make no

sense if the ladies and gentlemen of the South had been created
at the absolute expense of the rest of the population, white and
especially black, who themselves had been left dour dolts. But
this was not so. The ideal of manners and politeness permeated
the South, especially the Atlantic Seaboard South, where it had
longer to mature. You can see it even more sharply because more
brokenly defined among the very poor, who stand on their manners against the harsh inroads of necessity. And the ideal was by
no means simple gracefulness, the ability to dance, to tread
lightly in whatever situation; it was, in addition, an inner ideal of
integrity, of being all there, complete, at every moment. One
reason the early and innocent participants in sit-ins shook the
heart of the South was that they combined as never before so
massively the relaxed grace of manners and the quiet reserve of
dedicated hearts. They were really what the South had always
wanted to be. In the fullness of time they actualized for the South
that ideal of completeness which their very presence through the
long barren years had forestalled. They had reconciled, at least
within themselves, the often conflicting ideals of the Christian
and the gentleman. They had bridged the gap between the outer
and the inner worlds of the South.

This graciousness and grace was what the Southern social
order aimed at. How much of this it translated into religion we
shall see in a later chapter.

Where freedom is, God is. The Spirit blows through the
world on the winds of freedom and silently and unpredictably
touches the hearts of men. But there is freedom and freedom.
Even the image of freedom as a blowing wind misleads us unless
we bring it up sharply. What it immediately suggests is being
freed *from*. But to be freed from everything is to be entirely lost.
The Holy Spirit frees us "From the weary weight/ Of all this
unintelligible world" in order that we may know the real world,
and knowing it, may become part of it, may belong to it, not as
slaves, but as co-creators with God, as sons of God.

Undoubtedly the South has stressed order too much, freedom too little. This was due mainly to the presence of the black,
who was held—by force finally—in a subordinate position. It was
also due slightly to the lingering influence of the Middle Ages

with its stress upon an ordered society with a place for every man. But the ordered society of the Middle Ages culminated in God, who was free, and whose freedom, expressed in his grace, might appear at any moment in the order he had established. The South claimed to believe this, but it actually believed it in only a limited way: God's free grace might appear in the life of the individual, to shatter and remake that life, but it did not appear in the life of society. To admit this would have been too dangerous; a free God operating in and upon a slave society would be revolutionary. The leaders of the South recognized this, and so in their extremity they argued that the slave system had God's entire support.

So we end as we began, with belonging, with completeness. The South can be better understood under this term than under the related terms of reconciliation and freedom. Even the slave, the Southerner in his worst condition, though he belonged legally to his master, belonged more than legally to the natural world in which he lived and to the plantation, the human structure through which he was related to that natural world. And in this more-than-legal belonging lay whatever freedom he—and indeed all Southerners—had. As Flannery O'Connor says, the South is Christ-haunted. Or, as I have said, stressing a little more the presence and the presences in the South, it is simply haunted by God.

**PART
THREE**

The Church and the Culture

XVI

Centers of Order

Whatever else the church in the South is, it is a part of the culture; religious institutions are always a part of the culture to which they belong. A tribal religion belongs to the tribe in question; even world religions, including Christianity, take color from the cultures in which they are found. Christianity and Judaism have taken color from America, and without a doubt have taken deep color from the South. In itself this is no criticism. Human beings belong to particular times and places, and must be spoken to in their own language.

Whether supporting or opposing the culture, the church has existed in the South because it satisfied (or mollified) the needs of the people. We have to ask, then, the questions: What needs did the church satisfy? How well did it satisfy them? and What needs did it fail to take notice of?

The needs of men vary greatly according to place, time, and social structure. Yet finally men need God, and this is to need completeness, reconciliation, and freedom.

Looking back at the history of the South, one has to conclude that the greatest need was for racial justice. This, however, was so radical a need that its satisfaction would have demanded the virtual remaking of society. Even Jefferson, liberal and humane as he was, could not imagine the South as still existing with free Negroes instead of slaves. The churches consequently did not demand such a revolution, though by 1800 the small fringe sect of Quakers usually did. What the churches generally did in this matter was what society at large generally did: it tried to ignore it and to satisfy certain ancillary needs that were connected with the basic need for racial justice, e.g., the need to be kind to slaves and to be concerned about their souls.

I know there is a tendency to say that since the church did not have the courage to face this basic, essential problem, it had no justification for its existence. I do not agree. Granted it was far from what it called itself, a Christian church, and granted its basic cowardice resulted in ambiguity and confusion in other matters, yet it satisfied some needs, and not only for whites but for blacks also. Some of these needs may have been satisfied even at the cost of covering up a greater need, but if the greater need could not be met, there is some advantage in having met the smaller.

As we have already noticed, the frontier has been until fairly recently a powerful force in Southern life. As compared with long-settled areas, the frontier is always marked by disorder. Institutions are weak, fluid, and few, and men generally lack any great devotion to them, respect for them, or fear of them. It is every man for himself. This may result in deeds of great unselfishness, where a deep well of human goodness is touched in moments of sudden danger, or in much selfishness, as each individual strives to make a go of the new situation.

There is little doubt that the frontier needed order, felt this need, and had it in part satisfied by the presence of the churches. The wilder frontiersmen, of course, eager to express their licentious natures and materialistic desires, felt no need for churches and actively opposed them; but undoubtedly many of the people remembered with nostalgia the more formal lives they had left behind and welcomed the churches as bringing a little more order into a generally disorderly situation.

The need for order also depended upon the character of the settlers. During the eighteenth century the frontier of the South was its Piedmont. When the westward migration began after the Revolution, much of its source lay in the Piedmont. The chief settlers of the Piedmont were Scotch-Irish, who had arrived there after a stay of one to three generations in Ulster, where they had defended the English frontier against the Catholic Irish. They therefore came to America hardened in the individualistic ways of the frontier, ready to take and to hold what they wanted. The records show that as they moved southward down the Piedmont, they were in continuous conflict with the earlier English settlers to the east and the Indians to the west.

Their religion was the stern Calvinism of John Knox, a religion that laid stress upon God's sovereign power, upon an educated ministry, and upon a structured church with presbyteries, synods, and a general assembly. Sensing their own involvement in the material world, their passionate thirst for things, for power, and among the saintly, for goodness, they felt the need of a stern theology and a highly structured church to counter the disorder into which their desires and their circumstances led them. Under the influence of the Great Revival of 1800, churches began to have more influence and undoubtedly were centers of order along the generally disorderly frontier.

Finally, behind the disorder incident to the frontier and to the temperament of the Scotch-Irish settlers, there lay the vast, ordered disorder of slavery. Aristotle maintained that those men were enslaved who were by nature slaves. In this view slavery can be justified as a rational base for society. The South tried to do this—tried hard—but never could really convince itself. Its mind had been touched by nearly two millennia of Christianity, and it was in addition part of a vast physical world of apparently limitless freedom and of a human world in which the suggestions of freedom and democracy grew stronger with the passage of time. Therefore Southerners lived in a world which, for all its apparent order, showed strains and fissures both objective and subjective, a world where, not too far beneath the ordered surface, the Abyss loomed.

In such a world men need any suggestion of order they can find, and certainly the churches scattered throughout the South, especially those with clearer intellectual beliefs and more formal structures, did something toward satisfying this need.

It is clear that the slave did not need any assurance of order; he had too much already, as he indicated when he sang the moving words of Moses to Pharaoh, "Let my people go"—out of bondage into freedom. We shall consider also the religion of the slave and of the later freedman.

But if some assurance of order is necessary in the disorderly life of the frontier, this need grows less as the frontier becomes the settled community, in our case, as the frontier South passes into the modern South, becoming urban and industrial. In such a world the religious stress upon order serves mainly to rivet upon people the order which already exists, that is, to defend the status quo. What is needed now from religion is a stress upon freedom and creativity, and a shaking of the trust in order for order's sake.

The American church has always insisted upon a moralistic order, a private order, and an otherworldly order. It has been composed of maxims like "do not do this" and "do not do that." It has not been creative; it has seldom said, "Follow the light as you see it." The Quakers have done this, but they have always been a small group; the Baptists in their great concern for individual freedom seemed to be moving in this direction. What they usually meant, however, was the freedom of each congregation to go in whatever direction it wished, not the freedom of individual members of that congregation. The individual Baptist was as closely bound by accepted prohibitions—moralisms—as was the individual Presbyterian, and probably far more than the individual Episcopalian. As for the fringe sects, they have been moralistic in the extreme, often turning sharply against the usual customs of society but clinging tenaciously to their own moralisms.

I am raising no question here of the ethical values of Christianity. Christianity is an ethical religion, as the lives and teachings of the great prophets, including Jesus, attest. I am criticizing the tendency of the churches to reduce the great order of the universe to a few moralistic injunctions, good at times and in places, but entirely inadequate as a base upon which to build a life.

Far more fundamental and inclusive than the moral is the aesthetic order of the universe, wherein the individual parts—plants, animals, and men—all express their own desires, which, because the individuals are also parts of the whole, find some support by the whole and completeness in it. The aesthetic motive, says Whitehead, is at the base of all power. Jesus was too much of a Jew to lay much stress upon beauty. He was concerned with religious and ethical values, but he did recognize the beauty of the world as a part of God's creation, and his forebears, in the story of the Creation, said that God created man in his own likeness, a creative spirit.

The Episcopal Church does glimpse and attempt to express in its liturgy the great creative and saving quality of the world. So does the Catholic Church, though I'm generally omitting it in this discussion as being until recently insufficiently important in Southern life. But the Protestant churches generally have largely forgotten the unitary and inclusive significance of the aesthetic and have stressed an individualistic form of worship and exemplified a moral life based upon a few negative rules.

We should not confuse this doctrine of the unifying power of the aesthetic with the economic doctrine of the guiding hand, according to which, if every man will follow his own economic desires, a universal guiding hand will weave all this together for the good of the whole. The basic trouble here is that the economic man is a myth. Though men do act from economic motives, no man acts from economic motives alone. When man tries to do this, he splits the social fabric apart.

Again, the order insisted upon by the church has generally been a private order. This means it has been an order within individuals, not an order between individuals, that is, a social order. Undoubtedly this insistence made some individuals better individuals, more sober and steadfast; but also undoubtedly it made some individuals worse, raising their assurance to rude aggressiveness, their proper self-respect to pride of achievement and scorn of failure. As for the social order, this was supposed to be the natural product of orderly individuals. The individuals were made good by the grace of God and the persuasions of preachers; then they created the good society. This of course is at most only half the picture; the existing society creates individuals to fit and support it. The result of this insistence upon individual order was that the church usually supported the status quo by saying nothing, or occasionally when there was a strong consensus on some issue, by actively supporting this consensus, as in the Prohibition fiasco.

The church approved what society created, but if the church had been more Christian and less Stoic, it would have both approved and disapproved—approved justice, or integrity, in the individual and disapproved the failure to extend this justice throughout the social structure.

Throughout most of its history the church in the South—the white church—has been unable to consider the social teachings of the great prophets. The black church has, and with increasing vigor does. Born in injustice and bondage, it has always cried out for justice and freedom. Perhaps it is to the credit of white churchmen that they did not preach social justice; at least they saved themselves one hypocrisy.

In the third place, the order insisted upon by the church was not only moralistic and private, it was also otherworldly. The church taught the beauty of the spiritual life. This was the quiet ordered life of a Sunday morning, a Sabbath of the soul, a foretaste, they said, of the eternal Sabbath of the heavenly kingdom. The Southern church—and indeed the American church—fled to another world because it could not encompass the strains and the terrors of this world. In this regard the Southern church has indeed been the opiate of the people. The order of slavery was so hard to defend that the churches usually avoided the issue, saying it was a political or a police matter. So to men coming with passionate, disordered hearts from the disorders of the frontier and from the vaster disorder of a slave-based democracy, the churches could say little more than: "Peace. In this quiet hour, let us forget these troubles and rest in God. He will give us the peace that passeth understanding."

It passes understanding all right. The best you can say for the Southern church member is that he seldom accepted it with his whole nature, wholeheartedly. How could he? It was a product of the weary part of his nature, a mere shadow of the rich, dangerous life he often lived. Yet, by accepting it half-heartedly, he made a hypocrite of himself.

I have already told how for one Southerner, myself, this spiritual order was vague and unsatisfying, almost entirely detached from the daily world of disorder—and of order—that I knew. It had its own limited meaning, as any moment has, but it drew little strength from and cast little light upon the complex, difficult, and sometimes beautiful world which it was supposed, as a religious moment, to express and interpret.

Indeed, it was worse than inadequate; it was in its chief effect evil, for it tended to blind us to the real disorder of our lives, leaving us complacent and the disorder unchanged. Meanwhile our lives went on, with their great disorder occasionally and briefly illuminated by moments of order. The church, however, failed to judge the disorder even by the cultural standards of order which occasionally appeared. As for an inclusive divine order operative throughout the world, though the church—especially the Presbyterian Church—insisted upon the sovereignty of God, it didn't believe its own words.

Furthermore, the very form of worship, with the sermon as its core, pointed toward man rather than toward God. The liturgical churches—the Episcopal and the Lutheran—did attempt through their liturgies to bring the entire man, a sensuous, emotional, intuitive, intellectual being, into the universal neighborhood of man-and-God. But the nonliturgical services, though they did something of this, did relatively little. The form of the service said very little—and the very word "service" suggests the activistic, man-oriented quality. As Samuel Hill points out, in the Southern church worship is hardly "work done in God's service," but is humanly oriented—for producing fellowship, "for providing moral instruction, and for promoting the interests of the institutional church."[1] Though, as Hill says, gospel songs are preferred, something should be said about the hymns, especially the hymns of the more formal churches. These undoubtedly did something for religion, picking up the themes of man in nature, of his troubled life, and especially of his hopes of another and better world. I learned much of truth from this hymn:

> By cool Siloam's shady rill
> How fair the lily grows,
> How sweet the breath beneath the hill
> Of Sharon's dewy rose!
>
> By cool Siloam's shady rill
> The lily must decay;
> The rose that blooms beneath the hill
> Must shortly fade away.

These are utterly simple themes, simply expressed, of the beauty and transiency of life.

This suggests the emphasis of the Southern church upon images. Richard M. Weaver makes the following comment: "What the Southerner desired above all else in religion was a fine set of images to contemplate, as Allen Tate has shown in his *Religion and the Old South.* The contemplation of these images was in itself a discipline in virtue, which had the effect of building up in him an inner restraint."[2] Some important images were the rock in the weary land, the old rugged cross, the pilgrim and stranger, the mighty army, the golden strand. I think of my grandmother, a strong, resolute old lady, to the end of her long life singing quietly these songs of the church. As Weaver says, they may have taught restraint; they certainly taught acceptance; they seldom taught militant change.

The core of the religious service was not the hymn but the sermon, and its tone was often argumentative, rhetorical, in the broadest sense political, sometimes logical, sometimes highly emotional, and primarily directed toward men. The intention was to bring men to God, but the devices used were the devices of Southern public and political life—logic, argument, rhetoric— and the appeal was almost entirely to the will. Consequently, many a man, like my father, left the church arguing against the thrust of the sermon.

Samuel Hill remarks that religion in the South has been mainly a vertical affair—of man's looking upward toward God— not horizontal—of man's looking outward toward man. In a sense this is true, but it needs modification. The churches did attempt to turn men's eyes toward God and another world, away from the pains and the problems of this life. But, as I've just been saying, the methods used for this purpose were largely unsuccessful. For we come to God not by believing this or that moral injunction or this or that creedal statement, but by believing that he *is.* We believe that he is insofar as we know completeness—or recon-ciliation, or freedom—and we know completeness not through the brain or the will, but through the imagination. In religious services this means mainly through the liturgy. Imagination is the unifying force, not mind or will, and in religion the liturgy is both the expression and the source of imagination. The liturgy tells the worshiper not what he should do, but that he is a man expecting God, a man burdened and buoyed by human fears and hopes, a man reconciled to being a man, waiting for God.

So the Southern nonliturgical religious service (this applied also to the nation, but the South, more burdened with its humanity, needed aid more) left men largely where it found them —in the world. But instead of in the large, terrible, and splendid world out of which they had come, they found themselves briefly in a limited, private world, where the public problems were laid to rest and human life was touched with an aura of mystery. Perhaps this was the main benefit—the mystery; we again had the sense of being haunted by God, but it was in a twilight air, slightly sepulchral, far from the sunshine and the great winds of the world. We would carry back into the world a vague sense of uneasiness, similar, perhaps, to that uneasiness I felt as a boy when, returning home from pre-communion preaching on a Saturday, I saw men plowing in the fields and feared that God might break out of the church, where we had just left him, and rush upon the unsuspecting plowmen, and I might be the witness of the disaster. But the fear would fade with that day, made sacred by the service, and we would be faced once more with the world of everyday.

It was because of its deep-seated disorderliness that the South needed the order of a constitution strictly interpreted, of an inerrant Bible, and of a church which, however much it talked about grace, really stood for law and order. The basic trouble with the church was that its order remained largely immaterial to the order and disorder of society and consisted largely of private and otherworldly attitudes.

The church did not through any vision of a universal order in its liturgy complete the incomplete, disordered lives of its members; it merely clarified somewhat the individual disorder, but at the same time canceled this benefit by failing to relate individual disorder to social disorder. It did help to reconcile men—not to God, however, but to the evils of life and to their sinful participation in these evils. It may often have freed men from the burden of so-called private sins, but at the expense of leaving them burdened (however unconsciously) by public sins. They were freed temporarily *from* the world but not *for* it.

XVII

Release Through the Church

It was clear to the blacks that they had too much order of whatever kind; what they needed was freedom. This was not so clear to the more favored whites, especially those among the whites who clearly benefited materially from the prevailing order. Nevertheless, in a frontier society like that of the South—and to a lesser degree of the nation—the bond of necessity has often been so strong that the need for emotional release, through the church or some other institution, has been a powerful one. This need is related to the large place that pioneering has had in our life, to the hardships and loneliness of the frontier, to the paucity of social institutions through which men and women could express their varied human interests, and to the strength of that individualistic competitive drive, accentuated by the Puritan ethic, which drove men westward till the frontier was closed, and still drives them upward on the ladder of success.

In some of these matters the South has been more fortunate than the rest of the nation, in others less so. It was more fortunate in that it was never dominated by sheer individualism and the Puritan ethic, and less fortunate in that the frontier lasted far longer in the South than elsewhere and that it was usually a lonelier frontier, settled by individuals, not by groups, composed of scattered clearings in the forest, not of compact villages and towns.

The historian Clement Eaton particularizes the change in the manners and customs of the people of the South by the camp meetings so popular at the time. "The Great Revival of 1800–1805 changed the religious atmosphere of the age. The upper classes, particularly the Episcopalians, tended to look down upon the extravagances of the camp meetings. . . . Though the upper classes frowned upon the religious enthusiasm that brought thousands of ignorant and irreligious farmers into the evangelical churches, they too were deeply affected by the revival movement. By 1830 there were few deists and freethinkers left in the Southern states. . . . Indeed, a profound religious orthodoxy had settled upon the South."[1]

Though revivals continue even today, the outbreaking emotionalism of earlier times has disappeared except among some of the fringe sects and some of the more isolated Negro churches. What need does it express there, and how well is this need satisfied by such worship?

The need is essentially the same as that of the earlier frontier except that this is a human frontier while that was a physical one. Perhaps the word "backwash" is better than "frontier." Except when fleeing from justice, men went to the frontier willingly, though doubtless often urged forward by hard conditions at home. These modern frontiersmen have been swept into the backwaters of modern life; from these muddy coves they can only watch the world flowing by.

They suffer some of the physical hardships of frontiersmen: spare or monotonous diets, worn-out clothes, poor dwelling places. But the frontiersman always had a horizon, usually limitless; he always had hope. These people have no horizon. The rich world flows by in the shining cars, the neon signs, and on the TV screen, and the most they can do is to watch with glazed eyes. Now and again the glaze breaks in anger against the rich or even against themselves because, according to the American ethic, they too should have these things, and since they do not have them, they have been betrayed either by others or by themselves. Or, going a step further, they become proud of themselves because they are poor, seeing all worldly pleasures as devices of the devil and their poverty as a holy badge.

This describes mainly the whites of the backwash; it could not describe, except very recently, the blacks. There are several differences. First, the whites belong to the modern poor: those who have been impoverished, at least relatively, by our affluence. The blacks also belong to the modern poor, but they were poor a long time before the modern world pushed them aside, and they learned from those hard generations certain survival measures. Again, until recently, with the spread of education, the civil rights movement, and the rise of black nations, the blacks have not been bitten by the bug of success—indeed, they were not supposed to succeed—and therefore have been less inclined to bitterness at failure than were the whites of the same economic class. Also, because of this relative lack of concern for success—a concern rooted in part in the Puritan ethic generally foreign to them—the blacks have managed to enjoy life more than the whites in a comparable economic situation and have therefore been less frustrated and less in need of the release offered by highly emotional forms of worship.

Finally, race was more cohesive with them than class was with comparable whites. The whites were taught to think not of class but of race. Yet, though they were taught that they were bound to other whites by their race, they knew in their bones that they were separated from them by their failure. The blacks were bound together both by race and by failure, but since they had never had laid upon them the burden of success, they could more easily take failure as another evidence of the human predicament, not to be blamed upon anyone in particular, but simply one of "the troubles of our proud and angry dust." I am not saying that this attitude was best, and indeed, it is fading now under the attacks of the young and bitter blacks. I am simply saying that it existed and still to a degree exists, and that it affects the significance of the emotional release that was sought and found in highly emotional forms of worship.

Undoubtedly such forms of worship bring the worshipers together in a more cohesive group than does the hollow formalism of, say, a typical Presbyterian service, for emotions are deeper than thoughts, and—unless their intention is divisive—they unify more deeply than thoughts. But, in regard to the highly emotional togetherness of the type of worship we are considering, questions arise as to both its permanence and its cost in increased separation from all out-groups. The worship of the white fringe groups undoubtedly draws the members of the group close together, but this is partly because it teaches them that they form a select group, snatched from the unregenerate world and strongly opposed to most of the standards of that world. For remember, that world has both pushed them into a backwash and taught them that they are to blame for being so situated. So in their worship they are both drawn together by highly charged emotional ideas and at the same time separated from the unsaved world beyond the church doors. They gain a temporary and limited completeness—a completeness with and within the congregation—but at the expense of a completeness with mankind in the world. One reason they cannot find the larger meaning is that, like all Protestants, whether intellectual or emotional, they aren't consciously seeking it. They aren't really asking the meaning of human life in God; each is asking the meaning of his individual life in God. Each is trying to be saved or to push another into salvation. But salvation is into a kingdom, not into a chaos. God is the God of our fathers and of our brothers, not of our individual selves.

Undoubtedly many blacks have been falsely humble, with downcast eyes and whining voices, prostituting themselves for crumbs from the white man's table. But at their best, in their deepest religious moments—and the church aided them in this —they saw encompassing their own misfortunes the tragedy of human life. Thus some among them became Stoics, while many more became Christians and looked with compassionate eyes upon themselves and upon others, including the whites, as caught in the human predicament.

Similarities and differences between the worship of the white fringe groups and that of the blacks—who form as a whole a fringe group—are illustrated by a comparison of the mountain hymns of the whites and the Negro spirituals. The dominant tone of both is plaintive, as befits the religious music of an outcast group. True, the blacks were deliberately outcast, while the whites were bypassed incidentally as the frontier swept on westward, leaving them isolated and becalmed in their deep mountain valleys, but the effect is much the same: lonely people, living on the outskirts of society, largely cut off from the strong, sweet waters of the mainstream. But the plaintiveness of the hymns of the southern Appalachians is far more plangent than that of the Negro spirituals. The wavering, uncertain, unpredictable grace notes float out as if from a disembodied spirit. Their music and their meaning suggest lonely mountaintops away from other men, and worse than this, away from God, who may or may not be hovering in the mist. The spirituals, by contrast, rise out of the whole body of the singer and take their complex rhythms from the complexities of the body. In addition, the singer stands solidly upon the earth, which seems to sway with his swaying. Finally, though the spirituals may say *I,* they always imply *we*: the community on earth suggesting the community in heaven, the singers moving together into campground, the sweet chariots of heaven coming to carry them home.

The mountain hymns are Protestantism gone to seed—beautiful seed, but, like thistledown, ethereal, floating on vague currents of air. This is what happens when the individual pursues himself too far. He is lost to earth, to the natural and the human community, and consequently lost to the community of heaven. The Negro spirituals, though Protestant in their theology, are almost untouched by Protestant individualism. They express the hopes and fears of people who never lost their friendliness for, their trust in earth and in one another. In bondage to other men, suffering the heat and cold of earth, they still had some trust in mankind and in the natural world. (It has been claimed that the spirituals were used as signals, unintelligible to white masters. This makes no difference. Whatever they denoted, they connoted the deepest hopes and fears of the men who made them.)

To go back to our problem of the significance of highly emotional forms of worship, the basic question is whether a given congregation stands for (in place of) the world or against the world. The white fringe congregations tend to stand against the world, the black (fringe) congregations for it.

This is not all that must be said about highly emotional forms of worship. To modify McLuhan, the medium is also the message. We say, both to others and to ourselves, in part what the medium permits. The usual Protestant service, whether staid or emotional, is generally nonliturgical, and as such is far more individualistic, far less social than the liturgical service. The liturgical service is first of all a creation of the past, and participation in it implies one's willingness to forget oneself and to merge one's hopes and fears with the hopes and fears of those long gone. The spontaneity, the distinctiveness of the individual is diminished; the sense of the group is enlarged. Again, through its form the liturgy appeals to the imagination, which is a unifying force, and so reveals (or tends to reveal) to the participants their oneness in God. It reveals to men what they are: human beings bound together by the grace of God in sickness and in health, in loss and in salvation. If it urges anything upon them, it is merely that they become more what it reveals them to be: incomplete beings longing for completion, finding it—in the Christian view—in a being who, though indeed God, became incomplete as a man.

The ironic thing here is that the Southerner—and we shall consider the meaning of this later—brings to church a strong sense of community existing now, resting upon the past, growing into the future. But also, in partial opposition to this, he is an individualistic modern and as such is skeptical of liturgical worship. For liturgical worship sinks his individuality in the whole, asking him to yield himself, to suspend the driving will, the emotional outburst, even the analytical mind, and to contemplate the vision of man.

If the Protestant preacher is in spirit a priest rather than a pulpit politician, he may through his own poetic, imaginative outlook lead his people, at least for a moment, into such a vision. If he is such a person, he speaks not for himself and not to the individuals before him, but as their own voice reciting humble man's position before God. He says for them what they most deeply know.

But the Reformation clipped the wings of the priesthood. Reacting decisively against priestly corruption, it concluded that the whole matter was fol-de-rol and that any man could approach God without priestly mediation beyond that provided by the great High Priest, Jesus Christ. It phrased this conclusion in the words "every man a priest," thus expressing the modern individualistic attitude. Unfortunately, in abandoning the priesthood the modern world abandoned the very idea that made a priesthood possible: the idea of human oneness that permits one man to speak for many. Theoretically every man is a priest, equipped by his humanity to stand before God. But no man can be his own priest; only as he speaks for all other men, through his human voice, can he speak as a priest. Even the Great Priest, though he saved others, could not save himself, nor did he really try.

The modern preacher suffers from the same disease as the modern layman. As an individualist, the layman expects to be preached at, persuaded, or browbeaten; the preacher expects to preach at him. These preachers at their best are prophets, speaking the word of the Lord. But true prophets are always, by their very nature, in scarce supply, and a B.D. degree doesn't create one. The modern world has seen the rise of the common man; he has appeared in religious circles as the common prophet. The common prophet does the best he can. Lacking the searing vision of blessed completeness and sad incompleteness, he deals in platitudes and moralisms, perhaps persuading men more fully to support the status quo, whether that be good or bad. Living in a highly practical world, he wishes, like the layman, to get things done. He lacks the wide, contemplative, poetic vision of the priest, or even if he has it, lacks generally the liturgical form through which it might find expression, or where such form exists, lacks the understanding, even by the participants, of what the liturgy means.

The highly emotional services of some fringe sects among the whites and of some fringe sects and even churches among the blacks undoubtedly unite these groups within themselves in a warmer, more human fashion than do the more sober and thoughtful services of most of the old-line churches. And since these people need help (or appear to need it) more than the usual middle-class churchgoers, they receive more benefit from their churches. But how wide is the benefit, and how lasting is it? While such people are together, they are more closely together than more conventional worshipers, but to what degree are they together against the world, and to what degree for it, as representative of it? If much of this is a togetherness against the world, when they return to that world they will find their separation from it and their suspicion of it increased and themselves undefended by the warm sense of oneness that had supported them at church.

Too often, it would seem, such religious services are like

psychedelic "trips"—beautiful today, but offering little suste-
nance for the hard world tomorrow and no directions for grap-
pling with and improving that world.

We can consider from another angle this question of the
relative value of religion to these two groups, the fringe sects and
the main line churches.

In their emotionalism, the fringe sects represent the frontier.
They belong to the present social frontier, they represent best
the frontier religion which historically has been so influential in
the South. The life of the frontier is marked by the erratic, the
unusual, the unpredictable. Things have not yet settled down. It
is a place of great possibilities, both fortunate and unfortunate.
This is true not only of the physical frontier, but also in some
ways of the social frontier. On the social frontier men live from
hand to mouth. It is the present moment that counts. But,
whereas on the American physical frontier great fortunes could
be made and men lived in hope, hope is largely absent from the
present social frontier.

A natural question here is: How well does the unusual and
unpredictable life of the frontier serve as a seedbed for religion?
According to Émile Durkheim, poorly. "For religious concep-
tions have as their object, before everything else, to express and
explain, not that which is exceptional and abnormal in things,
but, on the contrary, that which is constant and regular. . . . Even
with the most simple religions we know, their essential task is to
maintain, in a positive manner, the normal course of life."[2]

Of course Durkheim's general opinion is that religion is
created by society. If the society itself is ill-formed, the religion
will be the same. In this view, religion has been relatively ineffective in the modern world because the inordinate thrust of the
individual has broken the community apart. Regardless of this
and regardless of the value of fringe-sect religion, it has to be said
that this religion, in its emphasis upon the unusual and the unpredictable, expresses a most important aspect of the life its
adherents live.

What of the religion of the main line churches? Though the
religious service is more quiet and reserved, the accent is the
same: upon the unusual, the critical moment, not upon the con-

tinuing life; upon conversion; upon justification, not sanctification; upon entering the church, not upon continuing to live in the church.

But the lives of these middle-class worshipers are not unpredictable frontier lives. They are settled lives, with day following day and season following season. The individualistic Protestant, however, has lost almost entirely the sacramental quality of the days and the seasons. Having devoted Sunday entirely to God, he can leave the world to the devil. As a consequence, his public worship, whatever the regularity of its form, does not pick up and justify and sanctify the rhythm of the world. It is therefore not poetry; it is therefore poor religion.

As to the relative value of this religion to that of the fringe sects, since the religion of the fringe sects is closer to their life than that of the main line churches is to theirs, it is a better religion. It adds at least some completeness to highly fragmented lives; the religion of the main line churches adds little to their more settled lives.

XVIII

Repentance and Reconciliation

Except for the mystic, and for him only momentarily, the need for completeness is not to be satisfied in this world. There exists therefore the need to be reconciled to incompleteness. Jesus did say, "Seek, and ye shall find," and those great seekers after God, the saints, have found him more than others, but finding him, they seek him still more passionately. They have tasted that water which, if a man taste, he shall thirst till death.

Saint Paul said that God was in Christ reconciling the world to himself. To be reconciled to God is to be reconciled to the nature of the world he has made, to the way he operates it, and to the nature of his creatures—oneself and other men.

This need for reconciliation is usually called by the church the need to repent. This includes the need to admit one's guilt, to confess one's sins. If we do, God is faithful, we are told, to forgive our sins.

It's easy for the church (especially a moralistic church like ours in the South—and in America) to get tangled up with particular sins. The problem is not *sins* but *sin*. Sin is the refusal, whether conscious or not, to be reconciled to the nature of life, that is, to God. All life is interdependent; he who fails or refuses to recognize this and tries to stand alone is still unreconciled. In the attempt to maintain this unreal posture, he may simply show scorn, or he may commit murder. The scorn or the murder is only the expression of his trouble; his trouble is that he is not reconciled to, is not willing to accept, the nature of life.

Suppose a friend has failed us or we have failed ourselves. To be bitter about this or to fall into indifference or sullenness is to refuse to accept man's poor, incomplete, imperfect nature. We should continue to forgive, said Jesus, even to seventy times seven. If we are reconciled to the nature of man, we can be reconciled to the actions of our neighbor and of ourselves.

To be reconciled to this is not the same as accepting it passively. It is not human nature to do so. For man is active, striving, as all nature is—Saint Paul heard the created universe groaning together. To sit with folded hands is to be unnatural; it is to fail to be reconciled to the drive toward completeness in an ever incomplete creature. This is part of the absurdity of life which we moderns make so much of. But the cross was also called absurd two thousand years ago.

Man is a son of the earth who believes on good authority that he is also a son of God, and the problem is how to be both.

The aspect of this problem we are dealing with here may be phrased as follows: What did the church in the South do to reconcile men to failure, to revive their burdened hearts?

The Southern church has always brought hope and strength to buffeted individuals, and it has usually tried to do this in a true though limited prophetic spirit by relating these defeats to the mysterious will of God and by urging acceptance of them as from God—an expression of his judgment and grace. This was called "improving the occasion," and insofar as the individual misfortune was related to the whole of man's life upon earth, that is, to wholeness, and detached from its painful focus upon the individual, such teaching did improve the occasion. Another method, often used, was less happy. This took the natural guilt which anyone feels when he has failed, and by interpreting the failure as punishment for sin, intensified the guilt and left the individual in a worse state than before. But at least the church did grapple with individual problems, attempting to aid, comfort, and warn those involved in them. It exhibited thereby a true though limited prophetic spirit.

As for the failure and defeat of the group, the white church said nothing; the black church, as we shall see later, did somewhat better.

In the defeat of the group, specifically in the loss of the Civil War, the white church had a typical Old Testament issue presented to it. Since the antebellum religion of the South had been predominantly the religion of the Old Testament, it may seem ironic that the church could not face this issue as the prophets had done. The irony disappears, however, when we realize that the Old Testament religion of the South was rooted in the patriarchal teachings of the earlier Old Testament. The prophets were hammering out the idea which Jesus, in his words and in his life, finally expressed: all men are God's children and therefore brothers. Some Southern churchmen paid at least lip service to this belief, but even these held that all Negroes were younger brothers to all whites, and it must be admitted that they treated these younger brothers pretty roughly. The dominant religious ideal in the South, however, was the tribal, patriarchal ideal in which there were grades of individuals held together under the strong will of a chieftain. The prophetic ideal of a "nation under God"—which today we acclaim but do not believe—wasn't believed by the Confederacy or by the defeated Southern churchmen who survived it.

Indeed, it was the preachers most of all who refused to see the defeated South as lying under the judgment of God. They found it hard to believe that God had so let them down. For it had been they most of all who, in the heated days before the war and in the furnace of the war itself, insisted that God was with them and would bless their fight. This doctrine, of course, was somewhat forced, considering how long these same men had taught the "spirituality" of the church and its lack of concern for the affairs of this world; it was not strange, however, since in a pinch men call in all the help they can, including God. But, having called him so loudly and with such assurance, they were particularly hurt that he had not brought them victory, and were probably more inclined than the average layman to view the Southern defeat through embittered eyes, unenlightened by understanding.

The general view which developed out of defeat and Reconstruction and which finally took on a mythical character was that, though chattel slavery was well done with, the Negro was either a child or a savage and must be both protected and restrained, that the war had had nothing to do with him but had been fought to defend the sacred doctrine of states rights, and that this cause had been defended by unsullied heroes, in rhetorical moments called the Chivalry. For this cause they had sacrificed their fortunes and their lives and were, like the ill-starred Confederacy, immortalized in defeat.

By adopting this view the church increased the sacredness of a memory already sacred and thereby made it more difficult for the South to reinterpret its tragic experience. If it had only been sufficiently Stoic, it might at least have seen the transitory nature of human institutions and so persuaded the South to let go what was gone and build as it could anew. But Stoicism is an individualistic religion, and though it can let institutions go, it isn't very good at building them. If the church could have developed from the heroic into the pre-Christian tragic attitude, it might have seen the whole matter not in the simple light of a heroic people striving purely against a foreign evil, but in the complex tragic light of good men on both sides through common human weakness plunged into a conflict in which brother destroyed brother. If it had been able really to adopt the Christian attitude or, to be more exact, the attitude of the Old Testament prophets, it might have adopted the view that even the deist Jefferson and the brooding skeptic Lincoln adopted—that men pay for their injustices. Lincoln was clearly aware that the North was implicated in the injustice, but even if it had not been, this wouldn't have fazed the prophets. They felt sure that the Israelites had been chosen by God as his peculiar people; yet God used the heathen Chaldeans and Babylonians to punish them for the sins they had committed.

The trouble here was that the South had never felt itself a covenanted, chosen people to the degree that the more strongly based Puritan North had. Many of the early Puritan groups had made covenants with God, according to which, in return for their obedience, they understood that God would bless them in the building of the kingdom of heaven in the New World. The South had been settled far more individualistically. Doubtless among the motives that settled the Southern frontier was the desire to spread the Christian gospel, but this was rarely a total community desire. Under pressure from the North during the late antebellum period, the South did develop a distinct sense of regional excellence—the Chivalry against the New England shopkeepers

—but this, though it became a form of religion, never had a clear-cut Judeo-Christian base, as in the covenants of early New Englanders. So when the Confederacy collapsed and the South was occupied by the enemy, there were no real grounds upon which to rest a prophetic explanation of their fate. If they could have been convicted of breaking their covenant with God, they might have repented and been blessed by his forgiveness. The comfort of God would have rested upon them even as it did upon the expatriated Israelites who sat weeping by the waters of Babylon.

On the contrary, what the South at its worst did with defeat was, as Robert Penn Warren describes it, to come up with the Great Alibi. This attributed the Southern defeat to fate and so laid upon the fathers all the inadequacies of the post-Civil War world: our fathers lost the war; what can we do now? This was the other side of the myth of Southern heroism: when we turned our eyes to the past, we saw a splendid heroic world and the war itself as a sunset blaze of glory; when we turned to the terribly inadequate present, we saw it as the result of a fated defeat.

If the lack of any clear covenant undermined the South in its defeat, the existence of such a covenant undermined the North in its victory. The most disastrous effect of victory upon the North, says Warren, was the creation in the Northern mind of the Great Treasury of Virtue. Living as it was in the mid-nineteenth century under the assumed blessing of God, attenuated by time but still half dormant, the North enriched beyond words this blessing by saving the nation and freeing the slaves. Either one of these accomplishments would have brought glory; the two together sealed the mind of the North against self-criticism for exactly a century. Complacency began to break down when racial troubles moved to the North in the 1960's.

It is clearly dangerous in victory to believe that you belong to God's elect. It might have been less dangerous in defeat. After all, the socially successful Pharisee belonged to God's people, the socially unsuccessful publican did not, yet Jesus said that the publican was closer to the kingdom.

As we have said, the South had not woven the idea of a universal God strongly enough into its self-picture to be upheld by him in defeat. Its regional god was a latecomer created under the pressures of adverse world opinion and finally of war. Yet even during the war, the god the revivalists preached and the soldiers sought was a moralistic god who was primarily concerned that men should refrain from swearing, drinking, whoring, and maybe card playing. It is ironic that at the height of this conflict in which brother was killing brother in a poor cause, the General Assembly of the Presbyterian Church in the United States—the Southern Presbyterian Church—passed a resolution condemning the swearing so common among soldiers. This was probably the wisest thing the soldiers did, though perhaps not the most effective. If they had been less human, more restrained, and more focused upon the sole purpose of winning the war, they might have been better soldiers. The greatest among them was Stonewall Jackson, a somber, straitlaced Puritan who, when asked how he proposed to handle the numerous blue coats massed against him, answered shortly, "Kill them, Sir! Kill them all!"

After all, since the white churches of the South had rarely spoken prophetically to the South before its defeat, they could hardly be expected to do so after that defeat. The Negro churches pursued a somewhat different course. We recall that the Negro church did not really exist in the South till after the Civil War. Before this Negroes had usually been members of white churches, occasionally in separate congregations, usually in the same congregation but segregated in the back of the church or in the gallery. As such segregated members, they had a certain kind of religious fellowship but no power. It was the desire to control their own religious life that caused them to organize their own churches in the years following the Civil War.

The enslaved Negro was born into failure; he did not suffer the catastrophic fall of the Southern white. Nevertheless, he too longed for freedom, as is attested, for instance, by the Underground Railroad and the spirituals. Primarily during slavery but also after emancipation, he found in the Old Testament his chief religious inspiration, especially in the great story of the flight of the Israelites from Egypt. He saw clearly in those enslaved people his own condition and in their escape from bondage his own hope. He found there not merely the ideal of justice as stated by the great prophets, but also the fact of a great injustice righted.

Furthermore, unlike the white, the black had not been defeated through any fault or weakness of his own; he had been born in bondage. Therefore the cause of his unhappy condition lay in fate or in God, and he did not have to blame himself or others for it; his quarrel was with God, and its theme was that God would free him from bondage as he had freed the Israelites in Egypt.

According to Joseph R. Washington, Jr., the origin of this religion is the passion for equality and justice.[1] Later on, however, and continuing into the present, the Negro church degenerated into a social club where members found togetherness, comfort, security, and some exercise of power. Washington recognizes that the Black movement began in the church, but doubts that its roots are really Christian. Nonviolence, he says, was adopted largely as a practical matter, not as a matter of basic belief. From the strict Christian point of view the Negro church lacks faith. But Washington tends to equate faith with theological belief and to discount the faith implicit in a struggle for justice.

The question we are considering in this chapter is: To what degree has the church in the South, white or black, interpreted the group or regional defeat in the light of Christian faith? The answer seems to be that the white church has done practically nothing here, the black church a great deal. Both offered strong support to individuals in defeat, but to its group as a whole the white church, controlled by an individualistic theology and representing a group less deeply and simply defeated and therefore less cohesive, offered little aid; the black church, holding less strongly to such a theology and in fact more socially adhesive, offered great aid.

To put it in other words, the Negro has been able to generalize his troubles far better than the white, to see them as a part of human life, not merely as an individual or group misfortune. In this way individual unhappiness becomes part of the tragedy of life, to be borne either stoically or, if one is a Christian, with joy. Through temperament possibly, certainly through training, the whites, generally of North European origin, were more stoical than the blacks, the blacks more expressive of both joy and sorrow, more ready to admit life's pangs and its ecstasies, more humble, therefore more acceptive of life, perhaps for all this more Christian. The Southern white, unfortunately, often made of his regional defeat a Great Alibi, thus to a degree generalizing his individual defeat, but only to a degree. He still saw himself as defeated by men, run over by massed enemies—he had boasted of being able to take care of ten, but they didn't stop at ten; they kept coming! He did not see himself as defeated by God. He did not generalize his defeat universally, did not see it in God. At this point his church was of no use to him.

XIX

The Personal God

Out of disorder men have sought order in the churches; out of a repressed emotional life they have sought some freedom of emotional release; because of inevitable failure they have sought some reconciliation. But now we come to their need for The Man, and we have to say that out of a world—at least a white world—which overemphasized the individual, they have sought in their churches not a structured society to balance that individual, but the very divinization of the individual himself. In this matter the culture clearly referred to the church or the church adopted from the culture the strength of the notable individual and the weakness of the social order.

With religion focusing so strongly upon the individual, called a person but lacking the social world necessary to personhood, we naturally end up with a so-called personal God. I say "so-called" because, though Christian theology provides for the personhood of God both by the idea of the Trinity and by that of Jesus the God-Man, the modern church, infected by individualism, has largely forgotten this. In the South, God (or Jesus) is The Man divinized. If you can get to him, all your problems are solved.

How desperately men sought him depended mainly upon how desperate their situation was in the secular world. The situation of the blacks, whether enslaved or segregated, was the most desperate of all, that of the poor whites less so, that of the middle- and upper-class whites, especially of the leaders among them, least desperate of all—if it can even be called desperate. A modifying word should be said about the blacks. Actually the most desperately situated, they did not necessarily feel the most desperate. First, rarely having been infected with the virus of success, they felt far less keenly the pain of failure. Second, not being responsible for the social order and suffering more from its injustice, they could more easily imagine its radical change. Consequently, God was to them not only the Great Consolator, but also the Great Liberator who would lead his people out of bondage as he had led the Israelites out of Egypt.

Whether the whites found in the God they sought a great dictator or a great paternalist depended mainly upon the degree to which their society still remained frontier, or to put it another way, the degree to which it had become settled and quiet. Upon the frontier, nature, as yet unbound, was more unpredictable and its violence more disastrous. There God was the Great Dictator, arbitrary and stern. Men needed most of all to avoid his wrath. In settled communities, where human relations were relatively more important and the power of The Man more firmly established, God tended to become, like his earthly representative, the Great Paternalist. In both cases he had sovereign power, but he exercised it more gently in the latter situation than in the former.

To some degree men got around this dual vision of God by holding that God himself, or Jehovah, was the Great Dictator, while Jesus was the Great Consolator, gentle and compassionate. This may have made verbal sense, but most men did not really believe in such an underlying unity. They did not see the awful power of God, apparent in his judgment, as related to the gentleness of Jesus, apparent in his forgiving grace. They said that these divinities were respectively Father and Son, but actually they saw little family resemblance between them. This is another way of saying that they saw little resemblance between the natural forces of the environing world and the frail human efforts that went on therein. They did not really believe in any inclusive kingdom of God.

So the South divinized uncritically its own social life. That it divinized it is no criticism; all cultures have to rest their world view upon what they are, for there is nothing else to sustain it. But Christianity as a world religion may serve as a check upon a particular culture. We are asking here what check it had through the churches upon the culture of the South.

For the most part—though not entirely—the church

strengthened the basic individualism and divisiveness of Southern life. Its view of life saw men as atoms scattered at random through the world, each related primarily and directly to the Great Atom, God.

The secular cohesiveness of Southern life is suggested by the fairly consistent attempt to build and maintain good will in a social structure not economically organized for good will: a status structure resting upon slavery in a world increasingly equalitarian. The words kindliness, courtesy, and consideration suggest what I mean. I know it has been charged that these words merely describe clever sentimental devices which hide from everybody's eyes the harshness of the system itself. I am willing to grant that this is a part of their intention. I am willing to grant also that the South began to value such attitudes partly because of the presence of whites and blacks together, especially in such dissimilar situations. But to the degree that Southerners became skilled in such manners, they came to value them not only for the added ease they brought, but also for themselves, as a skill which, when learned, one delights to practice.

The church merely accepted these usages with little attempt to evaluate them. It accepted courtesy, for instance, without ever judging it by the ideal of Christian courtesy. It accepted the "love" which Southern whites claimed to feel for Negroes without judging it by Christian love. As a consequence, Southern white church-people generally have assumed that the "love" they felt for Negroes is the same as Christian love and the "personal" relations they maintained were Christian relations. The church did not tell them because the church did not know. It had no ideal of a heavenly kingdom by which to judge an earthly society. The best it could do was to confront the atom, man, with the Great Atom, God. By so doing it made the Southerner even more individualistic than his culture inclined him to be.

I am not denying that this intense focus upon a personal and sovereign God—Jehovah or Jesus or both—has brought strength and courage and hope to great multitudes buffeted by the injustices and the cruelties of life. But we have bought this personalization of God at a great price. "When God became *a* person," says Tillich, "man's personality was driven into neurotic disintegration."[1] We have separated ourselves from God as we are separated from other persons. We have separated him from the world as we are separated from the world, both the world of nature and the world of men. We cease to share in it. We have both over-personalized life by separating personhood from its environment and under-personalized it by leaving the environment devoid of final meaning.

In brief, we no longer see the Lady in the Dawn or the Dawn in the Lady. Of course if we did, we would be in danger of becoming pagans again, or pantheists, but it might be a risk worth taking.

XX

Limited Commitment

As we noticed in discussing the culture of the South, one of the striking characteristics of Southerners is their ability, indeed, their propensity to commit themselves. This is seen even today in the futile defense of a segregated life, in willingness occasionally to take on the whole Federal Government again, and, a few years ago, in the beautiful nonviolent movement in which thousands of Negro Southerners were ready to "lay their bodies at the jailhouse door." It appeared historically as the Confederacy, in the defense of which men fought against increasing odds for two long years after Lee—as he later admitted—knew that the fight was lost. But he had to let them learn for themselves.

It is this desire for completeness, this desire to be more than a separate individual, to be rather a part of a larger whole, a community, a region, a world, which gives to the Southerner his power of commitment. Indeed, the experiential knowledge which he typically values is itself a commitment. Knowing the world in the way he likes to know it, experientially, as an extension of himself and himself as a part of the world, he is naturally committed to that which he knows, for it is a part of himself. Not to back up his knowledge would make him false to himself. Truth is not just what he knows conceptually; truth is what ought to be done.

Commitment is related to wholeness. To the degree that a man is himself, he is able to commit himself. The fact that commitment is a characteristic of Southerners indicates the social strength of the Southerner's life: he is part of a larger whole, of some community. In the feuds of the southern Appalachians, this community may include little more than the family, but within its limits it is almost absolute. Across the South generally, however notably among the whites, commitment has been to the family first, but beyond this to race and state and region. One reason for the Southerner's commitment is the same as that for the mountaineer's: his being excluded, cut off from the larger world, and even attacked by that world.

As we also noted, there is about this commitment a strange sense of humor. This serves to soften and set bounds to it, as we saw most beautifully in the case of Jackson's soldier who "hoped to God he'd never love another country." This same characteristic appears in what Cash calls the realism of the Southerner. When a thing has happened, it has happened. This is partly the wisdom of the farmer. No matter what he said yesterday, it's pouring down rain today and there's no plowing. Commitment to a cause yields to the force of events.

But not always. The Southerner can pursue a course to the bitter end of self-destruction. And one wonders whether at such times he isn't moved by a deep desire to fail, both because this is the meaning of the great image bequeathed him—the Gettysburg image—and also because he doubts the legitimacy of the American goals usually dangled before him.

Regardless of how we describe this paradox of commitment and detachment, or commitment and humor, the question that concerns us here is: What has the church done with it? Has it indicated its significance, its meaning? Has it merely assumed it as an inevitable part of life and by such assumption blessed it as it is, or has it attempted to use it without really understanding it?

However limited its scope, commitment is ultimately a religious matter. It speaks finally of the holy, of an ultimate concern, of something that commands complete loyalty. But the Southern church has not really understood this. To the loyalties to family, race, and region, the church has merely added another loyalty—to Christ or the church, which are usually considered interchangeable. The church says, of course, that these "religious" loyalties should supersede all others. Maybe they do among some members of the fringe sects. For here are people who have so little of the world to commit themselves to that commitment to a similar disadvantaged group—their congregation—and to Jesus, the friend of the poor, undoubtedly offers a real value. The Negroes are disadvantaged in somewhat the same way, though less greatly, for they have seldom disadvantaged themselves by puritanical scorn of the goods of earth which lie presently beyond their grasp. They can thus be loyal to the warm togetherness of their congregational meetings which, unlike the meetings of the poorer whites, extend and bless the warmth of their daily lives. So the friendliness of the church is an extension of the friendliness of the world.

But for the great majority of white church members the loyalties aroused by and within the church are, I'm afraid, a shadow of the more compelling loyalties of the world. If commitment to Christ meant commitment to the ever present and everlasting spirit of love, this would be no shadow. Unfortunately, it is far more apt to consist of a set of moralisms, a list of things not to do. On the contrary, the secular commitment shared by these worshipers consists in following a chosen leader, sticking to a course of action to the end, supporting a many-faceted way of life. I do not defend such inclusive loyalty; I merely say that the human being involved in this secular situation seems to me rich and vital, though often contradictory, while the participant in the nominally religious situation seems somewhat shadowy and unreal.

If this is so, it is a curious situation. For the church is supposed to distill the essence of life, to reveal its completion out of its many incompletions, and thus to serve as both the judge and the inspirer of the world. Here, however, the church is holding up a shadow against secular man.

If the secular Southerner is more solid than the churchly Southerner, it is because he is not isolated from other men or from the community; he is part of a larger whole, immersed in it. The Protestant Church has been trying to pull him, at least for Sunday, out of this larger whole and wash him down to a moral code. In brief, it has tried to skeletonize him. It has done this both because its individualistic bias has made it over-personal and because it could not face the dichotomy of racial life in the South. That life, though rich in certain community relationships, was also split down the middle. Instead of facing the enormously difficult task of healing this split—in part by revealing the rich and complex nature of Southerners white and black immersed in one world—it tried to save people by denying their tragic complexity and reducing them to a set of moral rules. True to its "spiritual" nature, it tried to save them *from* the world, not *for* it.

Yet under this cold moralism there was and is considerable fire, especially in the religion of the less cultured. They repent of their sins and throw themselves upon the grace of God. Stressing this point, Miss O'Connor says, "When [the Catholic novelist] penetrates to the human aspiration beneath [the individualistic religious forms], he sees not only what has been lost to the life he observes, but more, the terrible loss to us in the Church of human faith and passion."[1] But the sins so passionately repented of are very limited and personal, seldom clearly related to the social order in which the worshipers are daily immersed. That we are always involved in sin because of our tragic, divided nature, and in the South additionally because of the divided society we live in, is hardly realized. When a man is converted under such a regimen, he may become in a limited way morally better, though he may indeed become worse by the limitation of his ideal of goodness and by pride in having reached this limited goal. But even if he remains humble in his newfound moral goodness, he may be less human than he was when immersed in or perhaps even drowning in the rich, tragic welter of life.

So the church in the South has generally tried to induce men to commit themselves to a shadow, thus becoming shadowy themselves, instead of revealing to them the meaning of the rich though often contradictory commitments they already had, and by such revelation purifying and enlarging these commitments. The commitments of the church were thus separated from the commitments of the world, the separation of religion and life permitted to remain. It was worse, however, than this. Not only did the church fail to universalize these particular commitments; since it did not condemn them, it ended by blessing them. That is, it blessed the unhappy, divided life of the South, where belief in a racial code existed alongside individual kindness, where men in themselves disorderly were committed to public order for others. It could at least have said: You are not men who commit yourselves so thoughtlessly; you are still human fragments. It could have gone on to say that every commitment is a cracking of the individual's shell and a step on the way to complete commitment to all life, human and natural, including one's own. The light of this vision would have strengthened the Southerner in his longing to commit himself, to participate, to be a part of, while at the same time it would have revealed to him how incomplete his commitments as yet were.

The church might also have understood that half humorous, half realistic sense of limits which, as we have seen, has touched Southern commitment. Existing in a world terribly ambivalent and even contradictory, the Southern church has responded by being too sure of itself and self-righteous in its assurance. This may have helped certain people for a time, but in the long run it has been self-defeating. Doubtless its members, coming together out of a world confused by clashing currents of violence and tenderness, longed for absolutes and certainties expressed in an inerrant Scripture and an inflexible moral code. But with such a world around them, their longing to believe in absolutes was often stronger than their belief. To a degree this is always true. "Lord, I believe; help thou mine unbelief." In the South, however, more than usual, men repeated the assuring words without testing them by the actual world. Without knowing it, they were doing in church what they did in secular politics: listening to and participating in a flow of rhetoric which was only half believed.

Sensing this, they repeated the words more fervently, upheld the standards more fiercely, thus feeding their churchly pride. If only they had carried into the church a little more of that humor, that realism, indeed, that humility which softened their worldly commitments, if only they had not tried to make the church so unlike the world, they might have done better. But the world being so uncertain, they insisted upon certainty in the church. So they became sure, brittlely sure of themselves. Even the dictatorial Cromwell, writing to the General Assembly of the Church of Scotland, pled with that body, "Gentlemen, I beg you in the bowels of Christ to remember you may be mistaken."

In his best moments the Southerner knew this. He had learned it from history and from his own impulsive heart. Committing himself with too little thought, he had learned what failure meant. But the church did not understand these best moments and apply their lesson to itself. That lesson is simple: men must commit themselves. The final goal of commitment is God, but in the process of seeking him we are continually making commitments to false gods or half-gods. Even in the church, perhaps most dangerously in the church, this is what we do. No matter who our god is, it is well not to be too sure of him.

XXI

The Need for Complete Commitment

We've been considering for several chapters various human needs and what the Southern church has done to satisfy them. Some of these needs have been more clearly recognized than others, such as the need for forgiveness, or reconciliation, and the need for order in a disorderly world. Most of these needs come together in the need for complete community, which we shall now consider.

It is not of primary importance whether men naturally recognize this need or not. Perhaps the highest function of the great religions is this: to make men conscious of their deepest needs, and then to satisfy or at least assuage the needs so revealed.

Man is a social animal and always needs a community. The great religions, especially Christianity, teach that he needs a universal community. "Thou hast made us for thyself," said Augustine. Looking before and after, staring into the illimitable reaches of space, man can find complete security only through believing in such a universal community.

The essential strength—and weakness—of the South lies right here. The essential strength and weakness of any individual or group lie side by side. If you wish to find a man's essential weakness, look for his essential strength. The weakness is the corruption of the strength. The essential weakness of the South is not simply that it permitted slavery—and racial discrimination —it is that it permitted slavery under the dream and to a degree within the actualization of a human community. Slavery is the clear indicator of how far we missed our aims.

Some say that aims do not matter; only accomplishments matter. I do not agree. I know what hell is said to be paved with, but I also believe that one does not go to heaven unless he so intends. "Out of the heart proceed the issues of life." And—to come back to the South—this region has had more than good intentions; in spite of the race division, it did actualize its intentions in the creation of perhaps the richest communities this nation has seen.

The main question we are concerned with here is this: To what degree has the Southern church realized and made clear this great attempt and this great failure? But let us ask first a preliminary question: How does one come to realize his need for community, his need, that is, to become a complete human being?

One's realization of his need for community is directly related to such community as he has. If you can imagine a child without any community, you imagine a being who is continually driven in upon himself and is solely concerned to defend that self against everything else. But insofar as there exists for the child a community composed first of his mother, then of other relatives and close acquaintances, to that degree the child needs to extend his community into the world, whether he consciously wishes this or not. For only the world, or more accurately, the universe, is wide enough for security.

The growing child, like all of us, seeks what he has found. I remember a recurring scene from my boyhood. I see myself somewhere between the age of six and ten, at twilight, on the steps of my grandmother's summer house—the house where the family went in summer to escape the miasmas of the swamps. Seated behind me, just outside the rectangle of yellow light falling through the hall door, are my grandmother, my uncle, and several aunts. I can hear them talking in low tones about country matters—neighbors, crops, sicknesses, visitors—but my mind isn't on the words, and is only half on the tone. My mind is upon the deepening twilight. I note the fireflies flickering in the clearing and those steadfast lights, the stars, hanging in the branches of the pines; I hear the croaking of frogs and chirring of night insects, and I see in that strange world enveloping the lamplit house in the woods a slightly fearful but far more challenging image of the future. For I would go out into that world, carrying not the words but the tones of the group behind me, a family in depth, two generations, a center of love; and whether I knew it or not, I would be seeking in the world what I had already found, other communities like this, perhaps for the end a universal community like this. How far I would go would depend upon the depth of the suggestions I had received and upon my own ability to nurture these suggestions.

"Only by the handle of a community can we pick up the world." Whether we do pick up the world or only some fragment , of it depends upon our original community. For any community, in its movement toward world inclusion, can stop arbitrarily at any point: at the limits of the family, the neighborhood, the clan, the state, the nation, and even the church, though it may call itself universal, or as we usually say, catholic. It stops short of its destined end because it does not envisage that end and has no established institutions by which to attain it.

The South, carrying originally a stronger sense of the communal Middle Ages than the North, sensed more clearly than the North the need of communities, though less clearly their economic value. As we have seen, the plantation, perhaps the most influential institution of the South, was by intention strongly individualistic, in actuality unexpectedly social. Each plantation was a social unit within itself, a unit which by its prestige and power shaped the culture of the South. To what degree was the plantation a community that could serve as a model for larger human communities, finally of a world community?

The reply is very simple: not at all. (Beyond this, the plantation has now ceased to be viable even as an economic community.) As a human community it involved the vast disparity of masters and slaves in a world increasingly democratic. It did give to every member some place in the community, but the place for the slaves was fixed and pitifully low, the place of the poor whites, those hangers-on of the plantation, little better. Yet the fact remains that most Southerners have a strange sense of belonging to some community which they call the South. We have already examined certain aspects of the culture beyond the plantation itself that support this sense of belonging.

We have said that the plantation, supported by slavery and enriched by a complex family life, was the key institution of the South. As such it was a main producer of that sentiment within which the region has swathed its accustomed institutions and ways. I would suggest here that the church has been another center of sentiment, as important as, if not more important than, the plantation. Along the seaboard of the colonial South the church, then Episcopal, was clearly subservient to the plantation. It was the state church, and the plantation owners were effectively the state; the church was their local club. Some large plantations even established chapels for ease of local use. After the Revolution, with the disestablishment of the Episcopal Church and the spread of other denominations, especially along the westward-moving frontier, the church passed from such close dependence upon the plantation. It continued to express, however, perhaps even more strongly than before, the sentiment of the community. Further, with the strengthening of democratic forces—Jacksonian democracy—the effective membership of the church widened toward the whole community and away from the earlier handful of planters. As the center of, or if there were several churches, as centers in a community, the church, as a community institution, gathered about itself a rich veil of sentiment.

We have already seen how the Southerner is prone to bind himself to accustomed objects, places, and people by sentiments which, though vague, are complex and deep. The church was ideally suited to be such an institution. It was composed of a particular group, meeting on a given day—or days—in a particular building, and there performing together accustomed actions. Furthermore, in the graveyard which usually adjoined the church lay many of the kinsmen who had done these same things here in the past. So the living were bound both to one another and to the dead.

Expressing such a sentiment, my sister once remarked, "I don't belong to the Presbyterian Church; I belong to Brick Church." She spoke like a congregationalist, not a Presbyterian, but all Southerners, due to their love of the local, in religion tend to be congregationalists. A preacher from Nashville once told me that he knew many city people, recently moved from the country, who maintained their membership in and regularly attended their old churches. They found there the reassurance of old faces, forms, and places to set against the uncertain novelty of city life.

Here we have the Southerner, then, a man of sentiment—and this applies to whites and blacks together—whose daily life is rooted in sentiment, and who finds in religious services another sentimental tie, in many cases perhaps stronger than those that bind him to his home, for here many others are gathered with him to add their attachments to his, and in the nearby churchyard dead kinsmen bless these common attachments.

What should be the function of the church in this matter? It should universalize the sentiments. There is nothing wrong with this love of particular places, people, things—unless it is permitted to stop with particular places, people, and things. There is no hope of loving the world except as we love particular parts of the world. The problem is to love the world in the particulars, the particulars in the world—finally, everything in God. I know a man who fell in love with the earth because he had buried his beloved there. This is what should always happen. We lose—and find—the particular in the universal.

The church in the South has not so universalized the sentiments, which is to say that it has not universalized a considerable portion of Southern life, has not even tried to do it, and has indeed tried to do the opposite. For sentiments exist in community, by community, for community. They bind isolated parts together, man to man, man to nature. Their existence indicates community, however limited. But the Protestant Church is only in the most limited way a community. We speak of the communion of the saints, but in our understanding the saints are all dead, usually long dead, and we commune with them by withdrawing our minds from our neighbor in the next pew and projecting them, as the countryman said, "Way over in Jehovy." After this attempted flight, whose aim is to meet God and the blessed saints, we leave the church and become neighbors again, and neither the words nor the forms of worship have made us aware that these very neighbors and ourselves are the sainted sinners we have but a moment ago tried to reach heaven to meet.

The very structure of the Protestant service is intended to cut man's earthly and community attachments and—I suppose it is hoped—establish heavenly ones. But the heavenly ones have to be made out of the earthly ones, and the earthly ones we are talking about now are the ties of sentiment. The Southern church-goer brings them with him to church and swathes the place with them, and the church never tells him what this means.

It means, positively, that these attachments are the doors through which he might pass into spiritual freedom. What ties me to a given place is the same thing which, seen imaginatively—or in the spirit—ties me to the world, even the universe, and frees me in it. In the culture of the South the church has all this rich resource of sentiment, and it has done nothing with it. Worse than that, by being a part of it, it has blessed it just as it is, given it religious overtones, and so permitted men to think that when they loved their homes and their communities they necessarily loved mankind, when they loved "Brick Church" they loved the church universal. So the church, instead of opening for us the earthly doors to heaven, has left us locked behind them.

At best this is a happy bondage, for these ties of sentiment are ties of love. But since they are ties to particular things, places, people, we are bound to these particulars. Among these particulars the church has permitted itself to become just another particular, perhaps more loved than others because it gathers about itself the affections of a group, but still a particular—Brick Church in Salem community—rather than a moment of the church universal.

Permitting itself to become another particular, the church, because of its role as a community center and because of its imagined relation with another world, has blessed our love for particular things in themselves and thus deepened our bondage to them. If it had revealed the universal significance of these particular attachments, it would have translated sentimental bondage into spiritual freedom and thus revealed to its members the grace of God.

Yet it is something to be haunted by God, and the church has maintained this haunting. Our love of the church is not mere sentiment. Even while blessing the attachments of earth by itself becoming another such attachment, the church has also touched these attachments with mystery and with a hint of the universal and the timeless. This has resulted in part from the customary location of the graveyard nearby. Here lie those friends and neighbors who, usually under the protection of the church, have departed this life and have become in our minds frontiersmen on the margin of life itself. They live in our memories and more vaguely in our hopes. They bind us to the past and, again more vaguely, to the future. They are the best reminders of that sense of piety which is so strong in the Southerner.

Before discussing the sentiment of piety, let us consider a little further the sense of mystery that clings to religion in the South. Durkheim points out that this sense is not equally present in all religions, nor is it equally present in Christianity at all times. "For example, for the Christians of the seventeenth century, dogma had nothing disturbing for the reason; faith reconciled itself easily with science and philosophy, and the thinkers, such as Pascal, who really felt that there is something profoundly obscure in things, were so little in harmony with their age that they remained misunderstood by their contemporaries."[1] But the nineteenth century was the century of Romanticism and, in America, of the frontier, of newly-spawned and half-formed settlements and, especially in the South, of lonely frontier farms and plantations, of individual settlers and families almost lost in the vast forest. The whole world breathed mystery, a mystery both alluring and dangerous. That the nineteenth-century Southerner, romantic in other ways, should have found in religion most of all the essence of mystery is not surprising. Ironically, it was his romantic, individualistic sense which kept the Southerner from really finding God but which prevented him from ever forgetting God. He was haunted by God.

We return now to the sentiments, particularly the sentiment of piety. Piety may be defined as respect for the sources of one's being. Pious men remember with gratitude their parents, their families, their communities, the institutions that have supported their lives. Piety widens the individual's attention from himself and the present moment to other men and the past. It sets the individual in a community in time. Its strength in the South indicates the strong sense of community here. It is a form of sentiment which knits the present and the past together.

Though the word piety carries strong religious overtones there is a natural piety which, though essentially religious, is no commonly recognized as such. The poet Wordsworth emphasized this natural piety. It is a sentiment common to countrymen, especially to farmers, who sense the days flowing into the days, the seasons into the seasons, today the child of yesterday and the parent of tomorrow. The South, having been predominantly a farming region, has generally felt this sentiment. Also, as we have seen, the South has been conservative, tending to hold on to the past.

This tendency was greatly strengthened among the whites by the loss of the Civil War and the resultant nostalgic memory of antebellum days. Everything that had been tended to become sacred. When my uncle remarked to my aunt, "Ideals are a sin, Alice; we should love God," he was thinking of God not in the recesses of the soul but rather in the forms and structures of the world. He may not have intended to include segregation, but I'm sure he would have hesitated, if questioned, to exclude it. When another neighbor of mine said to a group of fellow churchmen, "If you take away the customs of my fathers, I have nothing left to live for," he was talking about segregation itself.

The question that arises here is: How could the white Southerner hold sacred the custom of segregation while at the same time attaching some sacredness to the person of the black demeaned by that custom? The quick, hostile reply is: He never felt any sacredness in the person of the black. Though there is truth in this, it is far too absolute. I am sure that my uncle and my neighbor would have honestly disagreed. Segregation was never intended to prevent all relations between white and black persons; it was intended to prevent all "social" relations. As to how "social" and "personal" are interdependent, the Southerner has never really known. The white at his best felt that the black was also a child of God, though indeed a brother younger than himself. In addition to this, his great—and necessary—stress upon order permitted him to see segregation as part of the order of the world, difficult to live with, maybe, but necessary.

By way of contrast to all this, consider Emerson's individualstic definition of sacredness: "Nothing is at last sacred but the integrity of my own mind," and again, "What I must do is all that concerns me, not what the people think." My uncle needed more of this, but Emerson could have learned something from my uncle, too.

The church has blessed uncritically this tendency to make the past sacred. Christianity has the strength of a historical religion but also its weakness. The church in the South has stressed the strength to the point of weakness. God so loved the world that he sent his Son; this, says the church, is a fact in history. But then, as most churchmen see it, God, having entered time, became a part of time, an historical figure. This is not the teaching of the Bible. Christ was crucified from the beginning of the world, says John. And he is crucified to the end of the world. God lives and dies among men. At every moment the flow of time is broken by eternity, or to put it the other way around, at every moment time blooms in eternity.

Just as the church has failed to see in the Southerner's love of the particular the doorway to heaven, so it has failed to understand the eternal burden of every moment. Instead of blessing the creativity of time, it has blessed time's creations. This has meant that the church in the South has been perhaps the strongest bulwark of conservatism. Of course the Christian church is always in danger of being this. The effect has only been more marked in the South because here we have a people made by their history strongly aware of the past, a people therefore to whom this awareness might have been made by the church a blessing instead of a handicap. On the contrary, the church by its approval has increased the burden of the handicap.

The Southerner has the strength of a man rooted in the past. He belongs to a community that has existed and that therefore may continue to exist. His culture has suggested to him this temporal step toward completeness. The church should have revealed the meaning of this step: we gather the riches of the past in order to imagine greater riches for the future, and we root these hoped-for riches in the soil of the present. Buoyed by memories of the past and hopes for the future, we may be lifted momentarily into the eternal present.

So far in this chapter we have been considering how the Southerner's need for community induced in him strong sentimental attachments to things, places, and people, and, in the mood of piety, to the past, and we have noted what the church did for these needs. But we usually think of community in a more general sense, as a certain relationship of individuals to one another, a relationship marked by definite social structures and carrying definite values—intellectual, emotional, economic, political, religious. In this more general sense, what has the church done for community in the South? What should it have done?

It should have revealed the eternal meaning of this temporal phenomenon. The church should have taught, by precept but more by example, how a universal, eternal community exists in space and time. It should have taken the cultural feeling for community which the South possessed and criticized it in the light of the Christian vision.

It never really did this. The church had neither the inclusive vision nor the polity nor, generally speaking, the liturgy with which to do it. On the contrary, it mainly gave its approval to such fragmentary class and racial communities as existed. It did approve the family—among whites, that is, hardly among Negroes —an excellent symbol of the human situation, as Jesus so clearly indicated in his images of the Father and the Son. But it did this for the most part verbally, moralistically, at times through disciplinary action, never truly and completely, for it could not: it was not itself a human family but a separate group selected on the basis of class and, most strikingly, of race.

So the church took a group of people already believing in a community, however limited, and instead of enlarging their faith, simply approved and blessed it as it was. At this point the blacks and whites were somewhat different, and their churches responded differently.

The whites, seeking community under the tutelage of their culture, were thwarted at two levels. First, on the actual level there were sharp divisions between rich and poor, and especially —and consciously—between whites and blacks. Second, they were thwarted on the formally religious level, where a universal, inclusive community was only talked about, not believed in and enacted in liturgy. Seeking to find in his inner world and in the church (supposedly expressive of that inner world) the meaning of such community as he had, the white Southerner came to a

dead end. This is the dead end, the Abyss, that apparently under-
lies Miss Welty's vision of the superficially easygoing and talkative society of the South. It is talkative and social in order to avoid
recognizing the unplumbed inner depths where community no
longer exists and every man is alone—not even alone with God,
just alone. For the God of the Christian faith is the God of our
fathers and of our brothers and can only be approached as *our*
father. The Protestant Church is but dimly aware of this. Consequently its membership, bringing from the culture the need for
community, finds no real community at the base—or the apex—
of things, and so in consternation turns back to such superficial
community as it already has and tries desperately to slake its
thirst therein.

We may note here the significance of personal relations in
the South. The Southerner is apt to boast, and indeed with some
justification, about the prevalence of these easy face-to-face
meetings between individuals. But what the perceptive new-
comer learns is that though first meetings are easy, understanding in depth is almost impossible. The Southerner wears an invisible shield to guard his inner life. It can be pierced by rude,
inquisitive men, but they pierce it at their peril, for, driven back
into those secret recesses, the Southerner will fight as for his life.

This could be merely the natural attempt of a provincial
people to protect themselves against outside interference. The
story is told of an African who had been responding freely to the
questions of a Western reporter, but who suddenly became silent. After insistent questioning he explained his silence by saying, "The Old Men told me never to tell anyone more than half
I knew; I have already told you more than that." And, by the way,
the reserve of the Southern black is notable. The reserve of the
Southern white, then, may be due merely to his life with the black
and to his provincial history. My guess is that it is more than this.
It is a part of the extreme individualism of Western man, but
more painful and frightening to the Southerner—though less
destructive—because he still retains a memory of some community, however limited and superficial. Ideally, our community-
minded outer world should be rooted within an inner community, mortised in granite, locked into the universe. Actually, i

finds no such support within, no such star-stretched inner landscape, but rather an abyss where, the church tells us, we are alone
with God. If we are thus alone, God is to us a demon, and we do
well to flee from him into the friendly vistas of the upper air.

It is this sense of inner vacancy which makes the Southerner
overly defensive of the privacy of his inner life. For that privacy
tends to be without form and void; he has to protect even himself
from it since it borders upon the Abyss. A truer vision would
make clear that his most private intuitions are indeed the most
public truths he could utter, and his reply to "May I ask you a
personal question?" would be "Surely." But, alas! if all he sees
in the depths is the Abyss, then he is also surrounded by an abyss,
however desperately he tries to hide it with a web of words.

In *The Fathers*, a story of the late antebellum South, Allen
Tate shows the Abyss in a somewhat different light. Here it
stands for the disorder of private life in contrast to the order of
civilization. George Posey was over-personal; Lacy Buchan says
of him, "Excessively refined persons have a communion with the
abyss; but is not civilization the agreement, slowly arrived at, to
let the abyss alone?" Civilization here is the complex culture of
the South coming apart under the personal revolt of men like
George Posey.[2]

I think Tate suggests that Posey's revolt, his turning toward
the Abyss, was in the South inevitable. The artificiality of civilization had become so great that the living forces within the individual were destroying it. But is this turning toward the Abyss always
inevitable, or did it happen in the South because the South did
not take sufficient cognizance of the Abyss, indeed tried to avoid
recognizing it? All the structures men build are built in part to
shut out the terrors of life—as roofs are built in part to hide the
cold eyes of the stars. Peter Berger, putting this more strongly,
suggests that "all human societies and their institutions are, at
their root, a barrier against naked terror."[3]

In spite of the fact that in critical moments we said it did, the
public life of the South, resting upon exploited black labor, neither rested upon nor culminated in God. In the quieter days of
the early Republic, we didn't even say it did; we admitted that
slavery did not belong to the order of the world; later, forced to

defend our "peculiar institution," we claimed that God had authorized it—as just the other day we were claiming that he had authorized segregation. As we said earlier, the whole hierarchical structure of the South was a pyramid without an apex. We *said,* of course, that God was the apex, but we did not really believe, as medieval man had believed, that he was the apex of the social order, only of the individual's aspirations—his aspirations as an individual, not as a social being. The God of Protestantism was the individual's god, not society's, and he could never really serve, therefore, as the culminating point of and justification for the human order of which society was the expression. He was rather the supreme individual, the distant god of the mountains or of the endless forests, arbitrary and uncertain, the Great Outlaw, the kind of spirit that would naturally be imagined by plantation owners, the "settlement outlaws" of the South. Or he was the compassionate Jesus, the friend of those whom life and the system had pushed to the edge of things. In neither case was he the apex of the structured life of the South.

If the South really could have seen God as the apex of the hierarchy, the order itself would have been touched with that freedom without which order cannot endure. Though men cannot survive without order, neither can they survive without freedom in that order. To think of God is to think of a freedom that men cannot possess. We often refer to this freedom as God's grace. If the hierarchical structure of the South had been felt, as was claimed, to be really his, it too would have been touched with, indeed changed by a freedom it never had. For a gracious God would have been part and apex of the order. He would not have found it necessary to retire within the walls of his church from a world he could not handle. The God of the South was an individualistic frontier god who cursed and blessed individuals as he pleased.

The blacks have been more fortunate. They too live in a fragmented world, but it is not they who have been its chief architects, nor is their religion as individualistic as that of the whites. Until recently they have been far more willing to compose one community with the whites than the whites have been to compose one community with them. Having been separated not chiefly by their own will, they suffer little from the poison of separation and can more easily see themselves simply as human beings suffering man's unhappy fate. So drawn together, they become a community of worshipers standing together before God. In brief, the sense of community which they, together with the whites, have received from the culture is strengthened, not weakened by their churches, and is given an eternal meaning.

Speaking generally but with more applicability to the whites, the communities of the South are too much of this world, too little of another. This gives them their sometimes feverish, sometimes unreal quality. For in any true community the individual must be able on occasion to stand quietly and firmly against the community. He can do this only as the earthly, temporal community is rooted in a more-than-earthly, enduring community in the light of which he criticizes the present community. Thoreau once described a true man as one whose foothold is mortised in granite, that is, one who stands solidly upon the solid earth. A Christian may be described as one who belongs to both an earthly and a heavenly city, whose earthly citizenship is backed by his heavenly citizenship. Paul always remembered that even though he was a Christian, he was also a Roman citizen.

In the South, white men in particular have generally been citizens of an earthly city, members of the culture of the South, but have held, each by the skin of his teeth, such claim as he hoped he had upon an omnipotent God. In spite of all his words, there was no real city, no community there. Consequently he had no assured standard by which to criticize his earthly city. When he rebelled against it, which was seldom, he was apt to do so with violent words and actions. Ordinarily he blew off steam by becoming a "character"—a fool, either plain or damned, but accepted.

In summary, the church in the South, among whites generally individualistic and Protestant, failed to recognize the grace of God in the general conditions of community life. Thus the church left the community little better than it found it; indeed, by giving its blessing to brokenness, the church sometimes made community problems worse. For its failures the church in the South has incurred God's judgment.

XXII

In Search of Grace

Perhaps man's greatest need—which he seldom recognizes —is the need for grace. I use the term here in its general religious sense. Grace is the free bestowal of God's gifts upon us. They come to us not because we deserve them or have worked for them, but because it is the nature of the Creator to bestow them. The only demand upon us is that we accept them.

But this is terribly hard to do, for each of us naturally wants to take care of himself, not to be beholden to anybody. Yet we cannot take care of ourselves; we have to be beholden to the entire environment. We have to do, therefore, what is most difficult: we cannot live without grace. Life itself is given to us, but this is hard for us to admit.

We may come at this problem in the South by considering closely the aspect of its culture whose ideal is grace, however worldly that ideal may be. Insofar as a culture stresses manners, the key words are gracefulness, graciousness, and grace. We think of gracefulness as primarily physical, of graciousness as primarily spiritual, and of grace as physical or spiritual or both.

Organic time, the sense of place, and manners go together in the South. In such a view truthful dealing is no longer merely a matter of stating and supporting certain universal moral truths, but of fitting such truths to the present situation. The ideal is a situation in which the participants create through fitting relationships the human truth. Truth exists in relationships. One may express this best by saying with Keats, "Beauty is truth, truth beauty."

I am not making the foolish claim that the manners of the South are always gracious. They are sometimes most rude or completely lacking. Though Flannery O'Connor is speaking in the following passage to the Southern writer, her comments about Southern manners are appropriate here: "Bad manners are better than no manners at all, and because we are losing our customary manners, we are probably overly conscious of them." The writer "should observe our fierce but fading manners in the light of an ultimate concern." Finally, "The South has survived in the past because its manners, however lopsided or inadequate they may have been, provided enough social discipline to hold us together and give us an identity."[1]

I am concerned here not with the social discipline of Southern manners, but with the fact that these manners strove—however ineffectually—for gracefulness, graciousness, and grace. This means that they accented the physical and the feminine. They began with the physical person, and, though in the case of some upper class females they may have sentimentalized the physical almost beyond recognition, Southerners generally remained solid men and women deployed in a solid, earthly theater.

What we are asking here is: What is the meaning in Southern culture of the desired characteristics—gracefulness, graciousness, and grace—and what is their relation, if any, to the grace of God? In other words, we are trying to sketch a theology of grace. We are doing this to determine whether the church, the prime exemplification of grace, has understood what it is supposed to exemplify.

The ideals of gracefulness and grace appear not only in the manners of the South; they are implied in the extensive interest in games and play. We have already noted this interest—in diversions, as critics of the South sometimes said. One distinction between play, at least physical play, and work is that play allows much more room for gracefulness. The worker is too often "bowed by the weight of centuries"; the movements of the player spring spontaneously from the moment. There is a fullness here, a sense of completeness, a touch of eternity. The same may be said of the dance, and to a lesser degree of the drama—two forms of play of which the South has been fond. At his best, the dancer is the dance; he is both himself and the moving pattern. "How," asks Yeats, "can we know the dancer from the dance?" The excellent player has style.

There is also playfulness and gracefulness among children and animals. To some degree this is nature's way of preparing the young for a more serious engagement with the world: they flex their muscles, become resilient, engage in mock combat. Whatever the final function, the immediate mood is playful, the action spontaneous.

I have mentioned children and young animals not to suggest any particular childlikeness or innocence among Southerners, though we have noted a strange quality of innocence in the South, but rather to remind us that grace, however spiritual or even divine it may become, is physical in its origin, or to put it more safely, physical at bottom. Santayana says somewhere, "All life is physical in its origin and spiritual in its possible fruits." One of the questions we are raising in this chapter is: Has the church in the South recognized this?

I described above the playful moment, or the game, as having about it a touch of eternity. This is another way of saying what Johan Huizinga says in *Homo Ludens* and Peter Berger in *A Rumor of Angels*: that games have their own time, different from the steady flow of the world's time; there are quarters and halves and innings, and fifteen more minutes to play doesn't mean fifteen minutes on the municipal clock. When one watches or plays a game, he detaches himself from the time of the workaday world.

So Southerners, with a strong sense of and desire for leisure, frequently detached themselves from the workaday world. Were they running away from reality or drawing nearer to it? It has been said that the modern world is based upon the discovery of the clock and of double entry bookkeeping. The South, with its simple agricultural life, didn't see much need for double entry bookkeeping; with its memory, however slight, of the more ritualistic formal and playful Middle Ages, the South didn't really see the point of breaking time into minutes and seconds. The South wasn't running away from the clock-ridden modern world; it was simply hesitant about accepting it. It still retained a memory of a less clock-ridden time.

I'm suggesting here that the clock-ridden time of the modern world isn't necessarily reality, and that in frequently turning from this to a more manageable game-time, the Southerner wasn't necessarily fleeing from reality. Even so, I am not satisfied that the great interest of the Southerner in games—in "diversions" of all kinds—is entirely a creative interest, a part of the animal's and the child's playfulness. It may also be a distraction from human problems too difficult to be faced.

Let us return for a moment to Huizinga and his philosophy of play. He maintains that man is essentially a playing animal and that all the structures of society rest heavily upon this playful, creative spirit. This is reminiscent of Whitehead's statement that at the root of all power is the aesthetic motive. Huizinga also maintains that what we usually call games may indicate by their nature and prevalence the breakdown of a culture, not its creativity. His classic illustration is Rome, where the late cry for "bread and circuses" tells how strong and how decadent the play motive was. Speaking of the decorative art of late Rome, Huizinga says, "All speaks of quiet and safety, allegories are gracious and shallow, and the whole betrays the would-be playfulness of an unquiet mind troubled by the dangers of a menacing reality but seeking refuge in the idyllic. The play-element is very prominent here, but it has no organic connection with the structure of society."[2]

The question that arises here about the South is: To what degree does the extensive play of the South indicate its creative spirit and to what degree, on the contrary, does it indicate its inability to face up to the critical problems that have always been present? Returning to the implications of Miss Welty's stories, did we play for the same reason we talked so freely and continuously—"the play of conversation" it may be called—to keep from remembering the work that had to be done, the questions that had to be asked?

The church in the South never grappled with this question. It took strong stands against some forms of play: gambling most consistently, to a lesser degree dance and the theater. For much of the nineteenth century and in most churches until now, it has supported "blue laws" and has denounced any suggestion of the "European Sabbath." It never saw the gracefulness of the dance as possibly related to God's grace, but tied it rather to the diabolical lure of the flesh. And it certainly never imagined that the Spirit of God might be at play in the world.

The playful element in Southern life is also suggested by the pervasive sense of humor. We have spoken of this and of some reasons for it. Neither whites nor blacks are inclined to take things too seriously. It would be disastrous; they would succumb under the burdens of life.

This element is apparent also, though perhaps less clearly, in the Southern propensity for role playing, for taking a part, for being in one's place on the stage of life. Keeping the Negro "in his place" is a degraded form of this attitude. To a lesser degree every man has his place and wants to do his part. Though it was Pope who wrote these lines, they found much agreement in the South:

> Honor and shame from no condition rise;
> Act well your part, there all the honor lies.

Even this propensity for role playing, which the church might have used to great advantage, was generally overlooked. Indeed, as it did with other communal aspects of Southern culture, the church tended to disintegrate this in its own individualistic atmosphere. Within these walls, it said, you play no roles; here you are just your poor, separate self, cut off from everything but God. You are your own priest; you cannot depend upon any priesthood to save you. But the function of the priesthood was not primarily to save the priest; it was to save the people. Thus, in the Protestant view, the individual worshiper, coming as a priest, comes with the burden of his people upon his heart. And who are these people? They are no particular church or group; they are anybody and everybody; they are mankind. He comes with the burden of man upon his heart.

Insofar as he does this, he is playing the part of man. Coming out of a culture where the part, the place, is emphasized, where he has responsibilities as a father, as a workman, as a leader or a follower, he could have been asked in and through worship to become now a man, to play the part of man. The great word here is Cranmer's dying cry to Ridley out of the flames: "Be a man, Master Ridley. By God's grace, we shall in England today such a fire light as shall never be put out."

It is the function of a liturgical service to aid the worshiper in becoming a man. Through words and deeds—spoken, performed with others, and observed—he enacts the human part of joy and grief, of failure and sin and repentance and trust in God. "*We* have done the things we should not have done and left undone the things we should have done."

But the Protestant Church generally has forgotten that to be a Christian is simply to be a man. Instead of asking men in the world to take on more manhood, to be more richly and completely what they are, to play better the roles they play, it asks them to forget the world and be estranged from it. I know there are supposed Christian grounds for this in the injunction of Jesus that his followers would have to hate their fathers and mothers, but I would point out first the figurative nature of Eastern speech, and second that Jesus had already done what Christianity intends: he saw his mother and his brothers all around him, and the woman taken in adultery was his sister.

His church, however, drawing men out of the world, has too often drawn them out of their manhood and made them in worship shadows of what they were in the world. The doctrine of the Incarnation is that God became—becomes?—man, taking upon himself the burden of humanity. The doctrine is also that we are Christ's brothers, God's sons, enjoined to be like our heavenly Father, and therefore to take also the burdens of mankind upon ourselves. This is what Christian compassion is. But we, especially we in the South, have been hypnotized by history. God has already saved the world, and therefore we may sit with folded hands, each in his own pew, awaiting the coming of the kingdom on some other, more startling Sunday.

We have now reached the point of declaring that it is proper to play before God. Indeed, it is improper not to; it is improper to be dead serious about your individual self. But Protestant worship generally is a pretty serious affair. You have to satisfy some intellectual and legal requirements among the Presbyterians, some moral ones among the Baptists and Methodists, and some emotional ones—a certain type of conversion—among the Pentecostal sects. Of course it is difficult to know to what degree all this is playacting. A Mississippi Baptist tells me that in his home church they were told they had to do certain things and avoid certain others, but they were also cautioned that all this might make no difference; you simply couldn't buy salvation. Do all the required works, but never trust them; depend at last upon grace (the playful spirit of the Lord?).

Such make-believe is a form of salvation insurance. Since you aren't absolutely sure what will guarantee salvation, you try several things, as a prudent man carries home policies against both fire and flood. But this is rather far from the essential role described above—playing the part of a man. For you don't make believe you are a man, you are one; the whole problem is to recognize this.

It is interesting that in the more critical moments of life we tend to become formal, to look beyond our separate selves and ask: What is my role in this occasion? Someone has remarked that when friends part they would like to speak poetry. The situation is too highly charged with meaning to be expressed in prose; the fluid words of prose need to be pressed into abiding form.

This is particularly true at those most critical partings, funerals. In such an unusual situation the bereaved, momentarily in the limelight, wants to do the proper thing, to act well his part. In some religions and churches where this demands violent weeping, whatever the personal feeling of the bereaved, violent weeping occurs. It is true, therefore, that not only do we play a part in grief; we are more concerned to play a part then than during the more placid, ordinary moments. And what we do then is not right or wrong; it is proper or improper. The judgment is aesthetic, not moral.

Here, then, is Cranmer playing the man at his own fiery death; here also is every bereaved person trying to play his part at the funeral of a loved one.

We have carried the discussion of play this far because gracefulness and grace are striking characteristics of play at the lowest level, among animals and children, and we are wondering whether they do not mark play at its highest levels. We have at least seen that at crucial moments men try to play their parts, to do the fitting thing, at best to do the beautiful, the gracious, or graceful thing. In other words, when the meaning of life seems almost beyond bearing, when men approach the presence of God even though they may not realize it, they try to act their parts well, to play out the game.

If as Huizinga believes, man is essentially a playful animal, and as the Christian believes, man is led by God's guidance toward the kingdom of heaven in this or another world, then God's kingdom might be defined as the place where everybody always plays. This is really what the image of the ever-sounding harps means.

From the graceful animal to the kingdom of a gracious God who watches his children at play, the path seems unbroken. Yet I must admit at this point that I find it a little difficult to relate the figure of a playful God to that of a suffering Redeemer who yielded for a time his completeness in order to give mankind the hope of completeness. But perhaps my difficulty results from an overemphasis in the Protestant world upon God as Redeemer, and an under-emphasis upon God as Creator. Perhaps we in the modern world have stressed God as Redeemer because we've been so busy losing ourselves in the abstract wilderness we have made. But this doesn't explain the South, the most concrete, least abstract part of the nation, where for more than a hundred years lost men in droves have turned to God as Redeemer. Perhaps the explanation is that there was still such a dream of completeness in the South that men knew they were lost; in the rest of the country that dream had disappeared in a mirage of abstractions wherein shadowy men pursued shadowy goals, pot smokers all before LSD was discovered.

Whatever the reason, modern Protestantism, the religion of the South, has seen God primarily as Redeemer, not as Creator. This is a part of the stripping, abstractive nature of the modern mind even in the South. And yet we have, especially in the South with its emphasis on home and woman, the means to correct it. For human love, sexual love, is creative. It begins in play, and play always remains a part of it at its best. But to create a being is at least for the woman painful, and to send this loved one out into the world, subject to its slings and arrows, is painful for both parents. If the child is to be saved in the world, more will depend upon the love of those parents than upon anything else. Creative and redemptive love are the same thing; laughter and tears come from the same source; the same Spirit that created the world and man and found the creation good wept over Jerusalem. But though the path from children at play to a gracious God seems unbroken, it was broken in Protestantism at the door of the church, and man, though he sought completion, had to stop playing there. In his accent upon play, upon diversions of all kinds, perhaps the Southerner has been more human than most Americans. In perhaps the most exciting moments of his life, he escapes from clock time and lives in the time of the game—innings, quarters, halves. He has become, if only briefly, a part of the game of life (if he's really playing, not merely observing a game). The churches of the South, certainly the formal churches of the South, have made no use of this, but have stripped the rich life of the region of all but its bare bones. In these churches we have had religion without poetry, which is religion without religion. It is a countinghouse religion, a religion historically more appropriate to Yankees than to Southerners, and indeed promulgated in the South mainly by the Scotch-Irish, those Yankees of the South. In this respect the Yankees have almost ruined us.

Ideally, men go to church and engage in worship in order to find more completeness in their generally incomplete lives. Yet the Southerner, except for the members of the fringe sects, may have found more completeness outside the church than within it.

If the playfulness and gracefulness of the animal and the child find completion in the grace of God; if, perhaps, both its beginning and its end are in God, how shall we define it? Let us begin not at the bottom but in the middle reaches of this progression, with the human trait of graciousness. The word may be used to describe the ideal of Southern manners, the usual image being that of the gracious lady. Only a few could reasonably aspire to this condition, and far too often the gracious lady was only, and ironically, the Lady Bountiful, who delighted in bestowing kind words and even things upon those below her primarily in order to feel herself above them. She was condescending.

But she did not have to be. There is an ideal of graciousness beyond condescension. How shall we define it? True graciousness belongs to him who can receive without pride or guilt and give without thought of gratitude. Though we usually recognize graciousness in the manner of giving, its key lies in the manner of receiving, for we receive life before we give it, and how we receive it is what matters most. As Eugen Rosenstock-Huessy puts it, *Respondeo, ergo sum*—"I respond, therefore I am." In responding we are in danger either of accepting as our own life's gifts, taking them as ours by right and being proud of possessing them, or on the other hand, of feeling guilty because they have been given to us and not to everyone. The gracious person, the person filled with grace, sees all the world as filled with gifts and gift bearers, and sees himself, in humility and without guilt, as another moment in the gracious life of the world, a temporary storehouse of gifts entrusted to him merely that they may be dispensed to others. He expects no gratitude in giving; he is merely doing the natural thing: passing on to others what has been temporarily given to him. This seems to him the nature of life. Since he did not receive life's gifts either coweringly or proudly, he dispenses them—himself chief among them—sweetly, without condescension and without guilt.

True grace in the individual, therefore, indicates a certain view of the world and of life. It sees the world as the field of grace, life as the great bringer of gifts. Seeing the world so, it is natural for such a person to see within and behind this world a gracious God. As human graciousness increases and expands, it rests itself finally and inevitably upon the graciousness of the world and of God.

This is a far cry from "nature red in tooth and claw," and it is meant to be. It is not a claim that cruelty does not exist in nature and, more terribly, in man. The truth remains, however, that up to the present there have been more gains than setbacks, more advances than retreats, more grace for gifts happily received than judgment for gifts refused. The gracious person is no Pollyanna. He is simply one who is on the side of the angels and who believes that the angels are on his side. The mystic Father Lawrence said, "A little lifting up of the heart is sufficient," meaning that a little lifting up of the heart will reveal God in the world about us. The gracious person believes in that little lifting up of the heart. In spite of all the evil—which he does not deny —he believes in goodness.

Gracious people—and those who approve of graciousness— should believe in a gracious God. But before considering what the South has believed about the graciousness of God, let us see if we can include the graceful animal within our definition of grace, for to leave him out is to fail to root grace in life itself. The graceful animal is not gracious; he has no choice in the acceptance or refusal of life's gifts or in the manner of receiving them. What instinct gives, he accepts. Man can make a choice—at the extreme, between fortune and disaster. Can we include animal gracefulness within the grace of God?

We can, if we define grace as the creative energy of the universe. When—in the language of today—you're with it, you have it; when you're against it, you've had it!

This assumes that God is still the creative artist, creating the world and enjoying his creation, even as the writer of Genesis said he did. The enjoyment of the floating antelope is his enjoyment, as is the richer enjoyment of the person who is filled with grace. If the antelope should have but a modicum of this gift of grace, or if, impossibly, he should refuse to accept that given him, he would almost certainly fall prey to some carnivorous animal. Insofar as the person refuses to accept or cannot accept life's gracious gifts and thus sets himself against life, he incurs what the Bible calls God's judgment: he has had it.

The South was composed of people who desired community and attained it somewhat, who valued manners as a cement of community and esteemed grace as the heart of these manners, and who in their religion talked at length about the grace of God. But they didn't really understand what they were talking about. They related but poorly the grace of God to the grace of the world.

The grace they were concerned with was a highly selective and limited grace, conferred by the whim of a dictator upon whomever he pleased, especially, as Flannery O'Connor delights to show, upon grotesque, far-out characters. This isn't quite fair to Miss O'Connor, who has said that instant by instant grace gives life to the soul. She would probably say that as a writer she searched for the dramatic, and the lurid salvation of a hell-bent sinner is more dramatic than the continuous upholding of a good man. My quarrel isn't really with Miss O'Connor but with the South. The South has been so concerned with the individual snatched from the burning by the grace of God that it has failed to translate into heavenly terms the gracefulness and graciousness of the best of its own life. As playful as the South was, and as seriously as it took its roles and its diversions, it could never see itself as "at play in the fields of the Lord."

Indeed, it hardly even tried. Having adopted the doctrine of the spirituality of the church, it attempted to separate religious man and the religious life from the world and to consider God's grace—and God's judgment—as operative only upon the individual. The grace it talked about appeared mainly in individual conversion and most strikingly in the lightning-stroke variety. It usually came on Sunday or during protracted meetings, and since protracted meetings were most commonly held in the summer after the crops had been laid by, it came naturally as a lightning stroke, matching the terrible lightning of the Southern summer. Like the lightning it fell directly from heaven—unlike the gentle dew distilled from the night air upon the flowers and grass of earth. Nor, in spite of the term "grace," was there much graciousness about it. You really worked to deserve it; you kept all the rules a prudent man would keep.

As for the world outside the church, it was in the religious view one with "the flesh and the devil," to be avoided, to be plucked as brands from the burning. That it was also God's creation, his continuing creation wherein his grace was always at work, was not recognized at all. And since men could not recognize his grace in the outside world, they could not recognize his judgment there. Events in the public world were political events; only the events of the private world were religious.

In his eagerness for individual salvation, the Southerner is also modern man: he has cut himself off from the natural world —and indeed from other men—with the conscious or unconscious intention of exploiting it and them. To the degree that he has cut himself off, he has lost Saint Francis' sense of our brother the Sun and our sister the Moon. Since there is no salvation, no creativity left there, in desperation and alone he repents of sin, not knowing that his chief sin consists of his proudly separating himself from the world and from men, and in sinful loneliness seeks salvation for himself alone.

The difference here is that the Southerner has not separated himself so completely from the community as has typical modern man, and therefore he still has visible about him evidences of the creative, the gracious power of God in the natural and the human world. But the pathos is that his religion is mainly the pseudo-religion of individualistic modern man, which tells him nothing of the grace of God striving to appear even in the gracefulness and graciousness that his own culture values. This graciousness was pleading to be divinized; his church was no help in the matter.

XXIII

Conclusion

We return to the main question of Part III: What has the church done with this haunted land?

It has kept it haunted. Without the church, men would have forgotten Christianity. With the church they remember it, but in seriously distorted ways. Perhaps this is always true. It is especially true in the South, for here the culture has most deeply penetrated the church, and the church, therefore, instead of transmitting the light of God as revealed in the Christian Scriptures, mainly reflects back upon the culture certain half-lights and shadows suggested by the culture itself. Indeed, the church has usually reflected more shadows than lights, more the divisions of society than its wholeness. Instead of being the culmination of the essential life of the South, the expression of whatever wholeness, whatever life it had, the church has usually been a mere aspect of that life, an aspect, unfortunately, which by its prestige lent dignity to the divisions of society. Its god was a god of the part, not of the whole.

I recall here a recurring scene from my boyhood. On the south side of old Brick Church there were two hand-hewn, moss-grown logs, one against the warm wall of the church, the other in the shade of a nearby oak, the sunny one for winter, the shady one for summer. Here during Sunday school the men sat while the women took the children inside. They talked quietly of what countrymen discuss: weather, crops, families, and politics. Then, when Sunday school was over, they went inside; and, though they sat in family pews, thus bringing some breath of the outside world with them, since this was a Presbyterian church they became reserved listeners to an expository sermon. More generally, since they were Protestants, they became individualists, having no real need of a priest or of anybody else, each man set to make his own bargain with God.

It was by no means a perfect community they had left outside: it was a white community, though there were blacks scattered all around; it was a provincial community with only the faintest hint of the world, but it was a community. Within the church it was every man for himself. They said they were united in God, were one in him, but he was abstract and infinitely far, "pinnacled aloft in the intense inane." I daresay he haunted them, but he must have found it very hard to save them, coming as they did one by one.

Yet he was something more than a force to them. Personal moral injunctions historically connected with him carried some weight in the community, though detached as they were from worship, they usually became moralistic. Also, some sense of a divine mystery spread outward from the church and touched the life of the community.

The god of that community was doubtless a pagan god, but he was powerful as far as he went. The god inside was often, I'm afraid, only a name. Perhaps the culture was more Christian than the church.

In fairness, however, it must be said that during at least the past fifty years the church in the South has become increasingly concerned with the community, increasingly social-minded. Churchmen and church bodies now speak prophetically, condemning the pride of the wealthy, admitting with shame the suffering of the poor and the outcast. Indeed, the church has gone beyond words into action, supporting such things as public housing and recreation.

This movement into the world has by no means been accepted by all churchmen. As it has increased, opposition has increased, so that today, for instance, there is extreme tension between the liberal and conservative wings of the Presbyterian Church in the United States (the Southern Presbyterian Church) the conservatives holding tightly to the old idea of the spirituality of the church, the liberals claiming that the church must be where the action is—in the streets, the markets, and the legislative halls.

There has even arisen now a strong radical opposition to thi

increasing concern of the church with public life. This is represented best by the Committee of Southern Churchmen and their
publication, *Katallagete: Be Reconciled.* This group believes that the
social-minded church has made politics a false messiah and that
it is trying to achieve through politics what can only be attained
through Christian conversion. Such conversion would be not to
the spirituality of the church, but to the spirituality of the world.
These churchmen are not agreed, however, as to how to spiritual-
ize the world, though they would not put it this way. They are not
agreed as to how God spiritualizes the world.

The essential point of this book goes beyond the old believers in a spiritual church, the new believers in a social gospel, and
the new-new believers who have renounced both the spiritualiz-
ers and the socializers and who stand, somewhat bemused, waiting for God to do his thing in the world. The essential point of
this book is that God has been doing and is always doing his thing
in the world, and we moderns are in terrible straits because we
do not recognize this. God is always spiritualizing the world, the
material is always reaching for meaning, the inner light never
goes out no matter how many lights go out all over Europe, or
indeed all over the world.

From this point of view, the true church is composed of those
who know this, maybe not clearly—maybe they only sense it—but
deep down they know it and live in eternal expectation of the
dawn, which comes on forever. Living thus, they celebrate that
dawn. The new-new churchmen make a great deal of the belief
that God has already reconciled men to himself through Jesus
Christ. I should prefer to say "is reconciling men." God recon-
ciles not only through the church—which, though I criticize, I
would not overthrow. Through every culture and through all the
secular life of man, the creative Spirit of God is drawing men
together within it.

At one time, a century and a quarter ago, there did creep into
American theology (but apparently without lasting effect) some-
thing of this sense of God's presence in the world. James H.
Nichols tells the story in *Romanticism in American Theology.* It is true
that the scene was in Pennsylvania, above the Mason and Dixon
Line, but the nation was still undivided, and, if I have read the

story correctly, the comment applies to the South as well. The banner was carried by two leaders of the German Reformed Church, John Williamson Nevin, the theologian, and Philip Schaff, the historian. Schaff felt that the evangelical focus on sin was unsound and that theology should focus on God, not on sin. Nevin "felt that praise and adoration were too generally crowded out by pulpit rhetoric or moralizing," and that "the natural creation was pervaded by the presence of deity and adumbrated invisible spiritual realities."[1]

But these were voices calling in the deepening wilderness of the modern world. The church continued and continues to spend too much time repenting of its sins, either personal or social, too little time celebrating the presence of the Holy Spirit in the world. The new-new churchmen say that only God in Christ can save us. This is true if we are speaking not of the Christ of two thousand years ago but of the Holy Spirit of today and forever, who saves us through men and through human institutions, of which the church is one. The Holy Spirit also speaks in the church. The great Stoic Marcus Aurelius said that one could be saved even in a palace. So one can be saved even in church, but only as the church gathers into one and cherishes and increases the myriad scattered lights that glow in the world.

The church is for the celebration of those myriad lights. The church of my boyhood used to offer me good moral advice and maybe—being Presbyterian—sound theology. I don't think any of it hurt me. But looking back upon it I have to conclude that it did not give me what I needed. I needed God, as all men need God: to solve the mysteries of this life; to adjust to its injustices; to complete its incompleteness. I needed to know that God had passed near me in the rustle of the corn last week and would speak to me in a human voice tomorrow. I needed to have his presence in the world recognized and celebrated.

But the Protestant Church was not made for celebration of life; it was made for repentance of having deferred or denied life. The Protestant Church is primarily the church of individualistic modern man who, in order to conquer and exploit the world, both of nature and of man, has cut himself off from that world. How can such a church celebrate the world? It can only repent for cutting itself off from the world. But it doesn't even know what it should be repenting of. It should repent of its lack of joy and its lack of ritualistic celebration of that joy. But how can it repent of the lack of what it does not have? Only as it has joy can it know that it lacks joy. And the only real joy it can have is rooted in the passing and the enduring world, no matter how much we attach it to the person of Jesus, who lived two thousand years ago.

Here is the irony of the whole Southern situation. We have evil and have had evils almost beyond compare; I have never denied this. But somehow we've never ceased being haunted by God. Somehow we've remained human. Somehow the stars of kindliness, of courtesy, of integrity, of courage, and indeed, of a strange kind of humility have never gone out. Somehow, though we've hated too much, we have loved somewhat. Somehow there has been a community, and men have taken some pleasure therein. These are all good things, however limited. It doesn't matter whether we intended them or whether they came by the lovely or—as Aeschylus said—the awful grace of God. They are here, and we should thank God for them. I say again: I sometimes wonder whether the Southern church has been as rich as the world surrounding it.

I was once on a program with my dear friend Will Campbell, director of the Committee of Southern Churchmen. Deep down I think I agree with Will, but he explains it one way, I another. On the program in question, Will spent his time frying segregationists on the fires of hell. He was clearly against sin. I began with the comment: "Will has been stoking the fires of hell; I shall try to polish, if but a little, the pinnacles of heaven."

These pinnacles rise all about us, though most of them stand hardly above the grass and may, like fairy castles, be crushed by a careless footstep. But they're all we have, and if we would cherish them and celebrate their existence, the church might then become a city set upon a hill, a light unto all the people.

Notes

II. The Southerner as American

1. William E. Dodd, *The Old South: Struggles for Democracy* (New York: The Macmillan Co., 1937), p. 70.
2. David Bertelson, *The Lazy South* (New York: Oxford University Press, 1967), pp. 244–245.

III. The Plantation

1. Edgar T. Thompson, "The South in Old and New Contexts," in John C. McKinney and Edgar T. Thompson, eds., *The South in Continuity and Change* (Durham: Duke University Press, 1965), p. 458.
2. *Ibid.,* p. 455.
3. *Ibid.,* p. 463.

IV. The Family

1. Edgar T. Thompson, "God and the Southern Plantation System," in Samuel S. Hill, Jr., ed., *Religion and the Solid South* (Nashville: Abingdon Press, 1972), p. 70.
2. Clifford Dowdey, *The Great Plantation,* reissue (Charles City, Va.: Berkeley Plantation, 1970), p. 99.
3. *Ibid.,* pp. 99–100, 179.
4. Allen Tate, *Essays of Four Decades* (Chicago: The Swallow Press, 1968), p. 588.
5. Frank L. Owsley, *Plain Folk of the Old South* (Baton Rouge: Louisiana State University Press, 1949), p. 94.
6. Tate, *Essays of Four Decades,* pp. 587–589.
7. Hannah Arendt, *The Human Condition* (Garden City, N.Y.: Doubleday & Co., 1959), p. 54.
8. Joseph Bryan, III, *The Sword over the Mantle* (New York: McGraw-Hill, 1960), p. 78.
9. Tate, *Essays of Four Decades,* p. 586.
10. Bell I. Wiley, *The Life of Johnny Reb: The Common Soldier of the Confederacy* (Indianapolis: Bobbs-Merrill Co., 1943), p. 77.

11. Andrew Nelson Lytle, *Bedford Forrest and His Critter Company* (New York: G. P. Putnam's Sons, 1931).
12. Francis Butler Simkins, *A History of the South* (New York: Alfred A. Knopf, 1953), pp. 388–389.
13. Margaret Jarman Hagood, *Mothers of the South* (Chapel Hill: The University of North Carolina Press, 1939), pp. 154–155.
14. John Temple Graves, *The Fighting South* (New York: G. P. Putnam's Sons, 1943), pp. 209–210.
15. Hodding Carter, *Where Main Street Meets the River* (New York: Rinehart & Co., 1952), pp. 10, 71.
16. Hylan Lewis, *Blackways of Kent* (Chapel Hill: The University of North Carolina Press, 1955), p. 103.
17. Catherine C. Hopley, *Life in the South*, Vol. I (London: 1863), p. 320.

V. The Black

1. James E. Sellers, *The South and Christian Ethics* (New York: Association Press, 1962), pp. 44–45.

VI. A Spacious Place

1. Tate, *Essays of Four Decades*, p. 581.
2. Émile Durkheim, *The Elementary Forms of the Religious Life: A Study in Religious Sociology*, trans. by Joseph Ward Swain (New York: The Macmillan Co., n.d.), p. 85.
3. Bertelson, *The Lazy South*, p. 20 and notes.
4. Francis Asbury, *The Heart of Asbury's Journal*, Ezra Squier Tipple, ed. (New York: The Methodist Book Concern, 1904), p. 487.
5. William Bartram, *Travels of William Bartram*, Mark Van Doren, ed. (New York: Dover Publications, 1928).
6. Bertelson, *The Lazy South*, p. 39.
7. James McBride Dabbs, "The Clearings," in Robert West Howard, ed., *This Is the South* (New York: Rand McNally & Co., 1959), p. 30.
8. Thompson, "The South in Old and New Contexts," p. 460.

VIII. The Inner Frontier

1. Paul Zweig, *Heresy of Self Love: A Study of Subversive Individualism* (New York: Basic Books, 1968), p. 62.
2. Tate, *Essays of Four Decades*, p. 581.
3. Walker Percy, *The Last Gentleman* (New York: Farrar, Straus & Giroux, 1966), p. 204.

IX. The Temporal South

1. J. H. Plumb, "Slavery, Race, and the Poor," *New York Review of Books*, Vol. XII, No. 5 (1969), p. 3.

X. INDIVIDUAL AND COMMUNITY

1. Pat Watters, "Keep on A-Walking, Children," *New American Review*, No. 5 (January 1969), p. 44.
2. Thompson, "The South in Old and New Contexts," p. 461.
3. Allen Tate, *The Fathers* (Chicago: The Swallow Press, 1960).
4. *Ibid.*, pp. 96–106.
5. Noni Jabavu, *Drawn in Colour* (New York: St. Martin's Press, 1960), pp. 13–19.
6. Jean G. Péristiany, ed., *Honour and Shame: The Values of Mediterranean Society* (Chicago: The University of Chicago Press, 1966), p. 43.
7. *Ibid.*, p. 110.
8. *Ibid.*, p. 212.
9. Melville J. Herskovits, *The Myth of the Negro Past* (New York: Harper & Brothers, 1941), p. 158.

XIII. WHERE FIRST I SAW THEM

1. Flannery O'Connor, *Mystery and Manners*, Sally and Robert Fitzgerald, eds. (New York: Farrar, Straus & Giroux, 1969), pp. 57–58.
2. James McBride Dabbs, "Beyond Tragedy," *Christendom*, Vol. I, No. 3 (Spring 1936), pp. 453–463.
3. O'Connor, *Mystery and Manners*, p. 234.

XIV. IN SPACE AND TIME

1. Philip Wheelwright, *The Burning Fountain* (Bloomington: University of Indiana Press, 1954), p. 162.
2. *Ibid.*

XV. AMONG MEN

1. O'Connor, *Mystery and Manners*, p. 44.
2. James McBride Dabbs, *The Southern Heritage* (New York: Alfred A. Knopf, 1958), pp. 266–267.
3. O'Connor, *Mystery and Manners*, p. 209.
4. A. E. Housman, *Last Poems* (New York: Henry Holt & Co., 1922), p. 25.
5. Max Lerner, *America as a Civilization* (New York: Simon & Schuster, 1957), p. 40.
6. O'Connor, *Mystery and Manners*, p. 234.

XVI. CENTERS OF ORDER

1. Samuel S. Hill, Jr., *Southern Churches in Crisis* (New York: Holt, Rinehart & Winston, 1967), pp. 94–95.
2. Richard M. Weaver, "Older Religiousness in the South," *Sewanee Review*, Vol. LI (April 1943), p. 243.

XVII. Release Through the Church

1. Clement Eaton, *The Growth of Southern Civilization: 1790–1860* (New York: Harper & Brothers, 1961), p. 14.
2. Durkheim, *The Elementary Forms of the Religious Life,* p. 43.

XVIII. Repentance and Reconciliation

1. Joseph R. Washington, Jr., *Black Religion: The Negro and Christianity in the United States* (Boston: Beacon Press, 1964).

XIX. The Personal God

1. Paul Tillich, *The Protestant Era,* trans. by James Luther Adams (Chicago: The University of Chicago Press, 1957), p. 63.

XX. Limited Commitment

1. O'Connor, *Mystery and Manners,* pp. 206–207.

XXI. The Need for Complete Commitment

1. Durkheim, *The Elementary Forms of the Religious Life,* p. 39.
2. Tate, *The Fathers,* p. 186.
3. Peter L. Berger, *A Rumor of Angels* (Garden City, N.Y.: Doubleday & Co., 1969), p. 93.

XXII. In Search of Grace

1. O'Connor, *Mystery and Manners,* pp. 29, 234.
2. Johan Huizinga, *Homo Ludens: A Study of the Play Element in Culture* (Boston: Beacon Press, 1955), p. 176.

XXIII. Conclusion

1. James Hastings Nichols, *Romanticism in American Theology* (Chicago: The University of Chicago Press, 1961), pp. 39, 294.

DAT